Logic Pro 101

To access online media, visit:
www.halleonard.com/mylibrary

Enter Code
4896-0184-5339-6559

Logic Pro 101
Music Production Fundamentals

Ryan Rey and Harry Gold

with Frank D. Cook and Eric Kuehnl

ROWMAN & LITTLEFIELD

Lanham • Boulder • New York • London

Published by Rowman & Littlefield
An imprint of The Rowman & Littlefield Publishing Group, Inc.
4501 Forbes Boulevard, Suite 200, Lanham, Maryland 20706
www.rowman.com

86-90 Paul Street, London EC2A 4NE, United Kingdom

British Library Cataloguing in Publication Information Available

Library of Congress Cataloging-in-Publication Data
Names: Rey, Ryan, author. | Gold, Harry, 1991- author. | Cook, Frank D., contributor. | Kuehnl, Eric, contributor.
Title: Logic Pro 101 : music production fundamentals / Ryan Rey, Harry Gold ; with contributions by Frank D. Cook and Eric Kuehnl.
Description: Lanham : Rowman & Littlefield Publishers, 2021. | Series: 101 series | Includes bibliographical references and index. | Summary: "Logic Pro 101 is a comprehensive guide to using a Logic Pro system for musicians and music creators. This book covers everything you need to know to complete a project in Apple's professional-level digital audio workstation; takes you through the fundamentals of music production; and includes exercises, projects, and downloadable media examples"— Provided by publisher.
Identifiers: LCCN 2021047618 (print) | LCCN 2021047619 (ebook) | ISBN 9781538158166 (paperback) | ISBN 9781538158173 (ebook)
Subjects: LCSH: Logic (Computer file) | Digital audio editors.
Classification: LCC ML74.4.L64 R39 2021 (print) | LCC ML74.4.L64 (ebook) | DDC 781.3/4536—dc23
LC record available at https://lccn.loc.gov/2021047618
LC ebook record available at https://lccn.loc.gov/2021047619

Contents

Acknowledgments

The authors would like to give special thanks to the following individuals who have provided assistance, input, information, material, and other support for this book: Eric Kuehnl, Frank D. Cook, Jules Fuchs.

Harry would like to thank his family, and musical mentors Steve Gannon and Michael Burks.

Ryan would like to thank his wife Audrey and daughter Olivia for their unconditional support and encouragement. Special thanks go to his mother-in-law Shushan for her immeasurable help throughout the process.

Introduction

Welcome to Apple Logic Pro

Congratulations on beginning work under the NextPoint Training Digital Media Production program. Within this program, you have the opportunity to pursue certification in Logic Pro and other digital media applications.

Apple's Logic Pro software is embraced the world over by hobbyists, musicians, recording artists, and audio production professionals. The material in this course book will help you discover Logic Pro's immense capabilities, expand your musical endeavors, and harness the power and flexibility of your own music creation system.

This book represents the first step on a journey toward mastering Logic Pro software. The information, exercises, and projects you will find here are written for Logic Pro systems running version 10.6.2 software or later. However, the book applies equally to software versions back to 10.5, and the vast majority of the discussions outside of the Live Loops Grid apply to all earlier versions of Logic Pro X.

Whether you are interested only in self-study or you would like to pursue formal training through a NextPoint Training Certification Partner, this book will develop your core skills and introduce you to the awe-inspiring power of Apple Logic Pro.

About This Book

This book is designed for the audio enthusiast with relatively little experience in Logic. Those who are new to the field of audio production can supplement this book with outside resources. We recommend the text *Audio Production Basics with Logic Pro X* by Ryan Rey and Harry Gold for learners who have knowledge gaps in the areas of computer usage, miking techniques, mixer signal flow, monitoring equipment, or MIDI devices.

This Logic Pro 101 textbook and the associated instructor-led training course were developed by NextPoint Training, Inc. (NPT) as part of our Digital Media Production program and certification offerings. While this course book can be completed through self-study, we recommend the hands-on experience available through an instructor-led class with an NPT Certification Partner.

For more information on the NPT Digital Media Production program, visit http://NextPointTraining.com and select our Certification Programs page (https://nxpt.us/DigitalMedia). For information on the classes that NPT offers directly to end users, select our Training and Education page (https://nxpt.us/training).

Logic Pro 10.6 Edition

This edition of the Logic Pro 101 course has been written to address recent software changes introduced to Logic Pro, including the Live Loops Grid. The material is focused on the principles that you need to understand to complete a Logic Pro project, from initial setup to final mixdown. Whether your project involves recording audio, preparing MIDI sequences for virtual instruments, or editing and mixing audio files, Logic Pro 101 will teach you the steps required to succeed.

The Download Media

This book makes use of media files for the included exercises and the final projects. The media files can be accessed by visiting www.halleonard.com/mylibrary and entering your access code, as printed on the opening page of this book. From there, you can download the **Media Files 2021-Logic101** folder for this course. Instructions for downloading the media files are provided with the exercises and final projects, as needed.

The downloadable **Media Files 2021-Logic101** folder includes three subfolders for use with this book.

Sample Project Files for Exercises

The **01 Completed Exercises** folder within the **Media Files 2021-Logic101** folder provides sample project files of each completed Logic Pro exercise (Exercises 4 through 10). These are provided primarily for reference purposes. Sample files 4 though 9 can also be used as a starting point for subsequent work in Exercises 5 through 10, as needed.

Exercise Media

The **02 Exercise Media** folder provides the audio and MIDI files you will import to complete the work in Exercises 5 through 10, following the instructions included in this book.

Files for the Final Projects

The **03 Final Project Media** folder provides content for the two final projects that you will complete in the second part of this book. This folder includes the project files and associated media required to complete the projects, following the step-by-step instructions in the two Final Projects at the end of the book.

Course Prerequisites

Most Logic Pro enthusiasts today have at least a passing familiarity with operating a computer. If you consider yourself a computer novice, however, you should review some basics before beginning this course. You will need to know how to complete such tasks as:

- Starting up your computer

- Using the mouse to navigate through folders and select files

- Using standard menus and menu commands

- Using common keyboard commands for standard operating system operations

- Locating, moving, and renaming files and folders

- Using standard cut, copy, and paste commands

- Opening, saving, and closing files

This course focuses on using Logic Pro in a digital audio recording and production environment. The work requires a basic understanding of MIDI and audio recording techniques, processes, and equipment, such as the following:

- MIDI devices

- Microphones and miking techniques

- Audio interfaces

- Mixer signal flow

- Audio monitoring equipment

If you are a beginner in the field of audio production, you can supplement this text with independently available literature or courses on audio recording tools and techniques. We recommend any of the books in the NPT *Audio Production Basics* series as a prerequisite, including *Audio Production Basics with Logic Pro X.*

Course Organization and Sequence

This course has been designed to familiarize you with the practices and processes you will use to complete a recording, editing, and mixing project.

Chapters and Exercises

The first part of the book includes ten primary chapters and ten associated short exercises. The first three chapters provide information on the background and history of Logic software, installation and startup procedures, and the current user interface. The subsequent chapters present specific processes and techniques, in the general order that you will use them to complete a project—from creating a new project file, to recording and editing, and on through to processing, mixing, automation, and completing a final bounce.

Each of the chapters is followed by a brief exercise that gives you practice applying what you have learned.

Final Projects

The second part of this book provides two final projects. This section includes instructions for completing the unfinished projects included in the **Media Files 2021-Logic101** folder. The projects in this section can be completed at any point as you progress through the ten primary chapters.

The NPT Digital Media Production Program

This Logic Pro 101 book has been written as a textbook for teaching and learning Logic Pro software. In addition to being an off-the-shelf guide for consumers, this book is also the official text for NextPoint Training's professional certification in Logic Pro. By completing the coursework in this text, you are taking an important step toward certification. Completing your certification just might help you land that next gig, find others with similar skills and interests, or even obtain your dream job in the industry.

To become certified in Logic Pro, you must register at **ElementsED.com**, where you can complete additional study in Logic, review coursework (as desired), take practice quizzes, and take the Logic Pro Certified Professional Exam. Detailed information on current requirements is available from the NextPoint Training website at http://NextPointTraining.com/certification-programs (or https://nxpt.us/DigitalMedia).

Curriculum and Certification Levels

NextPoint Training currently offers certification in Apple Logic Pro, Ableton Live, Avid Pro Tools, Reason software, and Steinberg Cubase software. (Visit NextPointTraining.com for the latest information.) The certification credential associated with the Logic Pro 101 course is Logic Pro Certified Professional I.

The Certified Professional program prepares individuals to operate an Apple Logic Pro system in an independent production environment. This certification requires successful completion of the Logic Pro 101 instructor-led course at an NPT Certification Partner school and a passing score on the associated Logic Pro certification exam.

Other Courses Offered in the Digital Media Production Program

NextPoint Training offers several additional certification courses to help you become proficient using a wide range of audio production tools.

- *Audio Production Basics.* This certification is available for a variety of digital audio workstations, including Avid Pro Tools | First, Steinberg Cubase, Ableton Live, Logic Pro, and Reason software. Each option teaches the basics of recording, editing, mixing, and processing audio using the applicable software. Each of the Audio Production Basics textbooks and courses offers an introduction to digital audio for students aspiring to work in music or video production, audio engineering, broadcast, or new media.

- *Ableton Live 101* provides the foundational skills needed to operate an Ableton Live system in an independent production environment. This course and certification will help individuals start working effectively on their own projects in Ableton Live software.

- *FL Studio 101* provides foundational information and skills needed to competently operate Image-Line's FL Studio software for independent productions. The goal of this course and certification is to help individuals work effectively on their own projects in FL Studio.

NextPoint Training Course Configuration

NextPoint Training uses a version–specific approach to course design, enabling students and educators to access classes based on the products and software versions that meet their particular needs and training environments.

Audio Curriculum

The NextPoint Training audio coursework includes programs supporting certification in several areas, including Apple Logic Pro, Ableton Live, Avid Pro Tools, Steinberg Cubase, and more. The Logic Pro certification path is described above. Course components are designed to be completed as individual product-focused classes; however, the content may be made available through different class configurations.

Other Media Courses

Details on of each of the courses offered through the NextPoint Training Digital Media Production program are available in the NPT Certification Program Guide and on our website at http://NextPointTraining.com.

How Can I Learn More?

Additional resources are available to help you explore the topics covered in this book, review key points in each chapter, and test your knowledge of the material.

The **Logic Pro 101 Study Guide** module available through the Elements|ED learning assessment platform (ElementsED.com) allows learners to review key concepts and information from this course through visual examples and to assess their learning using practice quizzes. This module is particularly useful to help students prepare for the Logic Pro Certified Professional exam.

If you have any questions about this textbook and included media files, the NPT Digital Media Production program, the Elements|ED platform, or the associated Logic Pro training and certification exam, please email us at info@nptteam.com.

Conventions and Symbols Used in This Book

Following are some of the conventions and symbols used in this book, and throughout the books in the NextPoint Training Series.

Keyboard Shortcuts and Modifiers

Menu choices and keyboard commands are typically capitalized and written in bold text. Hierarchy is shown using the greater than symbol (>), keystroke combinations are indicated using the plus sign (+), and mouse-click operations are indicated by hyphenated strings, where needed. Brackets ([ ]) are used to indicate key presses on the numeric keypad.

Convention	Action
File > Save	Choose the Save command from the File menu.
Command+N	Hold down the Command key and press the N key.
Control-click	Hold down the Control key and click the mouse button.
Right-click	Click with the right mouse button.
Press [1]	Press 1 on the numeric keypad.

Icons

The following icons are used in this book to call attention to tips, shortcuts, warnings, and reference sources.

 Tips provide helpful hints and suggestions, background information, or details on related operations or concepts.

 Shortcuts provide useful keyboard, mouse, or modifier-based shortcuts that can help you work more efficiently.

 Warnings caution you against conditions that may affect audio playback, impact system performance, alter data files, or interrupt hardware connections.

 Cross-References alert you to another section, book, or resource that provides additional information on the current topic.

 Online References provide links to online resources and downloads related to the current topic.

Chapter 1

Logic Pro Background

This chapter introduces you to the capabilities of Logic Pro software, including its uses for audio production, MIDI workflows, mixing, and video post-production. You will learn about the evolution of Logic Pro technology and get an introduction to the characteristics of analog and digital audio. You will also get an overview of the latest developments in Logic Pro software and learn about the different Logic Pro configurations available today.

✦ Learning Targets for This Chapter

- Identify common industry uses for Logic Pro software

- Recognize the contributions of historical developments in sampling and sound editing, MIDI technology, computer I/O, and recording technology to today's digital audio workstation

- Understand the relationship between sample rate and frequency response in digital audio

- Understand the relationship between bit depth and dynamic range in digital audio

- Recognize components and features of various Logic Pro configurations

Key topics from this chapter are illustrated in the Logic Pro 101 Study Guide module available through the Elements|ED online learning platform. Sign up at ElementsED.com.

The Logic Pro Digital Audio Workstation

Logic Pro is one of the most widely used applications for music and post-production (sound for film, video, and multimedia) on macOS today. A product of Apple Inc., Logic Pro integrates capabilities in audio and MIDI recording, composition, editing, and mixing, as well as support for desktop video. As such, Logic Pro software empowers both music and post-production professionals to easily achieve all of their production tasks in a familiar, Mac-based interface.

At its core, Logic Pro is a multi-track software-based music production and sequencing program. Since its initial release in 1993, Logic has set the standard for loop and pattern-based workflows.

Today's Logic Pro software offers audio recording, audio editing, MIDI sequencing, signal processing, and mixing through a single, integrated system. With the ability to incorporate video files within a project, Logic Pro has become a favorite tool for composing for visual media such as film, television, and video games.

Audio Processing

Logic Pro works with audio that is stored electronically in digital format. The software records audio performances and stores them as digital files. Similar to a digital camera, which stores a photograph as a collection of discrete pixels, Logic Pro stores recorded audio as a collection of discrete *samples*. Logic Pro records audio with resolutions up to 24 bits and sample rates up to 192 kHz.

Just as you can use an image editor to modify, enhance, and alter your digital photographs in creative ways, so you can use Logic Pro to edit and enhance your digital audio. Working in the digital realm makes editing and manipulating your media simple and intuitive. Logic Pro lets you trim waveforms, reprocess sections of audio, correct a compromised performance, replace drum sounds, rearrange song sections, and much, much more.

MIDI Production

Logic Pro has its roots as a MIDI sequencer. The built-in feature set enables you to record and edit MIDI data along with your audio recordings. MIDI recordings differ from their digital audio counterparts in that they capture performance data rather than sound samples. You can record MIDI signals from a keyboard controller (or other device) through a MIDI interface or USB port and then edit the data using the track displays or MIDI Editor windows in Logic Pro.

The MIDI features in Logic Pro include Software Instrument tracks, MIDI effects, grid and groove quantize functions, velocity editing, and more. Logic Pro also comes bundled with a huge library of royalty–free audio and MIDI loops, and several great-sounding virtual instrument plug-ins.

Notation and Scores

Logic Pro supports standard music notation display for MIDI notes. The Score Editor provides notation display functions, with options to see each region or Software Instrument track represented on a separate staff. From this window you can edit your MIDI data on a musical staff and print your arrangement as a score. The notation options in Logic Pro provide productivity and workflow enhancements for composers, songwriters, and others.

Mixing and Automation

Beyond recording, editing, and arranging, Logic Pro offers a software-based mixing environment that provides control over signal routing, effects processing, signal levels, panning, and more. The mixing operations in Logic Pro can be automated to store dynamic changes. When you save a project, all routing, automation, mixing, and effects settings remain exactly as you've left them, meaning you can easily recall, edit, and refine your mixes over time.

Additionally, Logic Pro software can be combined with hardware from third-party manufacturers in various configurations to provide all of the input and output connections you need for your Logic Pro sessions. Massive projects including hundreds of simultaneous Audio and MIDI tracks can be managed without audio degradation. Logic Pro systems can range from very simple to extremely advanced and powerful.

Audio for Video and Post-Production

Logic Pro also provides a powerful audio platform for video post-production tasks. You can import QuickTime movies and use the Movie Window for quick visual feedback or full-screen display for visual reference as you compose a music score, edit dialog, and/or create sound effects. Once you've completed your project, your finished movie file can be exported with the final audio embedded.

Logic Pro History and Evolution

Those who are new to Logic Pro may look at the line-up of Apple's programs and conclude that Apple developed GarageBand first, and eventually created the professional version, Logic Pro. However, Logic actually came out over a decade before GarageBand, gradually moving from a small German company to its position as a staple in Apple's professional software lineup.

Emagic Introduces Notator Logic

Logic's roots trace back to the days where music composition was done on Atari ST. In the late 1980s, a company called C-Lab released a MIDI sequencer developed by Gerhard Lengeling and Chris Adam, called *Creator*. Soon notation and score-writing functionality was added, using a program called *Notator*.

Figure 1.1 A Notator EBU/SMPTE sync box for C-Lab Creator

In 1993, the C-Lab programmers left to form Emagic and released the first version of Notator Logic for Atari ST, later arriving on Mac and Windows. Yes, Logic used to run on Windows! Eventually, "Notator" was dropped from the software's title, and it was then simply known as *Logic*.

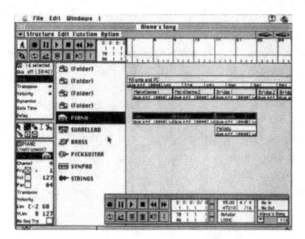

Figure 1.2 The arrange window in Notator Logic

What separated Logic from other programs at the time was its included library of virtual instruments. These instruments were available right out the box. Other DAWs on the market did not include virtual instruments; users either needed to connect a MIDI synthesizer (or other external sound module) and access its internal sounds or purchase third-party virtual instruments. Logic set a different standard, providing a huge set of sounds from its EXS24 sampler, and later several piano and organ instruments.

E-Magic is Purchased by Apple

In 2002, Apple acquired Emagic and quickly dropped Windows support for Logic. In March 2004, Apple released *Logic Pro 6*. This release bundled a bunch of Emagic software together—including several instruments and effects—into a single program. Apple also released new tiers of the software at this time. A slightly scaled-down version was introduced, called *Logic Express*, and a very simplified, free version of the software was released as the first version of *GarageBand*.

Apple Releases Subsequent Versions

With the Logic Pro 7 release in September 2004, Apple introduced the Global Tracks display, making it significantly easier for users to change key and time signatures, add markers, and adjust tempo in a project. This release also added the ability to import a GarageBand project directly into Logic. The Apple Loops collection of royalty free music loops came bundled with the release, along with three new instruments (including a drum synth and sequencer), and nine new effects plug-ins (including a guitar amp simulator).

In 2007, Logic Pro 8 was released. This update included a re-vamping to a lot of the built-in effects. Delay Designer was introduced, along with updated modeling for the compressors.

Logic Pro 9 was released in 2009 and introduced several pivotal features. Flex Time was added, allowing users to adjust the timing of a performance without using a separate application. EXS24 received added functionality with a quick context menu item allowing users to "convert to sampler track." Bounce-in-place and Drum replacer were also added at this time.

Logic Pro X is Born

With the version 10 release in 2013, Logic Pro became Logic Pro X, a designation it maintained until late 2020. However, that naming convention did not signal a lack of updates and new features over those years!

Figure 1.3 A demo session included with Logic Pro X ("Ocean Eyes" by Billie Eilish)

Logic Pro X Features through Version 10.4.8

Some of the features that were released over the span of Logic Pro X include:

- **Drummer** – A virtual session player that automatically plays along in a variety of styles, using simple controls to change complexity.

- **Flex Pitch** – A pitch adjustment equivalent to Flex Time.

- **Apple Loop Update** – A rebuild for the included loop library.

- **Folders** – A feature that groups a set of tracks into a single, top-level track displayed as a single region in the Main Window.

- **Orchestra** – A complete set of orchestral virtual instruments.

- **ChromaVerb** – A sophisticated new algorithmic reverb with a colorful, interactive interface for creating rich acoustic spaces.

- **Smart Tempo** – A feature that lets a recorded performance define your project tempo and allows you to easily combine content regardless of original tempos.

Logic Pro X 10.5 Features

In May 2020, Logic Pro X 10.5 was released, bringing some huge changes to Logic. Here are some of the most significant changes in that release:

- **Live Loops** – Lets you perform and capture free-form arrangement ideas into a new Live Loops Grid.

- **Sampler** (ESX24 makeover) – Lets you create a sophisticated multi-sampled instrument using a drag-and-drop workflow; includes a new, modern design that provides synthesis, mapping, and zone editing in a single window interface.

- **Quick Sampler** – Lets you import an audio file to instantly build a playable sampled instrument; Quick Sampler automatically identifies the root note and optimal loop points, and trims silence from the sample.

- **Step Sequencer** – A feature for creating and editing patterns, with control over velocity, repeats, step rate, and other parameters that generate pattern variations; lets you use any patch as a sound source, and includes a library of over 150 rhythmic and melodic patterns.

- **Additional Content** – Over 2,500 new loops in a variety of instruments and genres covering modern and classic hip-hop, electro house, reggaeton, future bass, techno, and transition effects.

The Logic Pro 10.6 Release

Introduced in November 2020, the 10.6 release offered stability improvements as well as support for the Apple M1 processor and macOS Big Sur. Apple also reverted the program name to *Logic Pro*, losing the X.

Using Control Surfaces with Logic Pro

Many third-party controllers will work seamlessly with Logic Pro. If you find a MIDI controller with knobs and faders on it, you can generally use that to control parameters on instruments or effects in Logic.

Figure 1.4 An Akai MidiMix MIDI controller

Logic Remote App

The Logic Remote app is a free app for iOS that can be used with GarageBand and Logic Pro on the Mac. It allows Multi-Touch gestures to help you mix, adjust plug-in settings, control transport functionality, and access virtual instruments from anywhere in the room.

Figure 1.5 A Macbook Pro running Logic Pro and an iPad running Logic Remote

Some of the features of the Logic Remote app include:

- Play any Logic instrument using a familiar piano keyboard or guitar fretboard
- Control Live Loops by triggering cells or switching between scenes
- Program beats, bass lines, and melodic parts in the Step Sequencer
- Operate basic transport controls like start, stop, record, and cycle
- Record-enable your system from another room
- Use Multi-Touch gestures to adjust Mixer volume, pan, solo, and mute controls
- Swipe to scroll or jump in banks to navigate through Mixer faders

Audio Characteristics: Waveform, Frequency, and Amplitude

To make the most of your experience working with sound in Logic Pro, it is helpful to understand what exactly sound is and what makes each sound unique.

When we hear a sound, we actually experience a variation in the air pressure around us. This variation results from vibrations in material objects—whether a knock on a tabletop, a running car engine, or a plucked guitar string. When a vibrating object moves through a back-and-forth motion, the variation in air pressure that it produces becomes an auditory event. If the vibrating frequency falls within the range of human hearing, we perceive the varying air pressure as a sound.

The nature of the sound we hear is determined by the waveform, frequency, and amplitude of the vibration.

Waveform: The Shape of a Sound

The waveform of the sound pressure variations that reaches our ears creates our perception of the sound's source, be it a tabletop, a car engine, or a guitar string. The waveform is the "shape" of the sound—or, more accurately, the shape of the vibration that produced the sound. As a vibrating object moves through its back-and-forth motions, its path is not smooth and continuous. Instead, the cycles of vibration are typically complex and jagged, creating a sound that is influenced by the physical material that the object is composed of and the resonance induced by the object's surroundings. Each object vibrates differently; the waveform of the vibration gives the sound its unique character and tone.

Frequency: The Pitch of a Sound

The frequency of the sound pressure variations that reaches our ears creates our perception of the pitch of the sound. We measure this frequency in *cycles per second* (CPS), also commonly denoted as *Hertz* (Hz). These two terms are synonymous—15,000 CPS is the same as 15,000 Hz. Multiples of 1,000 Hz are commonly denoted as kilohertz (kHz). Therefore, 15,000 Hz is also written as 15 kHz.

As the frequency of vibration increases, the pitch of the sound goes up—numerically higher frequencies produce higher pitches, while numerically lower frequencies produce lower pitches. Each time the frequency doubles, the pitch rises by one octave.

By way of example, the open **A** string on a guitar vibrates at 110 Hz in standard tuning. Playing the **A** note on the 12th fret produces vibrations at 220 Hz (one octave higher).

 The range of human hearing is between 20 and 20,000 cycles per second, or stated another way, from 20 Hz to 20 kHz.

Amplitude: The Intensity of a Sound

The intensity or amplitude of the sound pressure variations that reach our ears creates our perception of the loudness of the sound. We measure amplitude in *decibels* (dB). The decibel is a logarithmic unit used to describe a ratio of sound pressure; as such, it does not have a linear relation to our perception of loudness.

As the amplitude of pressure variations increases, the sound becomes progressively louder. Doubling the intensity of sound-pressure variations (acoustic power) creates a gain of 3 dB; however, we do not perceive this change as doubling the sound's loudness. An increase of approximately 10 dB is required to produce a perceived doubling of loudness. By way of example, the amplitude of ordinary conversation is around 60 dB. Increasing the amplitude to 70 dB would essentially double the loudness; increasing amplitude to 80 dB would double it again, quadrupling the original loudness.

Recording and Playing Back Analog Audio

The task of a recording microphone is to respond to changes in air pressure—the waveforms, frequencies, and amplitudes that make up a sound—and translate them into an electronic output that can be captured or recorded. A microphone functions as a *transducer*, converting acoustic energy into an electrical current.

The continuous electrical signal produced by a microphone is an alternating current with a waveform, frequency, and amplitude that directly corresponds to, or is analogous to, the original acoustic information. This electrical signal is thus a representation of the *analog audio signal.*

If this continuous signal is captured on analog recording media, such as magnetic tape, it can be played back by directly translating the electrical waveform, frequency, and amplitude back into variations in air pressure through the means of an amplifier and a loudspeaker.

Converting Audio to Digital Format

To record audio into Logic Pro, the electrical signal relayed by a microphone, guitar pickup, or other device must be translated into digital numeric information using binary data. This conversion is necessary so that the signal can be stored, read, and subsequently manipulated by a computer.

The process of translating electrical signals to binary data is referred to as *analog-to-digital conversion*, commonly abbreviated as *A/D conversion*. Two essential factors affect the A/D conversion process: *sample rate* and *bit depth*.

The Importance of Sample Rate

Sampling is the process of taking individual, discrete measurements of an electrical signal at various moments in time. Each measurement, or sample, is a digital representation of the signal voltage at that instant. Played back in succession, these samples approximate the original signal, much like a series of still images played back in succession approximates movement in a film or animation.

The sample rate is the frequency with which these digital measurements are collected.

Nyquist Theorem

The sample rate required for digital audio is driven by a fundamental principle of analog-to-digital conversion, referred to as the *Sampling Theorem* or the *Nyquist Theorem.*

The Nyquist Theorem states that in order to produce an accurate representation of a given frequency of sound, each cycle of the sound's vibration must be sampled a minimum of two times. If the sample rate is any lower, the system will read the incoming frequencies inaccurately and produce the wrong tones. (In concept, this is much like the effect seen in early motion pictures, where a wagon wheel will appear to rotate backward due to the low frame rates being used.) In digital audio, the false tones produced by this type of frequency distortion are known as *alias tones*.

Minimum Sample Rate

Because the range of human hearing is generally accepted to be 20 Hz to 20 kHz, the Nyquist Theorem tells us that a sampling rate of at least 40 kHz (twice the upper range of human hearing) is required to capture full-frequency audio.

Most professional digital recording devices today offer sample rates of 96 kHz or higher. The digital information on an audio CD is stored at a standard sample rate of 44.1 kHz.

The Importance of Bit Depth

Computers use strings of binary digits, or *bits* (0s or 1s), to represent each sample measurement that is collected. The number of bits used for each sample is referred to as the *binary word length*, or bit depth.

The more binary digits included in the bit depth, the greater the accuracy of each sample measurement. The relative amplitude (or loudness) of each sample is *quantized*, or rounded to the closest available whole-number value within the word length.

 The range of numeric values available for each sample at a given bit depth is equal to 2 to the nth power (2^n), where n is the number of bits in the binary word.

By way of example, consider a 4-bit binary word. This word length can represent only 16 different amplitude levels (2^4). As such, this 4-bit binary word would record audio using 16 discrete amplitude levels. By contrast, a 16-bit digital word could represent 65,536 discrete amplitude levels (2^{16}), creating a much more continuous dynamic response. A 24-bit digital word could define more than 16 million discrete amplitude levels (2^{24}).

Larger binary words are able to quantify variations in amplitude with much greater accuracy. Therefore, a 24-bit audio file will always more accurately reflect the dynamic range of the original sound than its 16-bit counterpart.

 Thirty-two-bit floating-point files represent discrete amplitude levels in the same way as 24-bit files. The 8 additional bits provide exponent biasing and allow for headroom above full-scale 24-bit audio.

Calculating Dynamic Range

A very general rule of thumb can be used to calculate the dynamic range capability of a digital system. By multiplying the word size by six, you can estimate the useful dynamic range of a fixed-point system.

For example, a system with an **8-bit** binary word would produce a dynamic range of about 48 dB (8 × 6), while a **16-bit** system would accommodate a 96-dB dynamic range (16 × 6). A **24-bit** system would have a theoretical dynamic range of 144 dB (24 × 6).

 In theoretical terms, the dynamic range (or signal-to-quantization noise ratio) increases by approximately 6 dB for each bit added to the binary word length.

Minimum Bit Depth

The useful dynamic range of speech and music is generally considered to be from 40 to 105 dB. To capture this range, an A/D converter must be able to accurately represent differences in amplitude of at least 65 dB; stated another way, it must have a minimum 65-dB dynamic range. This would require at least 11 bits in the binary word.

To provide an adequate dynamic range while minimizing the impact of the noise floor, and allowing a healthy amount of headroom, Logic Pro uses a minimum word length of 16 bits. Greater bit depths can be used to increase precision and accommodate a wider dynamic range.

Sample Rate, Bit Depth, and File Size

A consequence of files with higher sample rates and greater bit depths is the increased storage capacity required to record them. Each minute of 16-bit/44.1-kHz mono audio occupies about 5 MB of storage space. Higher sample rates increase the storage requirement. At 96-kHz, each minute of 16-bit mono audio requires about 11 MB of storage space.

Increasing the bit depth has the same effect. For example, one minute of 24-bit/44.1-kHz mono audio occupies about 7.5 MB of hard-drive storage space, while the same audio in a 32-bit float file (at 44.1 kHz) will require about 10 MB of hard-drive space per minute.

 Logic Pro supports audio recording at up to 24 bits and 192 kHz. When bouncing audio, Logic Pro supports resolutions of up to 32-bit floating point.

 Stereo files require twice as much storage space as mono files, since each file includes two channels of audio (left and right).

Recording in Digital Format

When you are recording into Logic Pro using an audio source that is already in a digital form (from a S/PDIF or ADAT input, for example), you don't need to translate the audio before bringing it into the system. The process of converting from digital to analog and back to digital can introduce distortion and degrade the original signal.

Digital Transfers

To prevent audio degradation, unnecessary conversions should be avoided. Audio kept in the digital domain while transferring between machines or devices will retain its sonic integrity and exhibit no discernible signal degradation.

Digital Audio Connections

On the rear panel of many audio interfaces are connections for accomplishing digital transfers. Common digital connections include *S/PDIF*, which uses RCA jacks (also called *coaxial jacks*), and *AES/EBU*, which uses XLR-type connectors. S/PDIF is the *Sony/Philips Digital Interface* standard, a consumer format, and AES/EBU is the *Audio Engineering Society/European Broadcast Union* digital interface standard, a professional format.

Although the formats are nearly identical in audio quality, if given the choice, you should use the AES/EBU format over S/PDIF. As a professional format, AES/EBU is technically more stable, and it filters out any copy protection encoded in the digital audio stream.

Logic Pro System Configurations

The requirements for your digital audio recording projects will determine the type of Logic Pro system that you will need to use.

Host-Based Systems Versus DSP-Accelerated Systems

Logic Pro systems can be either host-based, meaning they rely solely on the processing power of the host computer for routing, mixing, and processing of audio signals, or DSP-accelerated systems, meaning that the computer's processor is supplemented by additional processor chips dedicated to digital signal processing (DSP) for mixing and real-time processing.

DSP-accelerated Logic Pro systems involve the use of third-party products that feature DSP processing. The most common examples are the Apollo interfaces and UAD Satellite units by Universal Audio.

Audio Interface Options

An audio interface provides the analog-to-digital conversion required for recording to Logic Pro, as well as the digital-to-analog conversion required for playback from Logic Pro to your analog speakers or headphones. Logic Pro can be run without an audio interface, using your computer's built-in speakers or headphone jack for playback; however, recording options may be limited or unavailable.

Examples of Audio Interfaces

All versions of Logic Pro support a range of audio hardware:

- **Basic Interfaces**—Logic Pro supports a variety of hardware I/O options. Basic interfaces typically connect to your computer via USB. Most small interfaces are powered by the computer's USB bus, simplifying setup and enabling portability for laptop systems.

Figure 1.6 Focusrite's Scarlett 2i2 and 2i4 (pictured) are excellent entry-level interfaces

- **Mid-Range Interfaces**—Logic Pro supports a huge number of inputs and outputs, so larger interfaces (or combinations of interfaces) can be used. You should consider a mid-range interface if you need more than just a few of channels of input and output. You may also consider stepping up to a mid-range interface if you're looking for additional features, better quality microphone preamps, or higher quality convertors.

Figure 1.7 MOTU's UltraLite Mk3 is an affordable, mid-range interface

- **High-End Interfaces** – If you're looking for an interface with a large number of inputs and outputs, you'll most likely want to consider a high-end interface from manufacturers such as Antelope Audio, Apogee, Focusrite, or Universal Audio. These interfaces offer as many as 64 channels of input and output to accommodate the largest recording configurations. You may also want to step up to a high-end interface if you're looking for the absolute best quality in terms of microphone preamps and convertors.

Figure 1.8 Antelope Audio's Orion Studio is high-end interface with 32 channels of I/O

Shortcuts and Naming Conventions

Most Logic Pro controls, tools, procedures, and menus have a variety of shortcuts available. You'll find it helpful to familiarize yourself with common keys that are used in tasks you perform frequently.

Keyboard Commands

Many keyboard commands in Logic Pro use *modifier keys*. Modifiers are keys pressed in combination with other keys or with a mouse action. The modifier keys on available on Mac-based systems include:

- Command key
- Option key
- Control key
- Shift key

File Saving and Naming Conventions

You may encounter a variety of file types while working in Logic Pro. When you save a Logic Pro project, you have the option to save it as a package (which saves everything into a single large, self-contained project file) or a folder (which saves a smaller project file within a top-level folder, along with its associated audio files and other media assets in separate sub-folders).

File Name Extensions

Logic Pro projects use the *.logicx* file extension. Older logic projects used a *.logic* extension. WAV files have the *.wav* file extension, and AIFF files have the *.aif* file extension.

Incompatible ASCII Characters

Logic Pro file names cannot use ASCII characters that are incompatible with the operating system. The following characters should generally be avoided in order to maintain compatibility:

/ (slash)

: (colon)

You should also avoid any character typed while holding a modifier on your Mac system.

Review/Discussion Questions

1. Name and describe five types of production tasks that Logic Pro can be used for. (See "The Logic Pro Digital Audio Workstation" beginning on page 2.)

2. What is the frequency range of human hearing? (See "Audio Characteristics: Waveform, Frequency, and Amplitude" beginning on page 7.)

3. What does the frequency of a sound wave affect in terms of how we perceive the sound? How is frequency measured? (See "Audio Characteristics: Waveform, Frequency, and Amplitude" beginning on page 7.)

4. What does the amplitude of the sound wave affect? How is amplitude measured? (See "Audio Characteristics: Waveform, Frequency, and Amplitude" beginning on page 7.)

5. How does the sample rate of a system relate to the frequency of audio it can capture? What is the name of the law that specifies the relationship between sample rate and audio frequency? (See "The Importance of Sample Rate" beginning on page 9.)

6. How does the bit depth of a system relate to the dynamic range of audio it can capture? How can you estimate the dynamic range of a system? (See "The Importance of Bit Depth" beginning on page 10.)

7. What are some common digital connections that may be available on an audio interface? What type of connector jack does each use? (See "Recording in Digital Format" on page 11.)

8. Name some audio interfaces that are compatible with standard Logic Pro software. (See "Audio Interface Options" beginning on page 12.)

 To review additional material from this chapter and prepare for certification, see the Logic Pro 101 Study Guide module available through the Elements|ED online learning platform at ElementsED.com.

Selecting Your Audio Production Gear

🎧 Activity

In this exercise, you will define your audio production needs and select components for a home studio based around Logic Pro software. By balancing your wants and needs against a defined budget, you will be able to determine which hardware and software options make sense for you.

🕐 Duration

This exercise should take approximately 10 minutes to complete.

✦ Goals/Targets

- Identify a budget for your home studio
- Explore microphone options
- Explore audio interface options
- Explore speakers/monitoring options
- Consider other expenses
- Identify appropriate components to complete your system

Getting Started

To get started, you will create a list of needs and define an overall budget for your home studio setup. This budget should be sufficient to cover all aspects of your initial needs for basic audio production work. At the same time, you'll want to be careful to keep your budget realistic so that you can afford the upfront investment. Keep in mind that you can add to your basic setup over time to increase your capabilities.

Use the table below to outline your basic requirements and to serve as a guide when you begin shopping for options. Place an **X** in the appropriate column for your expected needs in each row.

Do not include MIDI gear in this table, as we will address that separately.

 This exercise assumes that you own a compatible computer with built-in speakers for playback. Do not include a host computer in this table.

Function or Component	Not Required	Minimum Configuration	Expanded Configuration with additional inputs and preamps
Audio Interface: Input Channels (Recording)	–	1 to 2 Inputs	4 to 8 Inputs
Audio Interface: Output Channels (Playback)	–	2 Outputs (for stereo playback)	4 to 8 Outputs (for stereo playback and output to external gear)
Input Device(s) (Microphones)	–	USB Microphone	XLR Microphone(s) (specify type and number)
Output Device(s)	Built-in Computer Speakers	Headphones	Stereo Monitor Speakers
Accessories and Other (List or Describe) (Stands, Soundproofing, Software Add-Ons, etc.)			

Available Budget for the Above: _____

Identifying Prices

Your next step is to begin identifying prices for equipment that will meet your needs. Using the requirements you identified above as a guide, do some Internet research at an online music retailer of your choice to identify appropriate options for each of the items listed in the table below. You may also want to browse some manufacturers' websites for more information.

Component	Manufacturer and Model	Unit Cost
Audio Interface		
Microphones		
Headphones		
Monitor Speakers		
Accessories/Other		
TOTAL		

Finishing Up

To finalize your purchase decisions, compare the total in the table above to the budget you allocated. If you find that your budget is not sufficient to cover the total cost, you will need to determine which purchase items you can postpone (or consider purchasing bundled option). On the other hand, if you have money left over in your budget, you can consider upgrade options.

Chapter 2

Getting Started with Logic Pro

This chapter covers basic requirements to get up and running with Logic Pro. It reviews the Logic Pro software components and installers, as well as the file structure used for Logic Pro projects. It also introduces the basic user interface for the software and reviews menu operations. The second half of this chapter provides an overview of the primary windows in Logic Pro.

⊕ Learning Targets for This Chapter

- Understand the components included with a Logic Pro system and how to access installers

- Recognize the basic Logic Pro project file structure

- Understand basic Logic Pro software and plug-in options

- Power up a Logic Pro system

- Navigate the Logic Pro menu system to locate common commands

- Recognize and work in the main Logic Pro windows

 Key topics from this chapter are illustrated in the Logic Pro 101 Study Guide module available through the Elements|ED online learning platform. Sign up at ElementsED.com.

This chapter presents an overview of basic Logic Pro operations and functions. You will be introduced to the filing structure that Logic Pro uses for its projects and backups, the steps required to start up a Logic Pro system, and the primary elements of the main Logic Pro windows.

Target Systems

Although the concepts discussed in this book are applicable to most versions of Logic Pro, the book is specifically written for Logic Pro 10.6. While any recent version of Logic Pro can be used with this book, certain menus, commands, and functions may differ from one configuration to another.

All descriptions are based on the user interface and functionality in Logic Pro 10.6, unless otherwise noted.

 You can try Logic Pro free for 90 days by visiting the Apple website at https://www.apple.com/logic-pro/trial/.

Software Installation and Operation

All Logic Pro software versions use the same software installation through the Mac App Store. Additional content included with Logic Pro can be downloaded and managed through the Sound Library Manager found within the software.

Installing Logic Pro

Installation of Logic Pro is available through the Mac App Store using your Apple ID. Essential content will download and install when Logic Pro is opened for the first time, and additional content can be installed when desired.

To download Logic Pro from the Mac App Store, do the following:

1. If you do not already have an Apple ID, create an account for free on the Apple website. If you already have an Apple ID, proceed to step 2.

2. Open the Mac App Store application and log in with your Apple ID.

3. Browse the App Store or use the search bar to locate Logic Pro.

4. Place your mouse over the blue price in the top right to reveal the **BUY** button to make your purchase. If you have already purchased the software, this button will be replaced by a **GET** button, **UPDATE** button, or cloud-download icon. (See Figure 2.1.)

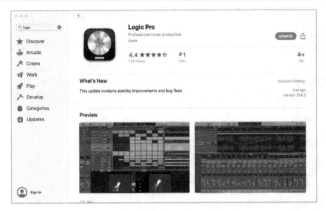

Figure 2.1 Logic Pro in the App Store

5. Once the blue button changes to a **GET** button or cloud-download icon, click the button to start the download. Logic Pro will begin downloading and will automatically install to your Mac.

    When complete, you will be able to launch Logic Pro from the App Store (by clicking the **OPEN** button) or from your computer's Applications folder.

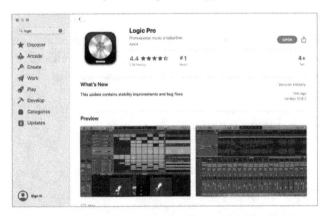

Figure 2.2 You can open Logic Pro from within the App Store.

Included Plug-Ins and Additional Content

Logic Pro comes with a large selection of Apple Loops, patches, drum kits, plug-in settings, sampler instruments and their settings, impulse responses, and legacy content that you can use in your projects. Essential content begins downloading on first launch of the software. You can select additional content to be downloaded at any time, using the Sound Library Manager. (See Figure 2.3.) To access the Sound Library Manager, choose **LOGIC PRO > SOUND LIBRARY > OPEN SOUND LIBRARY MANAGER**.

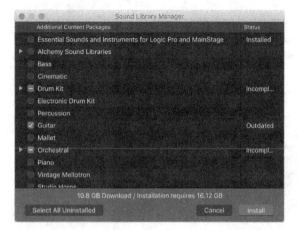

Figure 2.3 You can select additional content to download in the Sound Library Manager

 If you cancel the content download during the initial launch, you can restart it in the Sound Library Manager by selecting Essential Sounds and Instruments.

Plug-Ins

Plug-ins are special-purpose software components that provide additional signal processing and other functionality within Logic Pro. Logic Pro plug-ins can be used in two ways: for track-based inserts, which process audio in real time using the host computer's processing power, and for selection-based processing, which provide non-real-time, file-based processing.

Version 10.6 of Logic Pro includes the following additional software options:

- 70 effect plug-ins including Pedalboard, with 35 stompboxes

- 24 software instrument plug-ins

- 9 MIDI plug-ins

- 4,300 Patches for Audio, Auxiliary, Software Instrument, and Output tracks

- 10,500 royalty-free Apple Loops covering a wide range of genres

- 2,000 Sampler instruments

- 660 reverb spaces and warped effects for Space Designer

Audio and MIDI Effects

Logic Pro comes with an extensive collection of audio effects in these categories: Amps and Pedals, Delay, Distortion, Dynamics, EQ, Filter, Imaging, Metering, Modulation, Multi Effects, Pitch, Reverb,

Specialized, and Utility. The assortment covers commonly used audio effects for mixing and mastering, as well as more specialized effects designed for unique and creative results.

MIDI plug-ins can be inserted on Software Instrument tracks to process MIDI in real-time with effects like Arpeggiator, Chord Trigger, Transposer, and others. Custom MIDI effects can even be created with JavaScript using the Scripter plug-in.

Instruments

Logic Pro has an extensive collection of software instruments that use MIDI input to create sound. The assortment includes sample-based instruments (Alchemy, Sampler, Quick Sampler, and Studio Instruments), percussion synthesizers and instruments (Drum Synth, Ultrabeat, Drum Kit Designer, and Drum Machine Designer), vintage modeling instruments (Vintage B3 Organ, Vintage Electric Piano, Vintage Clav, and Vintage Melotron), synthesizers (Retro Synth, ES1, ES2, ES P, ES M, ES E, and EFM1), a modeling synthesizer (Sculpture), a vocoder (EVOC 20 PolySynth), and utilities (Klopfgeist and Test Oscillator). In addition to these, Logic Pro has an External Instrument plug-in that can be used to integrate hardware synthesizers or drum machines into a project.

Logic Pro Software Features

Version 10.6 of Logic Pro provides the following features:

- Up to 1000 Audio channel strips

- Up to 1000 Auxiliary channel strips

- Up to 1000 Software Instrument channel strips

- Up to 1000 External MIDI tracks

- Up to 256 busses

- Up to 15 inserts for internal or Audio Unit effects plug-ins

- Up to 8 inserts for internal or Audio Unit MIDI plug-ins

- Up to 12 sends per channel strip, pre- or post-fader, pre- or post-pan

- Audio file and I/O resolution up to 24-bit/192kHz

- Non-destructive, random-access editing and mix automation

- Ability to open GarageBand songs directly

- Support for all standard surround sound configurations

- ReWire support for Reason, Ableton Live, and other compatible applications

- 1929 definable key and MIDI commands

Logic Pro and GarageBand

Both Logic Pro and GarageBand are music production applications developed by Apple. While the two DAWs are separate, GarageBand is like a younger sibling and shares many of the same features and workflows as Logic Pro. GarageBand users can easily transition to Logic Pro and utilize the advanced tools and features if they desire.

Logic Pro File Structure

With all of the software components properly installed, you may be anxious to launch Logic Pro and get to work. But before you create your first Logic Pro document, or *project*, it is helpful to understand how the software interacts with the various files that are related to the project.

Logic Pro stores projects as either *Packages* or *Folders*. Project Folders store the project components separately, with the project file maintaining a roadmap to the external media files and assets it uses. Project Packages, on the other hand, have all the component contents packaged into a single, self-contained file.

 Additional information on creating Logic Pro projects is provided in Chapter 4.

File Organization

When you create a Logic Pro project as a Folder, the system sets up a standard hierarchy for the project and its associated files by automatically creating a top-level project folder. This folder contains the project file (*filename.logicx*) as well as subfolders for various supplemental files used for the project. (See Figure 2.4.) When you record, convert, import, or edit material, specific files can get stored in each of these subfolders.

Figure 2.4 Logic Pro project file hierarchy

Logic Pro keeps related files together in this hierarchy to facilitate project backups and transfers between different Logic Pro systems.

Project Components

The types of files that may be used in a Logic Pro project are described in the following sections. Many of these files are created automatically as you work, although some files are generated by export operations only. Project components can be saved directly in the project package or in subfolder locations within the project folder hierarchy. They can also be referenced from another location outside the project. The project configuration (package or folder) can be selected from the **SAVE AS** dialogue box and through the Assets Project Settings found under **FILE > PROJECT SETTINGS > ASSETS**.

Logic Pro Project File

A *project file* is the document that Logic Pro creates when you start a new project. When you select the Folder configuration option, Logic Pro creates this file along with various subfolders inside a project folder of the same name. Project files created in Logic Pro version 10.0 and later are recognizable by their *.logicx* extensions. (Projects from Logic 5 or later can be opened with current Logic Pro software.)

 The Package configuration option saves all of the project components described below within the *.logicx* package file.

The project file contains a map of all the tracks, audio files, video files, settings, and edits associated with your project. Project documents can be saved and reopened, recalling a given project with all of its edit information, input/output assignments, and links to the associated media files. You can easily copy and rename project documents to save alternate versions of a project without changing the source audio.

 Optionally, you can save alternate versions using Project Alternatives within a single project file. Project Alternatives are discussed in Chapter 4 of this book.

Alchemy Samples Folder

If the Alchemy Synth is used in a project, any audio data used for the instrument will be stored in this folder. This folder is created only when you use Alchemy in your project.

 When sharing projects with Logic Pro systems that have the same instruments and sounds downloaded, assets from Alchemy, Sampler, Ultrabeat, Space Designer, and Apple Loops are not necessary to include in a project folder.

Audio Files Folder

The Audio Files folder is where imported and recorded audio files are saved while working with Logic Pro. This is the only folder that is created automatically regardless of how assets are configured in a project.

When you record audio into an unsaved Logic Pro project, each recording is initially stored in a folder within a temporary Untitled Project Package located within the default Logic folder. Once the project is saved, the files are moved from the temporary location to the Audio Files folder of the project.

You can change the location of the temporary Project Package in the AUDIO RECORDING PATH section of the Recording Project Settings dialog box (FILE > PROJECT SETTINGS > RECORDING).

Logic Pro supports audio files in AIFF, CAF, and WAV (BWF) format for recording, and AIFF, WAV (BWF), CAF, SDII, Apple Lossless, eligible MP3, and AAC for playback.

 When you record Audio in a Logic Pro project configured as a Folder, the audio is saved *only* in the Audio Files folder, not within the project file itself. To transfer projects between systems, be sure to copy the entire top-level project folder in order to include all associated audio files and project components.

Note that when you import audio into Logic Pro, the imported files are not automatically copied to the Audio Files folder. Instead, Logic Pro will simply reference the files from their original location on your computer's connected drive. This is also the case for any Apple Loops used in the project.

Imported audio and Apple Loops can also be copied to the project package or folder. This copy behavior can be configured when first saving a project and can be modified later when using the **SAVE AS** or **SAVE A COPY AS** commands.

 It's a good idea to copy all media files to an archive when you finish a Logic Pro project to ensure that all required files remain available for the project.

 For details on creating a self-contained archive or backup project, see Chapter 10 in this book.

Bounces Folder

The Bounces folder is the directory that Logic Pro uses by default for files created using the Bounce function. If you do not use the Bounce operation, this folder will not be created.

Freeze Files Folder

When you freeze a track, the track is bounced to an audio file and saved in the Freeze Files folder. When you unfreeze a track, the bounced audio file will automatically be removed from the Freeze Files folder. If you do not use Freeze, this folder will not be created.

Impulse Responses Folder

If the Space Designer plug-in is used in a project, any impulse responses used by the plug-in will be stored in this folder. If you do not use Space Designer, the folder will not be created.

Movie Files Folder

The Movie Files folder is used when you import a video into a project. Logic Pro supports QuickTime video files (.MOV and .MP4). When importing a QuickTime movie, you have the option to import the audio as well. Imported audio will be saved to the Audio Files folder. If no video file is copied to the project, the Movie Files folder will not be created.

Samples Folder

If Sampler or Quick Sampler are used in a project, the associated instruments will have their samples stored in this folder. If you do not use a sample-based instrument, this folder will not be created.

Ultrabeat Samples Folder

If the Ultrabeat Drum Machine is used in a project, the associated drum samples will be stored in this folder. If you do not use Ultrabeat, this folder will not be created.

About MIDI Files

MIDI data is normally stored within the Logic Pro project file; as such, no MIDI files exist outside of the project document. However, MIDI files can be exported from Logic Pro using the **FILE > EXPORT > SELECTION AS MIDI FILE** command.

About Project Backups

Auto backups are enabled in Logic Pro by default. This function retains previously saved versions of the project, allowing you to return to an earlier saved state. Backups are not saved as separate files on disk, but rather as recoverable states within a project. You can restore an earlier version of an open project by choosing **FILE > REVERT TO** and selecting from the available backups.

 You can specify the number of backup files to retain under the PROJECT HANDLING tab of the General Preferences dialog box (LOGIC PRO > PREFERENCES > GENERAL).

Starting Logic Pro

Because Logic Pro systems are often composed of both hardware and software, preparing your system for use might involve more than simply turning on your computer and launching the Logic Pro application. The larger the system, the more important it becomes to follow a specific startup sequence.

Powering Up Your Hardware

When starting up your Logic Pro hardware, you'll need to turn on the system components in the proper order. Starting components out of sequence could cause a component to not be recognized. This could prevent the software from launching or cause unexpected behavior.

The recommended sequence for starting a Logic Pro system is as follows:

1.   Start with all your equipment (including your computer) powered off.

2.   Turn on any external hard drives that require external power and wait for them to spin up to speed.

3.   Turn on any MIDI interfaces and MIDI devices that require external power (including any MIDI control surfaces) as well as any synchronization peripherals, if used.

4.   Turn on your audio interface (if not bus powered). Wait several seconds for the audio interface to initialize.

5.   Start your computer and launch Logic Pro.

6.   Turn on your audio monitoring system, if applicable. This should always be the last component that you start up, to prevent any signal surges from reaching your speakers during the power-up process.

(i)   Many audio interfaces get their power from the computer (via a USB port or other connection); these interfaces do not need to be powered up in advance.

Launching Logic Pro

Logic Pro software can be launched by double-clicking on the application icon on the system's internal drive (see Figure 2.5) or by double-clicking on a shortcut to the application. Logic Pro is typically placed under Applications\Logic Pro.app, and an application shortcut is placed in the dock.

Figure 2.5 The Logic Pro application icon

The first time you launch Logic Pro, you will be prompted with a message box with links to additional information for beginners and descriptions of features of the current version. A collection of essential audio resources will also begin downloading. This download provides a selection of sounds, instruments, and loops that let you start making music immediately.

You can click the **DOWNLOAD LATER** button, if desired, to cancel the download and complete it at a later time, or wait for the download to complete.

Once you've proceeded past the initial dialog box, you will be presented with the Project Chooser. This dialog box lets you create a new project or open an existing one. For now if you'd like to explore, you can choose to create a new project. Details on working with projects are provided starting in Chapter 4.

Accessing Connected Audio Devices

When Logic Pro launches, it will generally be configured to use the default audio device or the last configured device. If no supported audio interface is found, Logic Pro will launch using the built-in audio capabilities on your Mac, meaning it will play back through the built-in speakers on your computer (if available) and record through the built-in microphone(s) (if available).

 If your supported audio interface is connected but not recognized by Logic Pro, you may need to install or update the device drivers. Check the manufacturer's website for the latest drivers for your interface.

To configure Logic Pro to use a specific audio device, such as a connected USB microphone or a separate audio interface, you will need to go to the Devices tab of the Audio Preferences dialog box by choosing **LOGIC PRO > PREFERENCES > AUDIO**. (See Figure 2.6.)

Figure 2.6 Logic Pro audio device settings in the Devices tab of the Audio Preferences dialog box

 Logic Pro limits the tools and features that are visible upon initial launch of the software. (This look is reminiscent of GarageBand.) To get the most out of Logic Pro, we recommend enabling the SHOW ADVANCED TOOLS option in the Advanced Preferences dialog box and clicking the ENABLE ALL button to access all features.

Optimizing Logic Pro Performance

The Devices tab of the Audio Preferences dialog box is also used to optimize the performance of Logic Pro software. Like most audio software, Logic Pro utilizes the computer's processing capacity to carry out operations such as recording, playback, mixing, and plug-in processing (effects and virtual instruments).

While the default system settings are adequate in some scenarios, Logic Pro lets you adjust a system's performance using the Sample Rate setting in the General tab of the Audio Project Settings dialog box (**FILE > PROJECT SETTINGS**) and the Latency setting in the Devices tab of the Audio Preferences dialog box.

Sample Rate Settings

The Sample Rate setting in the General tab of the Audio Project Settings dialog box will affect the quality of the audio that is going into or out of your system through a connected audio interface. The Sample Rate setting will also determine the sample rate of audio files that result from recording on an Audio track.

A higher sample rate requires more processing power than a lower sample rate and will reduce the number of tracks and plug-ins you can run on a particular computer. For this reason, many producers prefer to work with sample rates of 44,100 and 48,000. While high-definition sample rates (such as 88,200 and 96,000) will result in better fidelity in the studio, they don't necessarily translate to better quality in final mixes that are distributed as MP3 files or streamed on services such as SoundCloud or Spotify.

Latency Settings

The I/O Buffer Size setting in the Devices tab of the Audio Preferences dialog box controls the size of the buffer and the associated latency you'll experience when tracking. This buffer handles processing tasks such as plug-in processing.

- Low I/O Buffer Size settings reduce monitoring latency for recording or monitoring an active input.

- High I/O Buffer Size settings provide more processing power for mixing, at the expense of greater monitoring latency.

 CPU thread processing and other settings are available in the Devices tab of the Audio Preferences dialog box for further optimization.

As a general rule, the I/O Buffer Size should be set as low as your project will allow, in order to minimize latency when monitoring an active input. You may need to change the setting later as your project becomes more complex.

Low Latency Mode

Logic Pro offers an additional option for reducing latency on tracks with an active input. By activating Low Latency Mode, recorded audio will bypass any plug-ins that introduce latency in the signal path. The amount of allowable latency for this mode can be set in the General tab of the Audio Preferences dialog box.

Modifying Performance Settings

Adjustments to the Sample Rate setting can be made in the Project Settings dialog box, as follows:

1. Choose **FILE > PROJECT SETTINGS > AUDIO**.

2. From the **Sample Rate** pop-up menu, choose the desired sample rate.

Adjustments to the I/O Buffer Size setting can be made in the Audio Preferences dialog box, as follows:

1. Choose **LOGIC PRO > AUDIO**.

2. From the **DEVICES** tab, click on the I/O Buffer Size pop-up menu and select the buffer size in samples – lower the setting to reduce latency; raise it to increase processing power for plug-ins.

The Logic Pro Menu Structure

Before beginning to work on a project, you should have some basic familiarity with the Logic Pro software interface, including the menu structure and the primary windows.

Among the first things you see upon launching Logic Pro is the menu system across the top of the screen. (See Figure 2.7.) Learning how the menus are organized will save you a lot of time when you are trying to find a specific Logic Pro function. Following is a brief description of each menu.

Figure 2.7 Logic Pro Menu Bar

Logic Pro Menu

The Logic Pro menu lets you access preferences, set up control surfaces, edit key commands, manage the sound library, and quit Logic Pro.

File Menu

The File menu lets you perform various file-based commands. The File menu includes options for opening, creating, and saving projects and Project Alternatives; accessing project settings; bouncing tracks; and importing and exporting audio, video, and MIDI.

Edit Menu

The Edit menu allows you to edit and manipulate the media in your current selection. The Edit menu includes options for cutting, copying, and pasting; duplicating and shifting selections; trimming, splitting, and joining regions; and applying tempo operations.

Track Menu

The Track menu lets you perform track-based operations, such as creating, duplicating, grouping, deleting, and modifying tracks.

Navigate Menu

The Navigate menu allows you to move around within a Logic Pro project. The Navigate menu includes options for setting and moving the locator; creating, deleting, and managing markers; and adjusting playback options.

Record Menu

The Record menu allows you to configure settings for recording. This menu includes options for Metronome and Count-in settings; enabling and disabling Musical Grid, Quick Punch-in, Input Monitoring, and Low Latency Mode; Overlap Recording behaviors; and other Recording settings.

Mix Menu

The Mix menu allows you to adjust settings for Automation, Groups, and I/O handling. The Mix menu includes options for showing and hiding Automation; creating, deleting, and editing Automation and Automation Groups; adjusting Automation Preferences; configuring I/O Labels and Assignments; and toggling between Pre-Fader and Post-Fader Metering.

View Menu

The View menu commands affect the display within Logic Pro's Main Window. Most View menu commands show or hide parts of other windows as panes within the Main Window. Selecting a command will display a component part of a window, and deselecting the command will hide it. Other commands in this menu include view options for the control bar, Toolbar, and color palette. Most views can be toggled with the available buttons in the control bar.

 Though commonly confused, the View menu and the Window menu serve different functions. Commands in the View menu affect *parts* of a window or change how the elements within the Main Window are displayed. By contrast, commands in the Window menu show or hide *entire* windows on the screen.

Window Menu

The Window menu allows you to display various Logic Pro windows. The Window menu includes commands for displaying the Main Window and Mixer; Smart Controls and various Editor windows; MIDI Transform and MIDI Environment; Floating window options of the Main Window; various Keyboard windows; and others.

Screensets Menu

The Screensets menu allows you to access and manage Screensets for your Logic Pro project. The Screensets menu includes options for creating, deleting, editing, and selecting Screensets.

 The Screensets menu will display the current Screenset number. The default for a new project is Screenset 1, displayed as 1 in the menu bar.

 Screensets are stored configurations of the currently displayed windows in your project. Saving multiple Screensets lets you quickly toggle between different window layouts and onscreen views.

Help Menu

The Help menu allows you to show or hide the Quick Help display and provides links to important documentation and online resources, including the Logic Pro Manuals and Release Notes; Logic Pro Support and Discussion Communities; and more.

Logic Pro Windows and Views

Logic Pro software provides a host of windows you can use to perform a variety of tasks and functions. Many of these windows can be shown and hidden as displays within the Main Window. This allows you to access associated tools and views without needing to open separate windows.

The primary components that you will need to be familiar with to begin working with Logic Pro include the following:

- The control bar at the top of the Main Window.

- The two main views in the Workspace: the Tracks Area view and the Live Loops Grid.

- The Inspector on the left side of the Main Window.

Other windows and views that you will want to be familiar with are the Library, Loop Browser, Mixer, and Editors.

Figure 2.8 Main Window in Logic Pro showing the control bar (top), Inspector (left), and Tracks Area with regions (right)

Control Bar

The control bar runs along the top of the Main Window. (See Figure 2.9.) This area has several buttons to show or hide other displays and panels. It also includes transport controls for playback operations and information about the project meter, tempo, and key signature.

Figure 2.9 The control bar in the Logic Pro Main Window

 As mentioned earlier in this chapter, many of the available displays and panels have separate windows that can be opened if desired. These can be found under the Window menu.

The Library

The **LIBRARY** button on the control bar displays a panel that contains patches and FX chains for the selected channel strip or plug-in. Users can access this panel to quickly browse different presets and try out sounds. You can show or hide the Library panel by pressing the **Y** key on the computer keyboard.

Figure 2.10 The Library button selected in the control bar

The Inspector

The **INSPECTOR** button opens the Inspector panel allowing you to edit selected Region, Track, and Channel Strip settings. You can hide or show the Inspector by pressing the I key.

The image below shows the Hi-Hat track in the Inspector view. Region settings are visible at the top of the Inspector, and Track settings are collapsed and hidden from view. Below these settings are two channel strips. The right channel strip typically displays track information for hardware outputs or Auxiliary return channels. Here, the left channel strip shows the Hi-Hat track, while the right shows the settings for the **Stereo Output** channel.

Figure 2.11 The Inspector button selected in the control bar (top) and the resulting display

The Quick Help Button

The **QUICK HELP** button (circle with a question mark) displays coaching tips as you hover the mouse cursor over areas and tools. You can show or hide Quick Help by clicking the button or pressing **SHIFT+/**.

Figure 2.12 The Quick Help button selected in the control bar

The Toolbar

The Toolbar is an optional display that appears right below the control bar. Clicking the **TOOLBAR** button in the control bar will toggle this row of commonly used edit tools on/off. You can show or hide the Toolbar by clicking the Toolbar button or pressing **CONTROL+OPTION+COMMAND+T**.

Figure 2.13 The Toolbar button selected in the control bar

Figure 2.14 The Logic Pro Toolbar display

 You can customize the display in the control bar or the Toolbar by Control-clicking and selecting CUSTOMIZE CONTROL BAR AND DISPLAY or CUSTOMIZE TOOLBAR, respectively, from the pop-up menu.

Smart Controls

The **SMART CONTROLS** button opens a panel below the Tracks Area that enables you to edit a track's sound in a limited capacity without having to open up the current channel strip or effects chain. You can show or hide the Smart Controls panel by pressing the **B** key.

Figure 2.15 The Smart Controls button selected in the control bar

Mixer

The **MIXER** button opens the Logic Pro Mixer display below the Tracks Area. The Mixer display provides a mixer-like environment for working with tracks. In the Mixer window, tracks appear as mixer strips (also called *channel strips*). Each track displayed in the Mixer window has controls for applying inserts and sends, selecting input and output assignments, selecting an Automation mode, and setting pan and volume for the track. The channel strips also provide buttons for enabling record and toggling solo and mute on and off.

Figure 2.16 The Mixer button selected in the control bar

The Mixer display and the floating Mixer window provide the following controls:

- **Signal Routing Controls**—The top portion of each track's mixer strip provides controls for routing signals for the track. These include Audio or MIDI FX selectors for applying plug-in processors, Send selectors for routing to an output or bus, an Input selector for routing audio into the track for recording or processing, and an Output selector for routing audio out of the track for playback. At the bottom of this portion of the channel strip is an automation mode selector.

Figure 2.17 Signal routing controls

- **Record and Playback Controls**—The bottom portion of the mixer's channel strip provides controls for setting record and playback options. These include Pan controls for positioning the signal within the stereo field; a Volume Fader for setting the output level; and buttons to enable Input monitoring, Record, Solo, and Mute functions.

Figure 2.18 Record and playback controls

Editors

The **EDITORS** button opens a panel below the Tracks Area, giving you access to editing tools and options for audio, MIDI, patterns, or Drummer regions, depending on the type of region selected. You can show or hide the Editors by pressing the **E** key.

Figure 2.19 The Editors button selected in Logic Pro's control bar

Audio tracks have the following Editor displays:

- **Audio Track Editor**—The Audio Track Editor shows a closer view of audio regions used in your project. You can apply various non-destructive edits and functions, and perform Flex edits.

> Flex edits and Flex Time processing are discussed in Chapter 9 of this book.

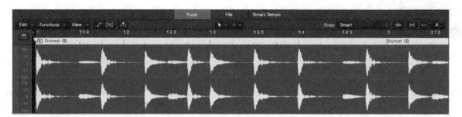

Figure 2.20 The Editor open on an Audio track showing the Audio Track Editor

- **Audio File Editor**—The Audio File Editor lets you perform destructive editing to audio files. This view also lets you edit transient markers, which is useful for time correction actions you perform using Flex Time.

> Destructive editing will permanently alter the original file on disk. Use this function with caution.

- **Smart Tempo Editor**—The Smart Tempo Editor lets you view and edit Smart Tempo analysis info. Smart Tempo actions can be applied to audio and MIDI regions, providing a convenient way to correct timing and synchronize content in your project.

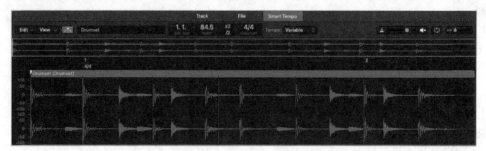

Figure 2.21 Smart Tempo Editor

Non-destructive editing leaves the original audio files unaltered, while destructive editing permanently changes the original files. Most edits should be applied using non-destructive editing, as it enables easy "recovery" of audio after an edit.

MIDI tracks have the following Editor displays:

- **Piano Roll Editor**—The Piano Roll Editor displays MIDI region events and provides various tools and functions for composing and editing MIDI performances. Multiple MIDI regions can be viewed and edited simultaneously. Additional tools include MIDI automation and quantization functions.

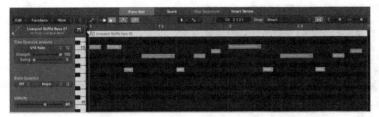

Figure 2.22 Piano Roll Editor

- **Score Editor**— The Score Editor lets you view, edit, arrange, and print MIDI data from your session as music notation. The Score Editor transcribes MIDI notes in real time and provides tools for navigating and editing in music notation. Tools for adjusting the layout and view are available in the Editor window. Additionally, various score symbols and notation tools are available in the Inspector.

Figure 2.23 Score Editor

- **Step Sequencer Editor**—The Step Sequencer Editor allows MIDI editing similar to a hardware step sequencer, using Pattern regions. MIDI notes and events are entered into a grid and can be manipulated in various ways.

Figure 2.24 Step Sequencer Editor

■ **Smart Tempo Editor**—The Smart Tempo Editor lets you view and edit Smart Tempo analysis info. Functionality for MIDI regions is similar to working with audio regions, as described above.

Drummer tracks have the following Editor displays:

■ **Drummer Editor**—The Drummer editor displays controls for the Drummer track. Drummer tracks use software drum kits and machines, but instead of editing MIDI regions, users can configure drum patterns based around drummers from various genre categories. Select patterns from presets or adjust performance settings in the editor. Preset pattern regions can also be accessed from the Loop Browser.

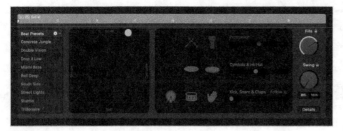

Figure 2.25 Drummer Editor

Transport Controls

The transport controls in the control bar provide buttons for various transport functions, such as play, stop, fast-forward, and rewind. These functions are available just to the left of the LCD in the control bar and are also available in a floating Transport window.

Figure 2.26 Transport floating window in Logic Pro

The LCD

The LCD in the Logic Pro control bar (and floating Transport window) displays helpful information about your project. You can double-click on any of the LCD sections to make changes for your project.

Figure 2.27 The LCD area in Logic Pro

  You can also open a larger floating bars and beats display or SMTPE time (timecode) display from the display mode pop-up by selecting **Open Giant Beats Display** or **Open Giant Time Display**, respectively.

By default, the LCD is set to **BEATS AND PROJECT.** This shows your project's playhead position, tempo, meter, and key signature. You can choose settings like **BEATS AND TIME** to display the playhead location in a combination of musical and absolute time formats.

The Beats and Project LCD view displays the following information:

■ **Playhead Position**—The left portion of the LCD indicates the position of the playhead, shown in Bars and Beats by default. It can also display smaller beat division and ticks, as well as absolute timecode/minutes and seconds values. You can click and drag on this display, or double-click and type in a new value, to reposition the playhead.

■ **Tempo**—The center LCD section displays your project's tempo. This can be set to follow your project's Tempo track in **KEEP** mode, or to adapt to detected tempo of recordings or imported audio with **ADAPT** mode. A third mode, **AUTO**, allows Logic to choose what best suits the situation.

■ **Project Information**—The right portion of the LCD shows information about your project, like its time signature and key signature. You can click on these values to change them.

(i) The LCD's current display can be changed by clicking on the display mode pop-up selector (down arrow) next to the project information section.

Replace

The **REPLACE** button lets you replace a recording or portion of an audio region during a record pass. The Replace button can be enabled/disabled by pressing the **/** key.

Figure 2.28 The Replace button selected in the control bar

Tuner

The **TUNER** button displays an onscreen tuner for any real instruments connected through your audio interface.

Figure 2.29 The Tuner button selected in the control bar

Solo

The **SOLO** button in the control bar lets you listen to selected regions in isolation from the rest of your mix. This Solo function can be enabled/disabled by pressing **CONTROL+S.**

Figure 2.30 The Solo button selected in the control bar

 If you unintentionally deselect regions while SOLO is enabled, the entire project will essentially be muted, and nothing will play. If you hear silence during playback, check to ensure that the SOLO button is disabled in the control bar.

Count In

The **COUNT IN** button is used in conjunction with the Logic Pro Metronome. The Count In feature gives performers a predetermined number of bars of click before recording starts. The Count In length can be specified by selecting **RECORD > COUNT IN** or clicking and holding down the **COUNT IN** button and then choosing the number of bars from the menu.

The Count In function can also be enabled/disabled by pressing **SHIFT+K**.

Figure 2.31 The Count In button selected in the control bar

Metronome

The **METRONOME** button activates a steady click during recording and/or playback. The tempo of the metronome click is determined by the project Tempo track. The Metronome can be enabled/disabled by pressing the **K** key.

Figure 2.32 The Metronome button selected in the control bar

You can click and hold the Metronome button to configure additional options from a pop-up menu.

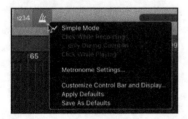

Figure 2.33 Additional metronome options in the Metronome button pop-up menu

Options available in the Metronome pop-up menu are discussed in Chapter 6 and Chapter 7 of this book.

List Editors

The **LIST EDITORS** button shows a list of markers, MIDI events, time signature changes, and key signature changes. Here you can view or add events to any of these lists.

You can show or hide the List Editors display by pressing the **D** key.

Figure 2.34 The List Editors button selected in the control bar

Note Pads

The **NOTE PADS** button displays a panel that lets users create, view, and edit text and image notes for the entire project or for specific tracks. You can show or hide Note Pads by pressing **OPTION+COMMAND+P**.

Figure 2.35 The Note Pads button selected in the control bar

Loop Browser

The **LOOP BROWSER** button displays a tabbed panel that lets you browse and add pre-recorded Software Instrument (MIDI) and audio loops to your project. Logic includes a large library of royalty free loops. Each loop has information about key, tempo, and length.

You can mark loops as favorites and browse using descriptors like genre or instrument type. You can drag loops onto existing tracks or onto cells in the Live Loops Grid (discussed later in this chapter). You can also drag loops into the workspace below your existing tracks to add them to a new track.

To show or hide the Loop Browser, press the **O** key.

Figure 2.36 The Loop Browser button selected in the control bar

Browsers

The **BROWSERS** button displays the Browsers panel. This panel lets you view any audio or media files that are currently in your project or search for media on your system. You can also import content from other projects.

You can show or hide the Browsers panel by pressing the **F** key.

Figure 2.37 The Browsers button selected in the control bar

Tracks Area

The Tracks Area provides a timeline display of audio, MIDI data, video, and mixer automation for recording, editing, and arranging tracks. (See Figure 2.38, below.) This view displays waveforms for Audio Regions, MIDI event data for MIDI Regions, pseudo-waveforms for Drummer Regions, and Step Sequencer Patterns for Pattern Regions.

Each Audio, Software Instrument, and Drummer track in the Tracks Area has standard controls, such as Solo and Mute buttons, a Volume fader, and a Panning knob. Tracks with recording functionality also have a Record Enable button.

Figure 2.38 Various track types in the Tracks Area of the Main Window

Tracks Area Menu Bar

Beneath the control bar in the Main Window is a thin area with additional controls and selectors known as the Tracks Area menu bar. This area contains menus that are specific to the Tracks Area. It also provides tool menus, controls for showing track automation, the Catch button, Snap and Drag pop-up menus, a Waveform Zoom button, scroll and zoom sliders, and Track Area and Live Loops Grid show/hide buttons.

Figure 2.39 Tracks Area menu bar in the Main Window

Rulers

Rulers are horizontal displays that appear at the top portion of the workspace area, right above your tracks. Logic Pro has two views for the primary ruler: Musical, which shows time in bars and beats, and Absolute, which shows time in minutes and seconds. To display the Absolute ruler (minutes/seconds) as a secondary ruler, you can click on the View menu in the Tracks Area menu bar and click SECONDARY RULER. Alternatively, you can use the shortcut COMMAND+OPTION+CONTROL+R.

Figure 2.40 Rulers appear below the Tracks Area menu bar and above the regions in the Tracks Area

Live Loops Grid

The Live Loops Grid introduced in version 10.5 of Logic Pro X uses cells to organize musical ideas and loops. You can start and stop playback or record freely while everything remains in sync with the project tempo. This view displays track content in two ways: looped and un-looped. Looped cells display region content in a circular pattern that visually progresses like a clock. Un-looped cells use a linear display similar to the Tracks Area view, but with the region content fitting within the range of the uniform cell. The standard track controls found in the Tracks Area view are laid out the same in the Live Loops Grid view.

 The Live Loops Grid and Tracks Area views can be shown or hidden individually on either side of a divider in the Workspace. Show/Hide buttons are available in the Tracks Area menu bar located at the top of the Workspace.

Figure 2.41 Logic Pro Main Window with split view of Live Loops Grid (left) and Tracks Area (right)

Cells

Tracks in the Live Loops Grid contain rows of cells. Cells within a given row utilize the same signal routing and channel strip settings as the associated track. Any arrangement of cells can be played, but only one cell per row may play at a time.

Scenes

Cells aligned in the same column are called Scenes and can be triggered simultaneous using the Scenes trigger at the bottom of each column in the Live Loops Grid.

Divider Column

The Divider column to the right of the Live Loops Grid gives you views and controls for handling regions between the Live Loops Grid and the Tracks Area Workspace. Button indicators in the Divider column show the status of cells. The buttons can be used to start, stop, and pause cells in corresponding rows or stop all with the Grid Stop button at the bottom of the Divider Column. Additionally, the Track Activation buttons set track priority to play back region content in the Tracks Area Workspace or Live Loops Grid. Track priorities can be set while viewing the Live Loops Grid, the Workspace, or both simultaneously in split view.

Review/Discussion Questions

1. Name some of the folders and files that Logic Pro creates as part of the project hierarchy. Where is the session file (.logicx) stored? (See "Project Components" beginning on page 24.)

2. Where are audio files stored in the project hierarchy? (See "Audio Files Folder" beginning on page 25.)

3. What is the Freeze Files folder used for? (See "Freeze Files Folder" beginning on page 26.)

4. Which components should you turn on first when powering up a Logic Pro system? Which component should you turn on last? (See "Powering Up Your Hardware" beginning on page 27.)

5. What does the I/O Buffer Size control? (See "Latency Settings" beginning on page 30.)

6. What kinds of commands can be found under the Logic Pro View menu? How does the View menu differ from the Window menu? (See "The Logic Pro Menu Structure" beginning on page 31.)

7. Which Logic Pro editor displays audio waveforms and can be used to work directly with audio non-destructively? (See "Logic Pro Windows and Views" beginning on page 33.)

8. Which Logic Pro editor allows you to compose and edit MIDI information? (See "Logic Pro Windows and Views" beginning on page 33.)

9. Which Logic Pro window(s) provides access to Pan controls and Volume Faders for each track? (See "Logic Pro Windows and Views" beginning on page 33.)

10. Which Logic Pro window provides access to cells that can be triggered individually or as Scenes? (See "Logic Pro Windows and Views" beginning on page 33.)

To review additional material from this chapter and prepare for certification, see the Logic Pro 101 Study Guide module available through the Elements|ED online learning platform at ElementsED.com.

Identifying the Primary Logic Pro Windows and Views

🎧 Activity

In this exercise worksheet, you will identify the primary windows and views in Logic Pro and their component parts. The information referenced in these questions is covered in Chapter 2.

🕐 Duration

This exercise should take approximately 10 minutes to complete.

⊕ Goals/Targets

- Identify the primary windows in Logic Pro
- Recognize the component sections of each window
- Identify the two options for viewing regions in the Detail view

Instructions

Answer the questions in this exercise by filling in the blanks on the following pages or by listing your answers on a separate sheet of paper or worksheet. Be sure to use the terminology referenced in Chapter 2 as you complete this exercise.

Questions 1 through 5 refer to Figure 2.42.

1. The window shown in Figure 2.42 is called the _____ window.

2. The area labeled **A** across the top of the window is called the _____.

3. The display area labeled **B** on within this window is called the _____.

4. The area labeled **C** on the left side of the window is called _____.

5. The area labeled **D** on the bottom of the window is called the _____.

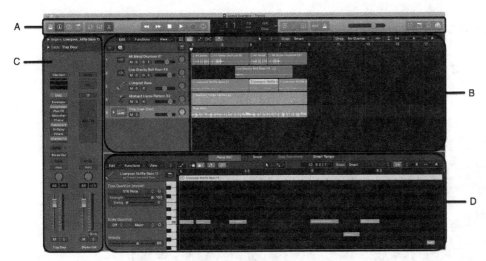

Figure 2.42 The Logic Pro window that displays regions

Questions 6 through 13 refer to Figure 2.43.

6. The button labeled **A** opens _____.

7. The button labeled **B** opens _____.

8. The button labeled **C** is called _____.

9. The button labeled **D** opens _____.

10. The button labeled **E** opens _____.

11. The button labeled **F** opens _____.

12. The button labeled **G** enables _____.

Figure 2.43 The Logic Pro display at the top of the Main Window

Questions 14 through 17 refer to Figure 2.44.

13. The content and spaces in this section labeled **A** near the top of the window are called
    _____.

14. This display labeled **B** on the right side is called the _____.

15. The section labeled **C** on the bottom of the triggers content in vertical columns called
    _____.

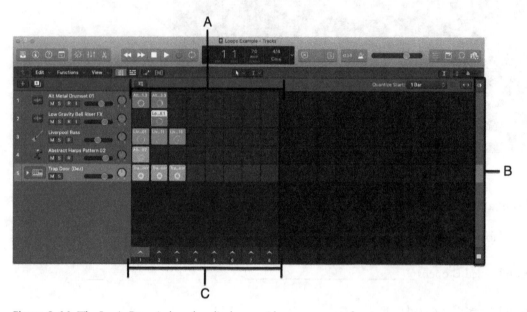

Figure 2.44 The Logic Pro window that displays a grid arrangement of region content

Chapter 3

Logic Pro Basic Controls

This chapter provides an overview of the edit functions, zoom options, and MIDI controls used in the Main Window. It also discusses the Grid available in Logic Pro, how to set the Edit Grid Value, and how to work with Rulers.

Learning Targets for This Chapter

- Recognize available editing tools and their functions

- Recognize various region editing operations in Logic Pro

- Understand zooming and scrolling behaviors available in Logic Pro

- Recognize various Rulers and Counter displays in Logic Pro

- Understand how to access Quick Help

 Key topics from this chapter are illustrated in the Logic Pro 101 Study Guide module available through the Elements|ED online learning platform. Sign up at ElementsED.com.

This chapter provides an overview of the controls available in the Logic Pro Main Window and Transport window. These primary controls are used day-in and day-out in Logic Pro for recording, playback, and basic editing of audio and MIDI material. Establishing some familiarity with the available tools, operational modes, and transport functions early on will help you in all aspects of the work you do in Logic Pro.

Playback in the Main Window

When you first create a Logic Pro project, you have two options under the New Project tab. If you select **EMPTY PROJECT**, a project will be created in the Main Window focusing on the Tracks Area in the Workspace. Selecting **LIVE LOOPS**, on the other hand, will create an empty project focused on the Live Loops Grid.

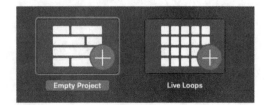

Figure 3.1 The Empty Project button (left) the Live Loops button (right) in the New Project tab

If you're working from a project focused in the Workspace area, activating playback will play all regions in the Tracks Area. However, if the project has Live Loop components and you activate playback of a cell or Scene, the Play function will generally switch playback of the selected track(s) over to the Live Loop Grid area. This may cause the regions on tracks in the Workspace to appear dimmed (grayed out) and to not play back as expected.

When this happens, the **TRACK ACTIVATION** or **DIVIDER COLUMN** buttons will display arrows to indicate that one or more tracks are currently not playing in the Workspace area, but instead are playing a cell or scene from the Live Loop Grid. These buttons are available whether you're displaying the Live Loops Grid, the Tracks Area, or both.

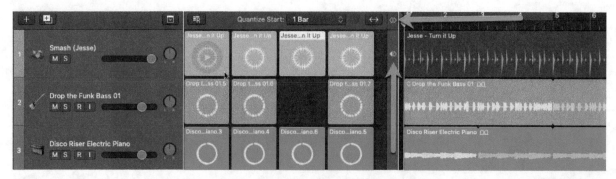

Figure 3.2 The Track Activation button (top) and Divider button (bottom) with the Live Loops Grid and Tracks Area displayed

To reactivate playback for the Tracks Area, click the **TRACK ACTIVATION** button to globally switch playback of all tracks between the Live Loop Grid and the Tracks Area. Alternatively, you can switch individual tracks' playback controls using the **DIVIDER COLUMN** buttons. A lit arrow will indicate where each track will play back. If the **TRACK ACTIVATION** button appears without a clearly lit arrow, this indicates that track playback is split, with some tracks active in the Live Loops Grid and some in the Tracks Area.

Region Editing in the Workspace

While several tools are available in Logic Pro, the majority of the time you'll be using the mouse to access the tools assigned in Left-click and Command-click Tools menu.

Figure 3.3 Tools menu for Left-click operations

Assigning Editing Tools

Logic has many tools available for working with regions. You can set a tool to your **LEFT-CLICK** mouse action (see Figure 3.3) and a second tool for a **COMMAND-CLICK** mouse action. The editing tools are available from dropdown menus in the Tracks Area menu bar of the Main Window.

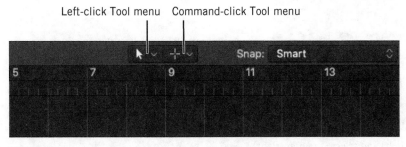

Figure 3.4 Use the Left-click Tool menu and Right-click Tool menu to assign mouse actions

Here are some of the options of tools you'll have to choose from under each menu:

- **Pointer tool**—Select, move, copy, resize, or loop regions and other elements. The appearance of this tool may change based on its function.

- **Pencil tool**—Create a blank region or event and edit its length; add and edit MIDI notes in a MIDI region or in the Piano Roll Editor.

- **Eraser tool**—Delete regions, events, markers, folders, and other elements.

- **Text tool**—Edit names of regions, events, markers, folders, and other elements.

- **Scissors tool**—Split a single region or event into two.

- **Zoom tool**—Click and drag to fill the workspace with a selection; click again to revert to the previous view.

- **Marquee tool**—Select regions or parts of regions for editing and playback by dragging across them. This tool can create selections across multiple tracks.

 To quickly switch between LEFT-CLICK tools, you can press the T key to access a dropdown list of available tools.

Selecting and Moving Regions

By default, Logic Pro gives you access to the Pointer tool for the **LEFT-CLICK** action and the Marquee tool for the **COMMAND-CLICK** action. Let's examine how you might use the Pointer and Marquee tools in the Main Window when selecting or moving a region.

To select an entire Region:

- **LEFT-CLICK** with the Pointer tool to select a region. The region will become outlined and the top of the region will invert to show the region name in dark text on a light background.

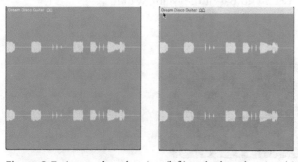

Figure 3.5 An unselected region (left) and selected region (right)

To move an entire selected region:

■ **LEFT-CLICK** on a region and drag with the Pointer tool to move it. Dragging horizontally (left or right) will move the region earlier or later on the timeline. Dragging vertically (up or down) will move the region to another compatible track.

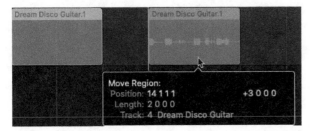

Figure 3.6 Moving an entire region by clicking and dragging

To select time within a region:

■ **COMMAND-CLICK** and drag with the Marquee tool to select a range of time on one or more tracks. (See Figure 3.7.) Using the Marquee tool will enable playback of the selected range, meaning playback will end at the end of your selection.

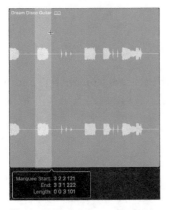

Figure 3.7 A Marquee selection made within a region

 Region editing is discussed further in Chapters 6 and 7 of this book.

Editing Regions

As you work with regions, you'll find many situations where you need to change the length of a region or move a portion of a region earlier or later in your project. You can do this by splitting regions with the

Scissors tool, separating on Marquee selections with the Pointer tool, and trimming regions using the Resize Pointer tool.

Splitting a Region

To split a region using the Scissors tool:

1.   Use the **LEFT-CLICK** tool menu in the Main Window, or press the T key, to select the Scissors tool.

Figure 3.8 Selecting the Scissors tool in the **LEFT-CLICK** tool menu

2.   Position your mouse where you'd like to split a region. You'll see the scissors icon change once you hover over a region.

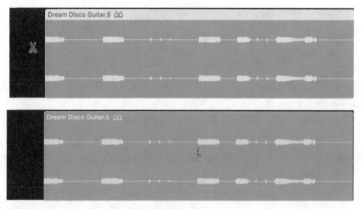

Figure 3.9 The Scissors tool placed next to a region (top) and on top of a region (bottom)

3.   Click with the Scissors tool active to split the region, creating a new region on either side of the mouse position.

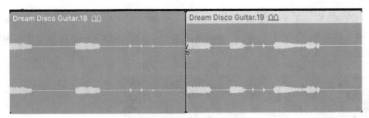

Figure 3.10 A region split with the Scissors tool

Separating a Selection

To separate a region at a Marquee selection:

1. **COMMAND-CLICK** and drag with the Marquee tool to select a range of time within one or more regions.

2. **LEFT-CLICK** on the marquee selection with the Pointer tool to separate the region to your selection.

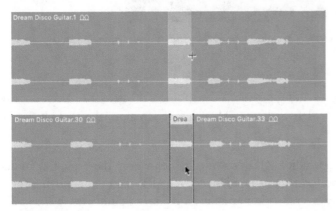

Figure 3.11 A Marquee selection made within a region, before (top) and after (bottom) being split with the Pointer tool

3. You can now move the selection earlier or later in the Tracks Area by clicking and dragging with the Pointer tool.

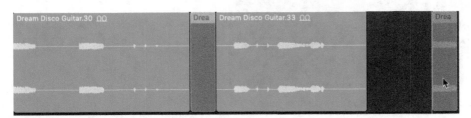

Figure 3.12 A split selection being dragged later on a track with the Pointer tool

To duplicate and move a selection within a region:

1. Make a selection within a region, as described above.

2.   Hold **OPTION** while dragging the selection with the Pointer tool. The mouse icon will display a green plus sign (+) underneath it, and a duplicate copy of the selection will be moved to the destination location. The waveform will remain unaffected in the original region.

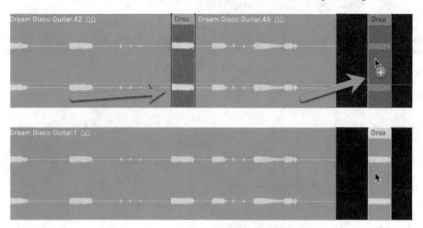

Figure 3.13 Holding **OPTION** while dragging a Marquee selection: before (top) and after (bottom)

Trimming a Region

The Pointer tool can adapt to provide other editing functions depending on where it's placed on a region. If you move the Pointer tool over the lower-left or lower-right edge of a region, the tool changes to the Resize Pointer.

You can use the Resize Pointer to trim excess audio, MIDI, or video content from the beginning or end of a continuous region. The Resize Pointer modifies regions nondestructively, leaving the underlying source file unchanged. This tool allows you to quickly crop a region or adjust a region's boundaries to hide or expose underlying material.

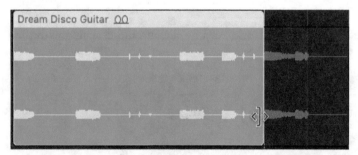

Figure 3.14 The Resize Pointer positioned on lower half of region

The first time you trim a region, Logic Pro automatically shows changes to the region in the Project Tab under the Browser. The darkened areas of the edited region indicate what has been trimmed from the source file.

Figure 3.15 The Project tab in the Browser displaying a trimmed region

Looping a Region

If you move the Pointer tool to the top-right edge of a region, it becomes the Loop Pointer tool. This tool allows you to create loop iterations of a region by dragging to the right. You'll see a small overlay indicating where the loop ends and how many repetitions have been created.

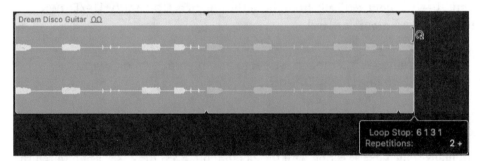

Figure 3.16 The Loop Pointer used to loop a region

Zooming and Scrolling in the Main Window

As mentioned earlier in this chapter, the Left-click tool menu includes a Zoom tool. With the Zoom tool enabled, you can simply click and drag across a selection on one or more tracks to fill the screen with the selected area. Clicking a second time will return to the previous zoom setting. Alternately you can temporarily activate the Zoom tool when another tool is active by holding **Option**.

You can also zoom in and out horizontally from the ruler by holding **Option** and dragging up or down. Dragging up zooms out, and dragging down zooms in.

As an additional option, you can click the **Vertical Auto Zoom** button or **Horizontal Auto Zoom** button to automatically fill your workspace vertically with all of your tracks or horizontally with the longest track in your project, respectively. You can also adjust vertical and horizontal zoom manually for all tracks by adjusting the Vertical Zoom and Horizontal Zoom sliders to the right of the Auto Zoom buttons.

Figure 3.17 Vertical and Horizontal Auto Zoom buttons (left) and Zoom sliders (right) in the Main Window

Alternate Zoom Functions

Logic Pro also provides keyboard shortcuts for zooming that can speed up your workflow when you need to quickly zoom in and out.

- **Zoom In/Out (Horizontal)**—To zoom horizontally from the keyboard, press **COMMAND+LEFT/ RIGHT ARROW**. Each key press zooms in/out one level.

 Hold **SHIFT+OPTION** while scrolling with a mouse wheel to zoom horizontally, or swipe horizontally on a trackpad while holding **OPTION**.

- **Zoom In/Out (Vertical)**—To zoom vertically from the keyboard, press **COMMAND+UP/DOWN ARROW**. Each key press zooms in/out one level.

 Hold **OPTION** while scrolling with a mouse wheel to zoom vertically, or swipe vertically on a trackpad while holding **OPTION**.

- **Toggling Zoom**—To zoom in on a selection on one or more tracks, press the **Z** key to activate Toggle Zoom to Fit, filling your entire workspace with the selection. This operation zooms in, both vertically and horizontally (much like selecting with the Zoom tool). Press the **Z** key again to return to previous zoom level.

Horizontal Scrolling

When zoomed in on your project, you will commonly need to scroll the Main Window to the left or right to access a desired location on screen. The following options can be used to scroll the Main Window horizontally:

- Drag left and right using the scroll bar at the bottom of the window.

- Press **RETURN** to jump to the start of the project.

- Press the comma and period keys (**<** and **>**) to move the playhead incrementally earlier or later; the window will scroll as needed to display the playhead location.

- Press the **HOME** or **END** key to scroll horizontally one page (screen) at a time.

You can also swipe left/right with a Magic Mouse, trackpad, or similar device to scroll the workspace earlier or later. When using a mouse with a vertical scroll wheel only, you can hold **SHIFT** while scrolling to move the screen left/right.

Vertical Scrolling

When working on a project with many tracks (or with tracks set to large display sizes), you will commonly need to scroll the Main Window up or down to access a desired track on screen. The following options can be used to scroll the Main Window vertically:

- Drag up or down using the scroll bar at the right of the window.

- Press the **PAGE UP** and **PAGE DOWN** keys to scroll up or down one page (screen) at a time.

- Swipe or scroll up/down with a Magic Mouse, trackpad, or scroll wheel.

Waveform Zoom

When you're working with audio, you can also zoom in on the waveform displays to see more detail. To do this, you can use the Waveform Zoom button in the Main Window to adjust the display of all waveforms in audio regions. (See Figure 3.18.) Note that this will not change the volume of the regions; it merely changes how the waveform data is displayed. Click and hold on the Waveform Zoom button until the vertical slider appears; then drag up/down to set the zoom level. The Waveform Zoom button will highlight in blue.

After setting the Waveform Zoom, you can click the button to toggle the zoom on/off.

Figure 3.18 Activating Waveform Zoom in the Tracks Area using the zoom slider

Selections and Rulers in the Main Window

When navigating a project to set locations for playback, recording, or editing, you'll find it useful to reference the playhead location indicators in the Logic Pro LCD area at the top of the Main Window. Additionally, the default display of Beats & Project shows you project information like the time signature, key signature, and tempo of your project.

Counter Displays

You can refer to the LCD to determine the current playhead location. You can click and drag on the Bar and Beat display in the LCD to move the playhead forward or backward. You can also double-click in the LCD and manually enter a desired location; pressing **RETURN** will move the cursor to the specified location.

 To enter a bar and beat position in the LCD, type the bar number followed by a period and then the beat number (e.g., type "15.2" to go to Bar 15, Beat 2).

Much like making changes to playhead location, you can click on the Tempo, Time Signature, and Key Signature displays to make changes as well. (See Figure 3.19.) The Tempo field lets you either click and drag to adjust the value up or down or double-click to manually enter a desired value. The other fields display pop-up menus when clicked.

Figure 3.19 Beats & Project LCD display showing the playhead location (left), tempo (center), and time signature and key signature (right)

The pop-up menu (down arrow) to the right of the LCD allows you to change the display format. For example, you can get a much more detailed view by selecting **CUSTOM** from the pop-up menu. (See Figure 3.20.) This option gives you Musical values (bars and beats) and Absolute values (Timecode and minutes and seconds). It also displays the selection or cycle area in/out points, as well as project information like tempo and meter information. Additional information in this display includes incoming/outgoing MIDI Activity and CPU/HD performance information.

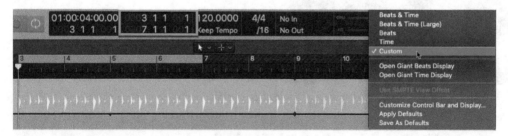

Figure 3.20 The LCD set to Custom with the cycle area in and out points highlighted

Ruler Displays

In Logic Pro, the primary ruler displays Musical time in increments of bars and beats by default. This can be useful for music production, allowing you to easily identify where Bar 8 ends and Bar 9 begins, for example.

For some projects, it can be helpful to display absolute time (minutes/seconds/timecode) instead. Doing so will change the Counter displays to show time in minutes and seconds, relative to the project start.

As mentioned in Chapter 2, you can display the Absolute ruler as a secondary ruler you by clicking on the View tab to the left below the LCD and enabling **SECONDARY RULER**. (See Figure 3.21.) Alternatively, you can use the shortcut **COMMAND+OPTION+CONTROL+R** to toggle the secondary ruler on/off.

Figure 3.21 Enabling the secondary ruler in the Main Windows view tab

 To change the primary ruler display, you can go into FILE > PROJECT SETTINGS > GENERAL and deselect the Use Musical Grid checkbox. The primary ruler will switch to showing Time, and the secondary ruler will display Bars and Beats.

Making Selections with Rulers

Two common ways of using the ruler displays include creating a cycle area and creating and adjusting marquee selections.

Creating a Cycle Area

You can enable loop playback by creating a cycle area. When enabled, the cycle area will be displayed as a yellow strip in the ruler.

 Cycle areas can also be used to record multiple takes over a selected part of the project.

 Recording techniques are covered in Chapters 6 and 7 of this book.

To set a cycle area you can click and drag in the upper portion of the primary ruler. To adjust the length of an existing cycle area, you can drag the left or right boundaries of the cycle area or Shift-click on either side to extend or contract the cycle area. You can also move the entire cycle area, while maintaining its length, by clicking in the center when the hand icon appears and dragging left or right.

 You can quickly create a cycle area based on an existing marquee selection by pressing COMMAND+U.

When a cycle area is active, playback will always begin at the start of the designated range. The playhead will return to the beginning of the range each time it reaches the end of the highlighted area, looping across the designated range.

Toggling the Cycle Area On/Off

You can enable/disable the cycle area behavior using the **CYCLE AREA** button (looped arrows) in the control bar. You can also toggle this function on/off from the keyboard by pressing the **C** key.

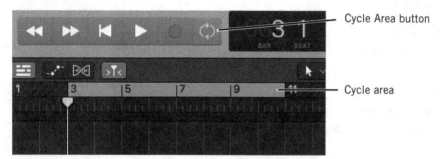

Figure 3.22 A cycle area in Logic Pro's primary ruler; the active Cycle Area button is shown in orange at the top

Using the Marquee Ruler and Marquee Stripe

As mentioned earlier in this chapter, you can select time ranges on one or more tracks using the Marquee tool (Command-click and drag). You can also enable the Marquee ruler in the Main Windows using the View tab.

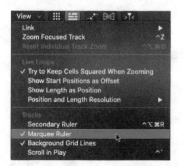
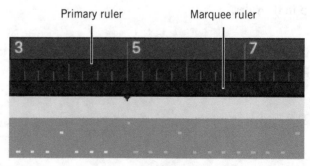

Figure 3.23 Showing the Marquee ruler (left) and the ruler display with the Marquee ruler showing (right)

With this ruler displayed, the Marquee start and end indicators will appear in the blank area just under your primary ruler. The blank Marquee ruler area can also be used to select across all tracks in a project: dragging within the Marquee Ruler will make a Marquee Stripe selection on all tracks across the selected range.

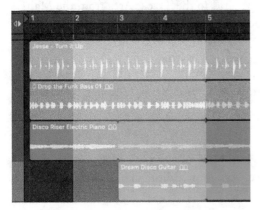

Figure 3.24 A selection created as a Marquee Stripe in Logic Pro's Marquee ruler

Quick Help Tips

The *Quick Help* button in Logic Pro's Main Windows can help you identify the various controls, tools, selectors, and functions in the software. When you hover the cursor over an unlabeled control or tool, or an abbreviated name or display, Logic Pro will display the full name of the control, function, or item, along with a brief explanation of how to use the control or item. This pop-up tip will also provide information on available shortcuts for buttons or functions, where applicable.

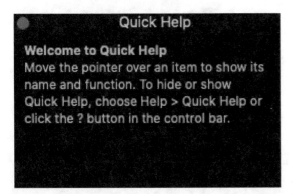

Figure 3.25 The Quick Help button enabled and the associated pop-up tip

Review/Discussion Questions

1. How can you switch a track's playback from the Live Loops Grid to the Tracks Area from the Main Window? How can you tell which area a track will playback from? (See "Playback in the Main Window" beginning on page 52.)

2. What Left-click tool lets you select and move entire regions? (See "Selecting and Moving Regions" beginning on page 54.)

3. Which editing tool lets you zoom in by clicking and dragging? How can you quickly return to the previous zoom setting after zooming in with this tool? (See "Assigning Editing Tools" beginning on page 53.)

4. Which editing tool lets you click and drag to make a selection across multiple regions, even on multiple tracks? (See "Assigning Editing Tools" beginning on page 53.)

5. What are some of the key functions of the Pointer tool besides region movement? (See "Editing Regions" beginning on page 55.)

6. How can you quickly zoom vertically to see all the tracks in your project? How can you quickly zoom horizontally to see the longest track in your project? (See "Zooming and Scrolling in the Main Window" beginning on page 59.)

7. What are some ways to scroll horizontally in the Main Window? (See "Horizontal Scrolling" beginning on page 60.)

8. What are some ways to scroll vertically in the Main Window? (See "Vertical Scrolling" beginning on page 61.)

9. How do you enable Custom LCD settings in the Main Window? What are some things you can display that aren't readily available in the Beats & Project view? (See "Counter Displays" beginning on page 62.)

10. What shortcut lets you create a cycle area based on your current selection? (See "Creating a Cycle Area" beginning on page 63.)

11. How can you enable the Marquee ruler? What is Marquee Stripe used for? (See "Using the Marquee Ruler and Marquee Stripe" beginning on page 64.)

 To review additional material from this chapter and prepare for certification, see the Logic Pro 101 Study Guide module available through the Elements|ED online learning platform at ElementsED.com.

Primary Tools and Controls

🎧 Activity

In this exercise worksheet, you will identify various Logic Pro controls and tools available within the Main Window. The information referenced in these questions is covered in Chapter 3.

🕐 Duration

This exercise should take approximately 10 minutes to complete.

◈ Goals/Targets

- Identify some of the controls available in the Main Window in Logic Pro
- Identify various edit tools and operations in Logic Pro

Instructions

Refer to Figures 3.26 through 3.28 when answering the questions below. Refer to the sections on "Playback in the Main Window" and "Region Editing in the Workspace" in Chapter 3 for assistance.

Questions 1 through 3 refer to Figure 3.26.

1. The button labeled **A** in Figure 3.26 is called the _____.

2. True or False: clicking the button labeled **B** in Figure 3.26 will toggle track between playing back in the Live Loops Grid and the Tracks Area.

   _____.

3. Based on this image, which two tracks will play back in the Tracks Area?

   _____ and _____.

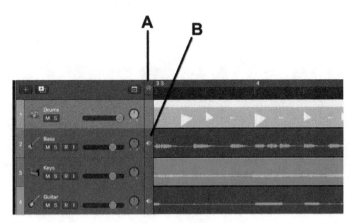

Figure 3.26 Tracks in the Main Window

Question 4 refers to Figure 3.27.

4. When moving a region with the Pointer tool, you can hold the _____ modifier key to create a duplicate copy.

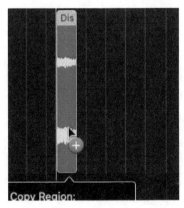

Figure 3.27 Copying a region in Logic Pro

Questions 5 through 8 refer to Figure 3.28.

5. The editing tool labeled **A** in Figure 3.28 is the _____ tool.

6. The editing tool labeled **B** in Figure 3.28 is the _____ tool.

7. The editing tool labeled **C** in Figure 3.28 is the _____ tool.

8. The editing tool labeled **D** in Figure 3.28 is the _____ tool.

9. The editing tool labeled **E** in Figure 3.28 is the _____ tool.

 A

 B

 C

 D

E

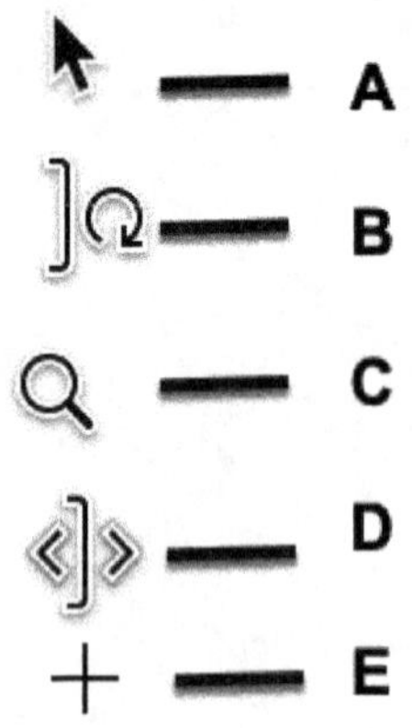

Figure 3.28 Editing tool icons in Logic Pro

Chapter 4

Creating Your First Project

This chapter covers the basics of working with Logic Pro projects. It introduces discussions on project configuration options, playback and navigation options, and project saving and opening operations.

 Learning Targets for This Chapter

- Choose appropriate preferences for Logic Pro

- Create a new project

- Create and name Audio and Software Instrument tracks

- Navigate your project for playback and editing

- Save, locate, and open projects

- Recognize the different Workspace views

Key topics from this chapter are illustrated in the Logic Pro 101 Study Guide module available through the Elements|ED online learning platform. Sign up at ElementsED.com.

Before you can begin working with audio or MIDI in Logic Pro, you need to have a Logic Pro project open. This chapter covers the basics of creating a Logic Pro project, adding tracks, using basic navigation for your tracks, and saving and reopening your work.

Project Chooser

When you open Logic Pro for the first time, the first thing you see after startup completes is the Project Chooser. If the Project Chooser doesn't open automatically when you launch Logic, you can choose **FILE > NEW FROM TEMPLATE** or press **COMMAND+N** to display the Project Chooser.

The Project Chooser is your springboard for creating a new Logic Pro project or opening an existing project.

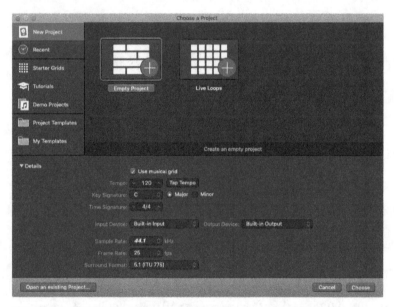

Figure 4.1 The Project Chooser in Logic Pro

From here, you can complete any of the following actions:

- Create a new Empty Project or Live Loops project.

- Open a project from a list of recently opened Logic Pro projects.

- Create a new Live Loops project from a selection of Starter Grids.

- Open a Tutorial and follow a step-by-step guide on basic workflows in Logic Pro.

- Open a Demo Project provided by a professional artist.

- Create a new Project from a selection of included Project Templates.

- Create a new Project from user-made Project Templates.

- Configure project settings such as tempo, key, time signature, I/O, and audio preferences.

- Open an existing Project from your computer or a connected storage device.

(i) **Startup behavior in Logic Pro can be configured in the Project Handling tab of the General Preferences by selecting LOGIC PRO > PREFERENCES > GENERAL. From the STARTUP ACTIONS pop-up menu, you can select your desired startup behavior.**

Feel free to explore and edit the options available in the Project Chooser, if desired. For the sake of simplicity, this chapter focuses on creating a new Empty Project, which will serve as a fresh starting point for expressing your creativity.

Creating and Configuring a Logic Pro Project

From the Project Chooser, you can create a new Empty Project by selecting the **CREATE** tab at the bottom right. By default, the Project Chooser will be configured to create an *Empty Project* document, as described in Chapter 2.

After creating a new empty project, the New Tracks dialog box will display. Logic Pro requires at least one track to be present in a project at all times.

Configuring Audio Preferences

Before you start creating in your new project, we recommend that you configure several important Logic Pro preference settings. These settings include selecting the audio device you will use with Logic Pro, and choosing the sample rate, file format, and bit depth for your audio. Most audio preferences apply globally to Logic Pro: once you have configured your audio preferences, Logic Pro will use them for all projects you create or open in the future.

A few audio settings are project-specific and will not remain active for new projects. If your audio needs or hardware devices change, you can modify your settings as needed at that point.

Global preferences for Logic Pro preferences are located under **LOGIC PRO > PREFERENCES**. Project settings are located under **FILE > PROJECT SETTINGS**.

 Templates store project settings, so these settings can be applied to new projects by using a template.

Audio Device and Sample Rate Settings

The Project Chooser gives you options for configuring details, such as the audio device and sample rate to use for a new project. After you've created a project, you can change these settings from the Audio and Recording Preferences and the Audio tab of the Project Settings.

Selecting an Audio Device

If you have a compatible audio interface connected to your computer, you can select it from the **INPUT DEVICE** and **OUTPUT DEVICE** dropdown menus in the Project Chooser or from the Device tab of the Audio Preferences once a project has been created.

 After making a selection in Audio Preferences, click APPLY to commit the change.

To get started recording and playing back through an audio interface, it's a good idea to make sure the **CORE AUDIO** driver is enabled. This will allow Logic Pro to recognize and communicate with an audio interface. The options should be enabled by default in the Audio Preferences window.

In Mac systems, the **CORE AUDIO** driver uses the built-in audio capabilities of the computer. Many audio interface options from third-party manufacturers are Core Audio-compliant. However, some interfaces may require that you download and install a specific driver.

 Consult your audio device manual or the manufacturer's website for information on the system requirements or required drivers.

Sample Rate

After selecting an audio device in the Project Chooser, you can choose from its available sample rates. Logic Pro supports sample rates up to 192 kHz with a compatible audio interface. To optimize the file sizes in your session, choose the lowest sample rate that meets the needs of your project.

 Once a project has been created, you can change the sample rate by navigating to FILE > PROJECT SETTINGS > AUDIO.

A sample rate of 44.1 kHz is often adequate for home- and project-studio recordings. Higher sample rates can be chosen for demanding projects, to capture a greater frequency response from the source audio, and to minimize sound degradation throughout the project life cycle. However, with higher sample rates come greater disk space requirements for your project. (See Table 4.1 later in this chapter.)

 For more details on sample rates, see "The Importance of Sample Rate" in Chapter 1 of this book.

File Type and Bit Depth Preferences

Within the Audio section of the Recording Preferences window, you can select the audio file format and the bit depth to use with Logic Pro. While you can mix and match audio files of varying formats and bit depths in your project, these preferences determine the format and bit depth of audio that you record or generate within your project (through Freezing or Converting, for example).

Supported File Types

Logic Pro stores audio recordings as WAV, AIFF, and CAF files in a project, without the need to convert formats. When recording audio, WAVE (or WAV) is the default file type. AIFF and WAVE are commonly used formats for most audio applications, but CAF (Core Audio Format) allows for extended periods of continuous recording. You can select a file format from the **RECORDING FILE TYPE** dropdown menu of the Recording Preferences.

Audio Bit Depth

Logic Pro records audio files in 16-bit or 24-bit audio resolution. The 16-bit option generates smaller files and is typically adequate for basic recording projects. The default in Logic Pro is 24-bit resolution. This provides greater dynamic range in your recorded audio and lowers the noise floor.

 For more details on bit depth, see "The Importance of Bit Depth" in Chapter 1 of this book.

Higher bit depth options should be used for high-end recordings, especially recordings that include very quiet passages (such as a classical orchestra), recordings that require intensive processing, and recordings intended for media that support high resolution audio, such as DVD and Blu-ray disc.

Bit depth can be adjusted in the Audio section of the Recording Preferences. By default Logic Pro records 24-Bit audio, indicated by a check box labeled **24-BIT RECORDING**. Deselecting this box will change the setting to 16-Bit Recording.

Figure 4.2 Recording Preferences in Logic Pro

File Size Considerations

A tradeoff of choosing higher sample rates and bit depths for your Logic Pro audio is an increase in the amount of disk space required to store your audio files. Table 4.1 shows the relationship between sample rate, bit depth, and disk space consumption for the standard configurations supported in Logic Pro.

Table 4.1 Audio Recording Storage Requirements (Approximate)

Session Sample Rate	Session Bit Depth	Megabytes/Track Minute (Mono)	Megabytes/Track Minute (Stereo)
44.1 kHz	16-bit	5 MB	10 MB
44.1 kHz	24-bit	7.5 MB	15 MB
48 kHz	16-bit	5.5 MB	11 MB
48 kHz	24-bit	8.2 MB	16.4 MB
88.2 kHz	16-bit	10 MB	20 MB
88.2 kHz	24-bit	15 MB	30 MB
96 kHz	16-bit	11 MB	22 MB
96 kHz	24-bit	16.5 MB	33 MB
176.4 kHz	16-bit	20 MB	40 MB
176.4 kHz	24-bit	30 MB	60 MB
192 kHz	16-bit	22 MB	44 MB
192 kHz	24-bit	33 MB	66 MB

Working with Tracks

Once you've created a new project, the New Tracks dialog box will display.

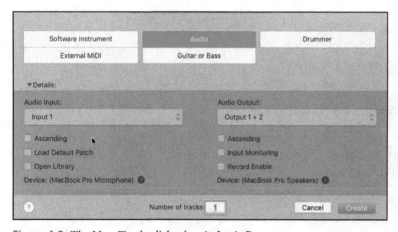

Figure 4.3 The New Tracks dialog box in Logic Pro

From this dialog box, you can choose a track type, set the number of tracks, configure input and output settings for the track(s), and specify other details. You will need to create at least one track in any Logic Pro project.

In Logic Pro, tracks are where audio, MIDI, and automation data are recorded and edited. Audio and MIDI data is stored in regions, which you can edit, arrange, and trigger in any order to create patterns and songs.

Supported Track Types and Channels

Like most audio applications, Logic Pro supports a variety of track types and channel strips that can be used for different purposes. The basic track and channel types supported in Logic Pro include the following:

- Audio tracks

- Software Instrument tracks

- External MIDI tracks

- Auxiliary channels

- VCA faders

- Master channel strip

- Output channel strips

Tracks versus Channels

When you create a new Logic Pro project, the Main Window will show any Audio, Software Instrument, and External MIDI tracks you've included as horizontal strips in the Tracks Area, where regions can be recorded, placed, and manipulated.

The project Mixer will include vertical channel strips for each of your tracks, as well as a Stereo Out channel strip and one or more output channel strips, representing the output options available on your audio interface. As you add audio, instrument, and MIDI tracks to your projects, corresponding channel strips will automatically be added to the Mixer.

Within the Mixer itself, you can add Auxiliary channel strips and VCA faders as well. By default, the Stereo Out channel, Auxiliary channels, and VCA faders are not represented as tracks in the Tracks Area; however, you can choose to create them from the Mixer > Options menu. Output tracks can also be shown in the Tracks Area by selecting Show Output Track under the Track menu.

Displaying tracks for your channel strips allows you to view and edit mixer automation for those channels in the Tracks Area.

Logic Pro also includes a feature known as track stacks. While not a track type in the traditional sense, a track stack provides a convenient system for summing and organizing tracks by packing them into a folder that can be revealed or collapsed.

The Function of Track Stacks

Track stacks are available in two types: Summing stacks and Folder stacks. Summing stacks are used to group tracks for submixing and effects processing. Folder stacks are used to group tracks and for nesting other existing Summing stacks. Neither Folder stacks nor Summing stacks can be nested inside a Summing stack.

To create a track stack, select the tracks you'd like to include in the stack and choose TRACK > CREATE TRACK STACK or press COMMAND+SHIFT+D to open the Track Stack dialog box. (You can also press COMMAND+SHIFT+F to create a new Folder stack or COMMAND+SHIFT+G to create a new Summing stack directly.)

Once created, you can add and remove tracks from a stack by dragging them in and out of the stack.

Audio tracks, Software Instrument tracks, External MIDI tracks, and more can be added to the Tracks Area of the Main Window using the New Tracks dialog box. Auxiliary channel strips and VCA faders can be created through the Mixer window.

 Selected Auxiliary channels and VCA faders in the Mixer can be added to the Tracks Area by choosing OPTIONS > CREATE TRACKS FOR SELECTED CHANNEL STRIPS or by pressing CONTROL+T. You can also COMMAND-CLICK any Auxiliary channel or VCA track and select CREATE TRACK from the pop-up menu.

Audio Tracks

Audio tracks allow you to import, record, and edit audio signals as waveforms within regions. Audio tracks can be mono, stereo, or any supported multi-channel format.

A Logic Pro project can have up to 1000 audio tracks. However, the project sample rate, the system hardware, and the continuity of audio all impact how many tracks can actually play back and record simultaneously.

 Logic Pro uses the computer's CPU to mix and process audio tracks. Computers with faster clock speeds and greater processor counts will support more tracks and audio effects than computers with slower CPUs or fewer processors.

Software Instrument Tracks

Software Instrument tracks store MIDI note and controller data within MIDI regions. The Logic Pro MIDI sequencer lets you import, record, and edit MIDI data in much the same way as audio. However, MIDI on its own does not generate sound; it is data that is sent to software instruments, which output sound in response. Tracks with MIDI and tracks with audio can coexist in one project.

A Logic Pro project can have up to 1000 Software Instrument tracks in mono, stereo, or any supported multi-channel format, depending on the output options of the instrument plug-in being used.

External MIDI Tracks

External MIDI tracks store MIDI note and controller data within MIDI regions similar to Software Instrument tracks. However, instead of using inserted instrument plug-ins on the channel strip, External MIDI tracks send MIDI data to external MIDI devices connected to the computer, such as synthesizers and sound modules. The sound output from the external devices can be returned to the computer through an audio input of a connected interface. This audio signal can be configured to play back through the External MIDI track, allowing it to function much like a Software Instrument track.

 In order to send MIDI data to an external MIDI device, you must have an interface that supports MIDI connectivity or use a USB connection for MIDI transmission.

Auxiliary Channels

Auxiliary channel strips allow you to route audio through your Mixer without recording the audio.

Auxiliary channels (or Aux channels) are commonly used as effects returns, allowing you to apply the same audio effect to the audio from multiple tracks. For instance, you could set up a reverb effect on an Aux channel and send signals to it from multiple Audio and MIDI tracks, thereby saving system resources and setup time.

Aux channels are also used as destinations for submixes of grouped tracks within a Summing stack. When you create a Summing stack, selected tracks are placed inside the stack and routed to an Aux channel that functions as the Main track. Aux channels can be mono, stereo, or any supported multi-channel format.

VCA Faders

Like Aux channels, VCA faders cannot be used for recording. But unlike on an Aux channel, audio does not get routed through a VCA fader. Instead, each VCA fader is associated with a VCA assignment, and the tracks in the assignment are then controlled by the VCA fader.

 A Master VCA fader is included by default in all projects. It is assigned to the Stereo Out track and cannot be removed.

Stereo Out Channel

The Stereo Out channel serves to control the overall level of the audio output for your project. A Stereo Out track is included by default in all projects. It can host audio effects, and its volume slider will control the level of Logic Pro's final output.

Adding Tracks

To add tracks to your project using the New Tracks dialog box, choose **TRACK > NEW TRACKS** (see Figure 4.4), and then choose the track type and the number of tracks using the dialog box controls. You can also configure the I/O and additional settings from the Details section, if desired.

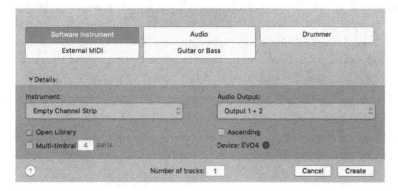

Figure 4.4 The New Tracks dialog box

Additional ways to add tracks include the following:

- Click on the **ADD TRACKS** button (plus sign) located just above the tracks list on the left.

- **RIGHT-CLICK** on the track header area and select a track type from the pop-up menu.

- **DOUBLE-CLICK** on the track header to create a new track. (The type is determined by the currently selected track.)

- From the **TRACKS** menu, select a track type from the upper portion of the drop-down menu.

 You can duplicate an existing track and its settings by selecting the track and clicking the DUPLICATE TRACK button located above the tracks list, next to the ADD TRACKS button.

Shortcuts for Creating Tracks

Various shortcuts are available to speed up the process of creating new tracks:

- Use **OPTION+COMMAND+N** to open the New Tracks dialog box.

- Use **OPTION+COMMAND+A** to create a new Audio track.

- Use **OPTION+COMMAND+S** to create a new Software Instrument track.

- Use **OPTION+COMMAND+U** to create a new Drummer track.

- Use **OPTION+COMMAND+X** to create a new External MIDI track.

- Use **COMMAND+D** to create a new track with duplicate settings.

 Regardless of the method you use to create a new track, the track will be inserted below the currently selected track. To rearrange tracks, click on the track within the tracks list and drag it to a new position.

Audio Input and Channel Mode

When adding Audio tracks using the New Tracks dialog box, you can choose an input format for the track or tracks. Input options will vary depending on your system or audio interface capabilities. Available input options include mono, stereo, and surround interface inputs, as well as bus inputs.

 You can change the input settings for an existing Audio track by selecting an option from the INPUT slot of the channel strip in the Inspector or Mixer windows.

You can switch mono and stereo settings on existing Audio tracks by clicking on the **CHANNEL MODE** button in either the Inspector or Mixer windows. This button will appear as either a single circle (mono) or two linked circles (stereo). Clicking the **CHANNEL MODE** button will toggle the track between mono and stereo.

Track Output Format

Within the New Tracks dialog box, you can choose an output format for the track or tracks you are adding. The default output setting is routed to your main Stereo Out. Other available options include mono (for Audio tracks), stereo, and surround interface outputs, and bus outputs.

A factor that affects whether or not a track will output in a certain format is the input setting for the track. By default, mono Audio tracks will output to both stereo out channels, and stereo Audio tracks will output separately to left and right channels of the stereo output. Software Instrument track outputs depend upon the capabilities of the inserted instrument to determine whether they will output in mono, stereo, or surround. Multi-channel surround outputs can be selected where available, but these will also require a compatible interface to correctly output sound for each channel.

Naming Tracks

When you create Audio, Software Instrument, and External MIDI tracks in Logic Pro, they are generally added to the project using generic names, such as Audio 1, Audio 2, Inst 1, and so on. When you create Drummer tracks, they are labeled based on the selected Drummer from the Library, with the default being *SoCal (Kyle)*. Often, you will want to rename your tracks with more meaningful descriptions.

To change a track name, double-click the track name within the Tracks Area, Inspector, or Mixer window. The track name will become highlighted, allowing you to rename the track. (See Figure 4.5.) Press Return when finished to commit the change.

Figure 4.5 A highlighted Track Name in the Tracks Area of the Main Window

  Press TAB or SHIFT+TAB when renaming a track to cycle forward and backward through your tracks and rename each without leaving the keyboard.

Deleting Tracks

You can delete a track from your project at any time. When you delete Audio tracks, your audio regions and data will *remain* in the project and can be accessed from the Project Browser, but your arrangement of the regions on the deleted track will be lost. When you delete tracks with MIDI instruments, such as Software Instrument tracks and Drummer tracks, the regions associated with the tracks will be lost. (A dialog box will warn you before this happens.)

If you inadvertently delete a track or tracks, you can undo the operation by choosing **EDIT > UNDO DELETE TRACKS** or pressing **COMMAND+Z**.

To delete a single track:

1. Click the track header to select the track.

2. Choose **TRACK > DELETE TRACK** or press the **DELETE** key on the computer keyboard.

To delete a contiguous range of tracks simultaneously:

1. Click the track header of the first track you'd like to delete.

2. **SHIFT-CLICK** on the track header of the last track you'd like to delete.

3. Choose **TRACK > DELETE TRACK** or press the **DELETE** key on the computer keyboard.

To delete a non-contiguous range of tracks simultaneously:

1. Click the track header of the first track you'd like to delete.

2. **COMMAND-CLICK** on the track header of each additional track you'd like to delete.

3. Choose **TRACK > DELETE TRACK** or press the **DELETE** key on the computer keyboard.

 You can also right-click on a track name and choose DELETE TRACK from the pop-up menu to remove all selected tracks.

If all selected tracks are empty, they will be deleted immediately; if any tracks contain data, you will be prompted with a verification dialog box. Click **DELETE** to permanently remove the selected tracks from the project.

Adding Audio to Tracks

Once you have created one or more Audio tracks in your project, you can begin adding audio regions, either by recording to your track(s) or by importing existing audio files from a storage drive or the Loop Browser. Audio content can be added to timeline locations on tracks in the Tracks Area (where they can be played sequentially) or to cells in the Live Loops Grid (where they can be launched in non-sequential order).

 Audio importing is covered in Chapter 5, and audio recording is covered in Chapter 7.

Adding MIDI to Tracks

Once you have created one or more Software Instrument tracks or External MIDI tracks in your project, you can create MIDI or Pattern regions and write MIDI data in the Editor. You can also add MIDI to a track by recording a performance from a MIDI controller or by importing a MIDI file from a storage drive or the Loop Browser. Like audio, MIDI regions can be added to timeline locations on tracks in the Tracks Area view or to cells in the Live Loops Grid.

 Various methods of importing, recording, editing, and working with MIDI data are covered in Chapters 5 and 6 of this book.

Adding Drummer Regions

Logic Pro includes a special type of track called a Drummer track. Drummer tracks are similar to Software Instrument tracks, in that they use software instruments (drummers) as instrument inserts. They differ from Software Instruments by using special Drummer regions that are edited through the Drummer editor window.

Drummer regions can be converted to regular MIDI regions for editing, but they cannot be recorded. You can add Drummer regions to a track by pressing the yellow plus button to the right of the Drummer track or an existing Drummer region. You also have the option of importing Drummer regions from the Loop Browser.

    Drummer tracks are discussed in more detail in Chapter 6 of this book.

Controlling Playback

How you go about playing your project is dependent on the mode you are currently using. You can choose between the Tracks Area and the Live Loops Grid as playback sources in the Main Window.

Playback in the Tracks Area

The Tracks Area in the Main Window displays a horizontal timeline of the regions in your project. Playback starts from the location of the playhead, which is indicated by a solid line that runs through one or more tracks and a position indicator that appears in the ruler above the Tracks Area. The playhead location is reflected in the LCD Display in the control bar of the Main Window.

Click the **PLAY** button in the control bar (or press the **SPACEBAR**) to begin playback from the location of the playhead.

Figure 4.6 Playhead in the Tracks Area of the Main Window

    The playhead can also be viewed and set in other time-based windows, like the Audio Track Editor and Piano Roll Editor.

To move or set the playhead position, do one of following:

■   Click a position in the lower half of the ruler.

- Click and drag the playhead to a new location.

- Use the **FORWARD** and **REWIND** Transport buttons in the control bar to reposition the playhead.

- Use the comma and period keys (**<** and **>**) to rewind and skip forward incrementally.

- Press **RETURN** to go back to the beginning of the project.

- **SHIFT-CLICK** in an empty part of the Tracks Area to move the playhead to that location.

- Click and drag a number in the LCD Display to update the playhead location.

- **DOUBLE-CLICK** the LCD Display and enter a new position to move the playhead to that location.

- If Markers are present, recall a marker location by typing the Marker number [1] through [9] on the numeric keypad.

 Markers and associated workflows are discussed in Chapter 8 of this book.

Cycle Area Playback

When the Cycle Area button is enabled, a yellow bar indicating the cycle area will be visible in the upper area of the primary ruler in the Main Window. By default, playback will start from the Left Locator position of the cycle area each time you press **PLAY**. When the playhead reaches the Right Locator position during playback, it will jump back to the Left Locator position to create a seamless loop until playback is stopped.

Cycle functionality can be toggled on or off during playback. When the Cycle Area button is enabled after playback has started outside the cycle area, the playhead will progress normally until it reaches the cycle area. Once the playhead crosses into the cycle area, playback will follow cycle playback behavior as described above. If the Cycle Area button is turned off after playback has started, the playhead will continue past the Right Locator until playback is stopped.

Figure 4.7 Cycle area enabled in the Tracks Area of the Main Window

Playback of Selected Regions

When you select one or more regions in the Tracks Area using the Pointer tool, you can start playback from the left-most region by pressing **SHIFT+SPACEBAR**. Playback will continue past the end of the last selected region until you manually stop the transport.

Playback of Marquee Selections

Another way to set playback positions is to use the Marquee tool. Holding **COMMAND** will activate the Marquee tool by default. The mouse cursor will display as a crosshair, letting you make selections anywhere in the Tracks Area. You can make selections outside the normal region boundaries, both inside and outside regions. When a selection is made with the Marquee tool, playback will begin within the Marquee selection, starting from the beginning position and stopping automatically at the end position.

With the Marquee tool active, you can also click anywhere in the Tracks Area to place the Marquee cursor without making a selection. A vertical line will be visible in the Tracks Area representing the Marquee cursor, and playback will begin from that point. Playback will continue until the project endpoint or until the transport is stopped manually.

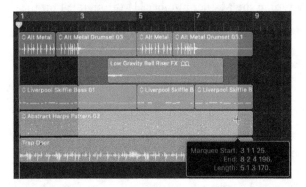 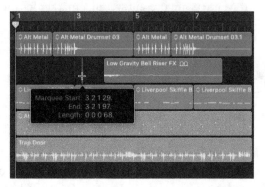

Figure 4.8 The Tracks Area of the Main Window showing a Marquee Selection (left) and Marquee placement without a selection (right)

Starting and Stopping Playback

You can set the playback point by clicking on the ruler in the Tracks Area to position the playhead. You can then start and stop playback by clicking the transport controls in the control bar or by pressing the **SPACEBAR**.

To play back a portion of your project, follow these steps:

1. Position the playhead in the Tracks Area. (See "Playback in the Tracks Area" earlier in this chapter.)

2. Press the **SPACEBAR** to begin playback from this point.

3. To stop playback, press the **SPACEBAR** again.

To move to a different playback point in the track, select a new position and press the **SPACEBAR** again.

Configuring Playback Behavior

The playback workflows discussed thus far use the default behaviors within Logic Pro. If you wish to configure playback differently, you can access options available within the **PLAY** button pop-up menu. (See Figure 4.9.)

Figure 4.9 Play button pop-up menu in the control bar

Toggling the Scrolling Mode

Logic Pro includes an option called **CATCH PLAYHEAD** that causes the display to scroll during playback, keeping the playhead visible in the Tracks Area. As the project plays, the window will scroll, page-by-page, to keep the playhead in view. You can enable this mode independently in the Editor windows.

To enable/disable **CATCH PLAYHEAD** mode, do one of the following:

- Click the **CATCH PLAYHEAD** button in the Tracks Area menu bar of the Main Window. The button will be highlighted in blue when active.

- Press the ` (backtick) key.

Figure 4.10 Catch Playhead button enabled (blue) in the Tracks Area menu bar

You can adjust **CATCH PLAYHEAD** settings in the **CATCH** tab under **LOGIC PRO > PREFERENCES > GENERAL**.

Locating the Playhead

At times, the playhead might end up off screen. For example, if the **CATCH PLAYHEAD** mode is disabled as described above, the playhead will move off screen after reaching the edge of the Tracks Area in the Main Window.

If the playhead is not visible in the Main Window, it can be located in the following ways:

- Press the **CATCH PLAYHEAD** button or press ` (backtick); the view will reposition to the playhead position.

- Zoom out until the playhead is in view.

- Locate the playhead position by reading the LCD display in the control bar.

Playback in the Live Loops Grid

While the Tracks Area view displays your project along a fixed timeline, the Live Loops Grid displays a grid of tracks and cells that you can play at any time and in any order. The Live Loops Grid is designed for improvisation and dynamic, non-sequential playback, so the layout of tracks and cells does not predetermine their playback order.

Getting to Know the Live Loops Grid

In the Live Loops Grid, content can be placed in a track's cell grid and triggered to play or stop independently. Each cell on a given track plays through the devices inserted on that track, so that the same instrument and/or signal processing is used by all cells on the track. You can also trigger an entire column of cells across all tracks simultaneously by triggering a Scene.

Because the Live Loops Grid features non-sequential playback, it can be useful for sketching out songs and performing them into the Tracks Area view. The Live Loops Grid is also a powerful live performance tool. It can be used to play backing tracks for a live band, to perform DJ sets that are free-flowing yet tightly synchronized, or to fire off music cues and sound effects for a theatrical performance.

Logic Pro also allows you to utilize both the Tracks Area and Live Loops Grid simultaneously. This makes for a unique experience that allows users to blend desired workflows from both views.

Starting and Stopping Cell Playback

Each cell that you load in the Live Loops Grid will display a **PLAY/STOP** button at its center when you hover the mouse over it. When the **PLAY** button is visible in a cell, clicking will launch playback for the cell at any time. Playback progress is indicated in active cells by an active animation in the cell. Looped cells display content in a circular pattern that progresses like a clock, and un-looped cells use a linear display. Launching a cell will also activate playback of the project, if it is not already in progress.

Figure 4.11 Cell Play button

To stop playback for a cell, click the **STOP** button on any cell in the track, or click the **TRACK STOP** button in the Divider column to the right of the grid area.

Figure 4.12 Cell Stop button (left) and Track Stop button (right)

When you stop playback for a specific cell in the Live Loops Grid, the **PLAY** button in the control bar will remain engaged and the Playhead Position field of the LCD display will continue running. These fields maintain a continuous flow of musical time so that you always know your position in song-time during playback or while recording cells into an arrangement.

You can stop playback by clicking the **STOP** button in the control bar or by pressing the **SPACEBAR**. Clicking the **STOP** button a second time (or anytime while playback is stopped) will return the playhead to the start of the entire project.

 The Stop button will display as the GO TO BEGINNING button when playback is stopped. When the playhead is at Bar 1, the button reverts to the standard Stop icon.

Cells aligned vertically can be launched using the **SCENE** triggers at the bottom of the Live Loops Grid. (See Figure 4.13.) The **GRID STOP** button at the bottom of the Divider column will stop and queue all cells in the grid, effectively pausing playback. Pressing the **GRID STOP** button a second time will dequeue the cells, effectively resetting the play position.

Figure 4.13 Scene Triggers and Grid Stop button in the Live Loops Grid

Additionally, cell playback behavior can be configured in the Cell Inspector. A variety of options are available, such as play modes, play from positions, looping, quantization, and more.

 The Cell Inspector is available in the Inspector tab on the left side of the Main Window. Press I to display the Inspector, if it is not currently showing.

Track Activation

Logic Pro gives users the option of alternating between or interacting with both the Tracks Area and the Live Loops Grid simultaneously. You can enable both views in the Tracks Area menu bar. The **TRACK ACTIVATION** buttons (left and right arrows) determine whether tracks will play back regions in the Tracks Area or cells within the Live Loops Grid. Track priority can be set individually or globally with the Divider column positioned between the Live Loops Grid and the Tracks Area.

Tracks can play from either the Tracks Area or the Live Loops Grid, but not from both at the same time.

The **TRACK ACTIVATION** button at the top of the Divider column, just below the Track Area menu bar, sets global priority. Use this to choose either region playback in the Tracks Area or cell playback in the Live Loops Grid. The **TRACK ACTIVATION** buttons on each track row determine individual assignments, allowing you to select either area for playback.

Track priority is indicated by a solid arrow pointing at either view. If a cell is playing or queued, a progress display will be visible in the Divider column instead of the **TRACK ACTIVATION** arrows.

Figure 4.14 Cells and regions playing in both the Live Loops Grid and the Tracks Area

Saving, Locating, and Opening Logic Pro Files

As with most software applications, Logic Pro provides commands for saving and opening your files under the **FILE** menu. The following sections describe the options for saving, locating, and opening your Logic Pro project files and other files related to your Logic Pro project.

Saving a Project

While working in Logic Pro, it is important to save your work often. Note that when you save your progress using one of the commands described below, you are saving only the Logic Pro document file, not the other associated files. (Audio regions in a project either reference existing files on disk or are recorded directly to disk within the project folder, so you don't have to save them independently.) This means even very large projects can be saved quickly.

Save Command

Saving can be done manually by choosing the **SAVE** command from the **FILE** menu. This saves the changes you have made since opening the session (or since the last time you saved) and writes the project in its current form over the old version. You cannot undo the Save command.

 If you need to return to an earlier state after completing a Save command, you can use the UNDO command to work backwards through previous actions; however, the file on disk will not be reverted.

Save As Command

The **SAVE AS** command is useful for saving a copy of a project under a different name or in a different drive location. Because this command leaves the original project unchanged and allows you to continue working on the renamed copy, it is particularly useful for experimenting and saving successive stages of your work. You can save each stage under a different name, such as Edit Session-Day 1, Edit Session-Day 2, and so on. By working this way, you can always retrace your steps if you should want to go back to an earlier stage of the project.

To use the Save As feature, follow these steps:

1. From within an open project, choose **FILE > SAVE AS**. The **SAVE AS** dialog box will appear.

2. Type a new name for the project in the dialog box.

3. Optionally, adjust settings and/or navigate to a new drive location.

4. Click **SAVE**.

The renamed, newly saved project will remain open for you to continue your work.

 Optionally, you can select or change which types of assets are copied into a project by using the CONSOLIDATE command. To consolidate project assets, choose FILE > PROJECT MANAGEMENT > CONSOLIDATE.

Save A Copy As Command

The **SAVE A COPY AS** command simply saves a copy of the current project with a different name or within a different directory location without affecting the currently open project. After saving a copy, the original version of the project—not the copy—will remain open for you to continue your work.

 The SAVE A COPY AS command allows you to save a copy of a project under a different name, giving you similar benefits to the SAVE AS command for projects.

To use the SAVE A COPY AS feature, follow these steps:

1. From within an open project, choose FILE > SAVE A COPY AS. The SAVE A COPY AS dialog box will appear.

2. Type a new name for the project version in the dialog box.

3. Optionally, adjust settings or navigate to a new drive location.

4. Click OK.

Save As Template Command

If you find yourself regularly creating projects with similar settings or production elements in Logic Pro, you may find it beneficial to save a template. Templates can store display options, playback behaviors, audio settingss, track layouts, and more, making templates incredibly powerful for more effective workflows. User templates can be saved and accessed from the Project Chooser display.

To use the SAVE AS TEMPLATE feature, follow these steps:

1. From within an open project, choose FILE > SAVE AS TEMPLATE. The SAVE AS dialog box will appear with the Project Templates directory selected.

2. Type a name for the template in the dialog box.

3. Click SAVE.

 User created templates are located in the user's profile under MUSIC > AUDIO MUSIC APPS > PROJECT TEMPLATES.

Project Alternatives

As mentioned previously, you can retrace your steps to an earlier stage of a project if you have saved interim versions using the SAVE AS command. Project Alternatives serve a similar function within a Logic Pro project, allowing you to store multiple save states that can be accessed within an open project. A benefit of this process is that the various alternatives remain accessible within the project file rather than as a series of individual files saved elsewhere.

To create a Project Alterative, follow these steps:

1. From within an open project, choose FILE > PROJECT ALTERNATIVES > NEW ALTERNATIVE. The SAVE A NEW ALTERNATIVE dialog box will appear.

2. Type a new name for the project version in the dialog box.

3. Click OK.

To open a Project Alterative, do the following:

1. From within an open project, navigate to **FILE > PROJECT ALTERNATIVES**.

2. Choose an alternative from the list.

 If you have made changes that haven't been saved, you will be prompted to save your project before opening the alternative.

Locating and Opening a Project File

If you know the location of a project file you want to open, you can open it directly from the **FILE** menu. In addition, Logic Pro makes it very easy to open recently used projects regardless of their location.

To open a project, do one the following:

- Choose **FILE > OPEN**.
- Press **COMMAND+O**.

To open a recently saved Project, do the following:

- Choose **FILE > OPEN RECENT** and select the file that you wish to open from the submenu.

 You can also open projects from a storage drive by **DOUBLE-CLICKING** on the project file in a Finder window.

Regardless of which method you choose, the project will open with all tracks and regions appearing exactly as they were when last saved.

Review/Discussion Questions

1. What kind of actions can be completed in the Project Chooser? (See "Project Chooser" beginning on page 72.)

2. What does Logic Pro require you to do in order to create a new project (what is required to be present in a project at all times)? (See "Creating and Configuring a Logic Pro Project" beginning on page 73.)

3. What is the maximum sample rate supported in Logic Pro? (See "Audio Device and Sample Rate Settings" beginning on page 74.)

4. What audio file types are supported in Logic Pro? (See "Supported File Types" beginning on page 75.)

5. What is the maximum bit depth supported in Logic Pro? (See "Audio Bit Depth" beginning on page 75.)

6. Describe some track and channel types supported in Logic Pro. (See "Supported Track Types and Channels" beginning on page 77.)

7. What shortcut command lets you add Audio tracks to your project? What shortcut lets you add Software Instrument tracks to your project? (See "Shortcuts for Creating Tracks" beginning on page 81.)

8. What happens to the audio and MIDI regions on a track when the track gets deleted from your project? How can you access the audio regions and data from a deleted track? (See "Deleting Tracks" beginning on page 82.)

9. What are the two different Workspace views you can use to interact with a project? (See "Controlling Playback" beginning on page 84.)

10. In the Tracks Area, what is the playhead? How does it appear in the project? (See "Playback in the Tracks Area" beginning on page 84.)

11. How does playback differ between the Tracks Area and Live Loops Grid? (See "Playback in the Live Loops Grid" beginning on page 88.)

12. Describe some ways to play back cells in your project from the Live Loops Grid. (See "Starting and Stopping Cell Playback" beginning on page 88.)

13. What is the purpose of the Save As command? Which project will be open after completing the Save As command—the original or the renamed copy? (See "Save As Command" beginning on page 91.)

14. How do Project Alternatives differ from projects saved using the normal Save or Save As commands? (See "Project Alternatives" beginning on page 92.)

15. What are some ways you can open a project from within Logic Pro? (See "Locating and Opening a Project File" beginning on page 93.)

To review additional material from this chapter and prepare for certification, see the Logic Pro 101 Study Guide module available through the Elements|ED online learning platform at ElementsED.com.

Creating a Project

🎧 Activity

In this exercise tutorial, you will create a new Logic Pro project, configure your Logic Pro preferences and project settings, add and remove tracks for the project, name each of the tracks you are keeping, and save the project for use in subsequent exercises.

🕐 Duration

This exercise should take approximately 15 to 20 minutes to complete.

⊕ Goals/Targets

- Create a new Logic Pro project
- Configure audio devices and sample rate
- Choose an appropriate file type and bit depth
- Add and rename Audio and Software Instrument tracks

Downloading the Media Files

To complete the exercises in this book, you will need to use various media files included in the **Media Files 2021-Logic101** folder. If you haven't done so already, you can download the media files now. Be sure to save the files to a location that you will have ongoing access to as you complete the exercises and projects in this book.

To download the media files, point your browser to www.halleonard.com/mylibrary and enter your access code (printed on the opening page of this book). Next, click the **Download** link for the **Media Files 2021-Logic101** listing in your **My Library** page. The Media Files folder will begin transferring to your Downloads folder.

Getting Started

To get started, you will need to open Logic Pro and create a new project, configuring its audio settings (audio device, sample rate, bit depth, and file format) to suit your needs.

Launch Logic Pro and create a new project:

1. Power up your computer and any connected hardware.

2. Do one of the following to launch Logic Pro:

    *   Click the **LOGIC PRO** icon in the Dock.

    *   Double-click on the **LOGIC PRO** icon in the Applications folder.

3. In the Project Chooser, select **EMPTY PROJECT** from the New Project tab.

 If the Project Chooser isn't visible, choose File > New from Template. This will open the Project Chooser. Then select Empty Project and proceed.

Configure Logic Pro's audio device and sample rate:

1. In the **DETAILS** section at the bottom of the Project Chooser, choose an Input Device and Output Device. If you do not have a dedicated Audio Device, you can choose your computer's built-in Audio Device.

(i) You may need to expand the Project Chooser by clicking on the Details heading, if the device and sample rate settings are not visible.

2. Select **44.1 KHZ** for your Sample Rate.

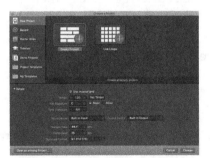

Figure 4.15 Project parameters configured in the Project Chooser

3. Once the parameters are configured, click the **CHOOSE** button at the bottom. Logic Pro will prompt you to create a new track before continuing.

4. For this exercise, select an Audio track type from the New Tracks dialog box and click **CREATE**.

Configure the Logic Pro file type and bit depth:

1.   Open the Recording Preferences window by selecting **LOGIC PRO > PREFERENCES > RECORDING**.

2.   Set the **FILE TYPE** to WAVE (BWF).

3.   Make sure the box is checked for **24-Bit Recording**.

4.   When finished, close the Preferences window.

Creating and Naming Tracks

For this part of the exercise, you can work in either the Tracks Area or the Live Loops Grid. Using the **SHOW/HIDE** buttons in the Tracks Area menu bar, you can choose a view or display both views simultaneously. Here, you will add and remove tracks as needed and give your tracks meaningful names.

Adding Tracks

At this point, you have only one Audio track in your new empty project. In the next series of steps, you will add some new tracks, delete unneeded tracks, rename the tracks you will use in the project, and reorder the tracks.

Create additional tracks for the project:

1.   Choose **TRACK > NEW AUDIO TRACK** to insert a new Audio track. The **Audio 2** track will appear below your existing Audio track.

 Try using the keyboard shortcut to add an Audio track: OPTION+COMMAND+A.

2.   Choose **TRACK > NEW SOFTWARE INSTRUMENT TRACK** to insert a new Software Instrument track. The **Inst 1** track will appear below your other tracks.

 Try using the keyboard shortcut to add a Software Instrument track: OPTION+COMMAND+S.

3.   Select the **Inst 1** track and press **COMMAND+D** to duplicate the track. The **Inst 2** track will be added.

4.   Duplicate the Software Instrument track once more to make a total of three software instrument tracks.

You should now have a total of two Audio tracks and three Software Instrument tracks, along with the default Stereo Out channel and Master channel.

 The Stereo Out channel and Master channel are visible only in the Mixer window (or Mixer view), by default.

Deleting Tracks

For this project, you will only need two Audio tracks and two Software Instrument tracks. The third Software Instrument track (Inst 3) should be deleted from the project.

Delete the above track using one of the following techniques:

- Select the track and press the **DELETE** key on the computer keyboard.

- Right-click on the track and choose **DELETE TRACK** from the pop-up menu.

- Select the track; then choose **TRACK > DELETE TRACK**.

Naming and Organizing Tracks

Next, you'll need to rename the remaining tracks to prepare for producing some music.

Name the four remaining tracks:

1. Double-click on the track name for the first track so that the track name becomes highlighted.

2. Change the name for the first Audio track to **Chords**.

3. Change the name for the second audio track to **Bass**.

 Try using the TAB key to move between tracks while renaming, to rename multiple tracks in succession.

4. Change the names for the Software Instrument tracks as follows:

   - Name the first Software Instrument track **Drums**.

   - Name the second Software Instrument track **Melody**.

The last step is to make sure the tracks are in the correct order for the next exercise. You will need to move the Drums track to the top of the Tracks Area.

Move the Drums track:

- Click the track name at the head of the Drums track and drag it to the top position in the Tracks Area.

- Reorder the other tracks as needed. The final track order should be as follows (see Figure 4.16):

   - Drums

   - Chords

   - Bass

   - Melody

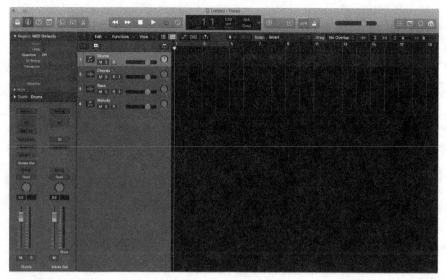

Figure 4.16 Track layout in the Tracks Area view

Finishing Up

To complete this exercise, you will need to save your work under a new name and close the project. Note that you will be reusing this project in Exercise 5, so it is important to save the work you've done.

Finish your work:

1. Choose **FILE > SAVE AS** to save the project and create a project folder structure containing the associated Logic Pro project files.

2. In the **SAVE AS** dialog box, rename the project as *Exercise04-XXX* (where *XXX* is your initials), and select an appropriate save location. Under **ORGANIZE MY PROJECT AS A:** choose the Folder radio button and click **SAVE**.

  DO NOT move the renamed projects to a different save location as you work through the exercises in this book. The exercise revisions you create should all remain within the same original project folder to avoid duplicating the media files.

3. Choose **FILE > CLOSE PROJECT** to close the project (or click the red button on the top left of the Main Window).

(i) You can close a Logic Pro project by closing the Main Window as long as there are no other active windows associated with your project.

4. If desired, you can press **COMMAND+Q** to quit Logic Pro.

Chapter 5

Importing and Working with Media

This chapter introduces various processes for importing audio and video files into a Logic Pro project. We describe file formats and types that can be imported and cover how to use the Browsers in Logic Pro to locate and preview audio files. We go on to discuss methods for importing audio and video files in both the Tracks Area and the Live Loops Grid.

⊕ Learning Targets for This Chapter

- Understand the file resolutions and formats that can be imported into Logic Pro

- Locate supported audio and video files using Logic's Browsers

- Use both the Tracks Area and the Live Loops Grid to import audio files as regions on tracks

- Import video files

Key topics from this chapter are illustrated in the Logic Pro 101 Study Guide module available through the Elements|ED online learning platform. Sign up at ElementsED.com.

As a music producer, composer, sound designer, or engineer, you'll encounter many situations in which a project will start with some kind of existing media. You might find inspiration in a previously created musical loop—such as a drum loop or a chord progression—and want to use that as a starting point for a new song. A collaborator might send you tracks they created so you can continue to develop or mix the idea in your own studio. You might receive video from a director whose film needs a score. Perhaps you just want to browse and use your own samples and sound effects.

In these situations and many others, you will be working with existing media files—and you will need a way to get them into Logic Pro. In this chapter, you will learn the types of files you can import into a Logic project, as well as how to import them.

Considerations Prior to Import

Logic Pro allows you to add audio, MIDI, and video files from any available storage location to your project. There are multiple ways to get media files onto tracks in your project, including dragging and dropping files from a Finder window and locating files through Logic's built-in Browsers. Logic Pro can read some file formats directly and can convert many other audio formats on import.

Prior to importing a file to your project, you need to consider whether the file is compatible with Logic Pro.

File Characteristics

Logic Pro supports audio, MIDI, and video files of various resolutions, types, and formats. In order for a media file to be recognized in a Logic project, it must meet certain criteria.

Supported Audio Bit Depth and Sample Rate

The bit depth of a Logic Pro project will always be either 16-bit or 24-bit, but Logic also supports 20-bit files for import. Project sample rates can be anywhere from 44.1 kHz to 192 kHz. These settings can be specified when the Logic Pro document is created and after by accessing the preferences and project settings. (See "Creating and Configuring a Logic Pro Project" in Chapter 4.)

Although the bit depth of the Logic Pro file can be different from the audio files it references, the sample rate must match between the session and its audio files. This means that any imported audio files must match the session sample rate, or be converted, in order to play back correctly.

Supported Audio File Formats

Logic Pro features native support for three audio file formats: Audio Interchange File Format (AIFF), Waveform Audio File Format (WAV), and Core Audio Format (CAF). WAV, AIFF, and CAF are the only audio file formats that Logic can load without conversion.

To determine the bit depth and file format of an existing open session, choose LOGIC PRO > PREFERENCES > RECORDING. To determine the sample rate, choose FILE > PROJECT SETTINGS > AUDIO.

Logic Pro also utilizes Apple Loops that come in multiple file types including audio and MIDI. All WAV, AIFF, and CAF files can coexist in a session without requiring conversion. However, any files in another format—as well as any files that have a different sample rate from the session, regardless of format—must be converted.

Logic Pro can also import Sound Designer I and II files, ReCycle files, and compressed formats such as MP3 and AAC. These formats are converted into the WAV format by default when imported. The converted file is stored in Audio Files folder of the Logic project.

Here is an overview of the types of audio files that can be imported into Logic Pro:

- **Audio Interchange File Format (AIFF).** This file format is used primarily on Macintosh systems and can be recorded directly or imported without requiring conversion. The AIFF file format is commonly used with media programs such as Final Cut and QuickTime software.

- **Core Audio Format Files (CAF).** Core Audio Format files are containers that support a variety of internal formats including WAV, AIFF, AAC, and Apple Lossless Audio Codec (ALAC). CAF files allow for unrestricted file sizes, making very long recording times possible.

- **Waveform Audio File Format (WAV).** Logic Pro reads and plays back any standard WAV (WAVE) format files. However, it records and exports WAV files in the Broadcast WAV or BWF format. (Like other WAV files, BWF files are denoted by the *.wav* extension.) BWF files are ideal for file interchange operations, due to the way they store timestamps. BWF is the default file format for all Logic Pro systems. BWF files can be recorded directly and imported without conversion, allowing seamless audio file exchange between Mac and Windows.

- **Apple Loops.** Audio loops found in the Loop Browser commonly contain additional identification information about project settings and transient markers. When Apple Loops are added to a project, they will adapt to match the project settings (such as key and tempo) for seamless synchronization.

- **Sound Designer I and II (SD I and SD II).** Sound Designer I and II are mono or stereo file formats supported on Macintosh systems only. This format supports sample rates up to 48 kHz.

- **MP3 (MPEG-1 Layer-3).** MP3 files are supported on all common computer platforms and employ file compression of up to 10:1, while still maintaining reasonable audio quality. Because of their small size and cross-platform support, they have traditionally been popular for email messages, portable music players, and social media. MP3 files must be converted for import into a Logic Pro project.

- **Advanced Audio Coding Format (AAC).** AAC files were created as a successor to MP3. This format generally achieves better sound quality than an MP3 at the same bit rate. AAC is the standard audio format for platforms such as YouTube and iOS devices.

■   **ReCycle Format (RCSO, RCY, REX, and REX2).** ReCycle is a loop editing software manufactured by Reason Studios (formerly Propellerhead). RCSO, RCY, REX, and REX2 files contain original audio, slices (or edits), and signal processing, where applicable. Using the REX Shared Library, added files will be aligned to a project similarly to the behavior of Apple Loops, although not as seamless.

Supported MIDI Files

Logic Pro can import Standard MIDI Files (SMFs) in both common formats—type 0 and type 1. Supported MIDI files are recognizable by their *.mid* or *.smf* file extensions.

Type 0 Standard MIDI Files (SMF0)

In type 0 SMFs, all MIDI data is stored in a single track, separated by the MIDI channel. When imported into Logic, all MIDI data will appear in one track.

Type 1 Standard MIDI Files (SMF1)

In type 1 SMFs, individual parts are saved on different tracks within the MIDI sequence. When imported into Logic, each part will appear on its own track.

Supported Video File Formats

Logic Pro supports video files in Apple QuickTime format (MOV and MP4), allowing you to perform sound design and scoring to video within a Logic project. Supported video files can be imported by dragging them into a Logic project when working in the Tracks Area.

Import Methods

Logic Pro provides several methods for bringing audio and MIDI files into your project: you can import from Logic's built-in Browsers, use the **IMPORT > AUDIO FILE** and **IMPORT > MIDI FILE** commands under the **FILE** menu, drag and drop files from the Finder, or import included content from the Loop Browser.

The following sections provide details for importing audio, starting with a focus on files in Logic's Browsers, as they offer useful search and organizational features.

Loop Browser and Apple Loops

Logic Pro comes with 10,000 Apple Loops. These include drum beats, rhythm sections, phrases, leads, and much more that can be added to any project. Whether for a professional production or drafting an idea, Apple Loops can be used as is or edited to suit your needs without limitations.

Four types of Apple Loops are available: Audio Loops, Software Instrument Loops, Pattern Loops, and Drummer Loops. Audio Loops and Software Instrument Loops function exactly as discussed earlier in this book. However, Drummer Loops are a little different. Drummer Loops are like software instruments that use a special interface to customize their performance.

Drummer tracks are discussed in Chapter 6 of this book.

Showing the Loop Browser

To show or hide the Loop Browser, click the Loop Browser button on the right side of the control bar (or press the **O** key). The Loop Browser will display on the right-hand side of Main Window. The top of the browser displays categories and search tools. Listed below are all available Apple Loop files.

Figure 5.1 Loop Browser in Logic Pro

The Loop Browser has two sections:

- **Apple Loops.** This section contains Apple Loops that are categorized, searchable, and will follow the project tempo and key.

- **Untagged Loops.** In this section, users can add their own content. User content will not contain the same type of embedded information (like categories) as Apple Loops.

Browsing the Loop Browser

To browse categories and narrow down the list of loops available in the browser, users can make selections in any of the following ways:

- Click the **BUTTON VIEW** to see category buttons.

- Click the **COLUMN VIEW** to see a column file directory similar to the Finder.

- Choose a Loop Pack from the pop-up menu at the top of the browser.

Once you have selected a category, you will be able to navigate the selection of loops listed below the category area. To clear out a category selection, click the **RESET** button (orange square with an **X**) at the top of the browser.

Figure 5.2 Loop Browser Category Reset button

You can filter your choices further by arranging the results according to loop type, name, beat, favorites, tempo, and key.

Searching the Loop Browser

To search for Apple Loops by name, type into the **SEARCH** field just below the category area of the browser. In the Untagged Loops section, the **SEARCH** field is located below the file path selector area at the top of the browser. As you type in the **SEARCH** field, Logic Pro will begin filtering results to display any file containing the search text. To clear the results, press the **CANCEL** button to the right of the **SEARCH** field.

Figure 5.3 Loop Browser Search field (top right)

Previewing Audio Files in the Loop Browser

By default, when you click on or select an audio file name, Logic Pro automatically previews the audio. After selecting an audio file, you will also see its waveform display at the bottom of the browser window, below the list of loops. You can click anywhere within the sample waveform to start playback from that specific location.

To stop the preview, you can do any of the following:

- Click on the file a second time.

- Click the **PREVIEW** button to turn off audio previews altogether.

- Press **OPTION+SPACEBAR**.

When previewing loops in an empty project, loops will play at their original tempo. Once a project tempo has been established and regions are in the Tracks Area, previewed loops will play back following the project tempo.

By default, loops will preview in the project key. You can change preview behavior to play in the original key or other keys by selecting an option from the **PLAY IN** pop-up menu at the bottom of the browser that resembles a gear.

You can adjust the preview volume using the **VOLUME** slider at the bottom of the browser.

Project and All Files Browser

Another way to import audio and MIDI files into Logic Pro is to use the built-in browsers, which have two variations: the Project Browser and the All Files Browser. These browsers work like Finder windows embedded within Logic Pro.

Showing the Browsers

To show or hide the browsers, click the **BROWSERS** button on the right side of the control bar (or press the **F** key). The browsers will display on the right-hand side of Main Window. The top of the browsers display categories and search tools. Available content will be listed below.

Figure 5.4 The All Files Browser in Logic Pro

There are two types of browsers:

- **Project Browser.** Use the Project Browser to browse for files within an open project.

- **All Files Browser.** Use the All Files Browser to browse or search for files on any mounted volume on your computer.

Navigating the Browsers

Once you have selected a browser option, content will be displayed in the bottom section of the browser as folders that can be opened by double-clicking or folders with disclosure triangles that expand and collapse. If a listing has additional folders, depending on how they are displayed, you can either expand and collapse them using the disclosure triangles next to each folder name or open by double-clicking folders and using the **FORWARD** and **BACK** buttons.

Alternatively, you can use the Right Arrow and Left Arrow on your keyboard to expand and collapse folders or move forward and back through folders. You can use the Up Arrow and Down Arrow to move your selection through the list of folders and files.

Searching the Browsers

To search for content by name, type into the **SEARCH** field, similar to this operation in the Loop Browser. In the All Files Browser, the **SEARCH** field is located above the File list. The Project Browser does not have a **SEARCH** field.

Previewing Audio Files in Browsers

Previewing files in the Project and All Files Browser works the same as in the Loop Browser.

Importing Audio from the Browsers

After you have located an audio file (or files) in a browser that you would like to use in your project, your next step is to get the audio onto an Audio track. You can import files to existing tracks or create new tracks for the audio as you import files.

Importing Audio to Existing Tracks

You can import to existing tracks in either the Tracks Area or Live Loops Grid; either way, Logic Pro will create an audio region that you can edit in any way you see fit.

Importing to Tracks in the Tracks Area

When you're working in the Tracks Area, you'll see a linear, timeline-based view of your production.

To place audio from a browser onto an audio track in the Tracks Area:

1. Select an audio file in the browser.

2. Click and drag the audio file onto an existing Audio track. You can drag the region anywhere in the arrangement.

Importing to Tracks in Live Loops Grid

When you're working in the Live Loops Grid, you will have access to a series of scenes and cells. You can trigger cells and scenes in any order to generate performances without being tied to a linear timeline.

The process of placing audio files as regions on tracks in the Live Loops Grid is very similar to that for placing audio files.

To place audio from the browser onto an Audio track in the Live Loops Grid:

1. Select an audio file in the browser.

2. Click and drag the audio file to a cell on an Audio track. You can drag the region to any cell in the track.

With the region added to a cell, you can launch the audio file using either the cell's play button or the associated scene trigger button.

Importing Audio to a New Track

If you wish to import audio to a blank track, you can skip the step of manually creating a destination track.

To automatically place an audio file on a new Audio track, drag the file from a browser to any position below the last track in your project. Logic Pro will create a new Audio track at that position and will place the region on the track.

Batch Importing Audio to Tracks

At times you might find yourself in a situation where you'd like to import multiple audio files simultaneously. In these cases, you can quickly send a set of selected files to one or more tracks.

Batch Import in the Tracks Area

The Tracks Area offers several different options for importing audio files to tracks. You can import the audio to new tracks, to existing tracks, or as a contiguous string of regions on a single track.

To batch import files, follow these steps:

1. Select the audio files in the browser:

    *   Hold **SHIFT** to select a contiguous range of files, or

    *   Hold **COMMAND** to select non-contiguous files

2. Drag the audio files onto the target Audio track or below the last track.

    The **ADD SELECTED FILES TO TRACKS** dialog box will open.

Figure 5.5 Add Selected Files to Tracks dialog box

3.   Select one of the following options:

- **Create new tracks.** This will create a new track below the selected track for each of the imported files. Each audio file will be placed at the same start position.

- **Use existing tracks.** This will place the imported files on the selected track and any available tracks that exist below the selected track. New tracks will be made for any files that aren't placed on existing tracks, and each file will be placed at the same start position.

- **Place all files on one track.** Files will be placed back-to-back on the same selected track or on a newly created track.

4.   Optionally enable the **ALL SELECTED FILES ARE STEMS FROM ONE PROJECT** checkbox. This causes a set of multitrack files to be linked together so they will be analyzed as a group when using Smart Tempo. Enabling this option makes it possible to do tempo operations that affect or follow the multitrack set rather than the individual tracks.

Batch Import in the Live Loops Grid

The Live Loops Grid also offers different methods for importing multiple audio files to tracks. You can import the audio into subsequent cells on a single track, or you can place each audio file on a separate track in the same cell position.

To place the audio files into subsequent cells on the same Audio track:

1.   Select the audio files in the browser using one of the methods described above.

2.   Drag the audio files onto a cell on an Audio track. As you drag, a preview will indicate where the regions will be imported.

3.   Release the mouse to add the regions to successive cells on the track.

To place the audio files into cells on separate tracks:

1.   Select the audio files in the browser using one of the methods described above.

2.   Drag the audio files to a desired cell in the Live Loops Grid and press **SHIFT** before releasing the mouse. A preview will indicate where the regions will be imported.

3.   While holding **SHIFT**, release the mouse. The regions will be added to successive Audio tracks, at the same cell position on each track. (See Figure 5.6.)

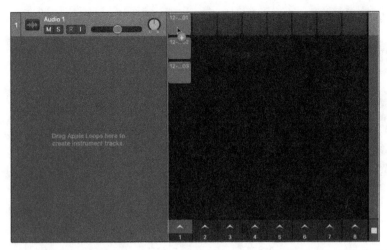

Figure 5.6 Batch importing audio files to separate tracks in the Live Loops Grid

Audio, MIDI, and Tempo Changes

Although Audio and MIDI tracks can coexist in projects, they can respond differently to changes in tempo because their source material is different – Audio tracks contain samples from a waveform, while MIDI tracks contain performance data. MIDI regions easily conform to changes in your project tempo, as the MIDI data is flexible. Audio regions, on the other hand, can be absolute, meaning Logic Pro will continue to play them back at their original speed regardless of the project tempo. This can be desirable for non-rhythmic audio, such as spoken words or ambient textures, but it can cause rhythmic audio to fall out of sync in the context of a song.

Flex and Follow

With Flex algorithms, Logic Pro is capable of time-flexing audio regions while streaming them from disk so as to synchronize them to the project's tempo. Tempo matching is done without affecting the pitch of the audio. As such, you can mix and match audio files from various sources with MIDI data, and your project can remain flexible to tempo changes.

One way to enable Audio tracks to follow the tempo of a project is to enable the **FLEX & FOLLOW** option in the Region Inspector. If an audio file contains tempo information, this will be detected by the Flex algorithm and inform playback behavior when Flex is enabled.

 The Region Inspector is available in the Inspector tab on the left side of the Main Window. Press I to display the Inspector, if it is not currently showing.

To enable Flex & Follow, use these steps:

1. Select one or more audio regions from a given track.

2. If the Inspector is not already open, press the I key.

3.   Set the **FLEX & FOLLOW** pop-up menu in the Region Inspector to **ON**. (See Figure 5.7.)

Figure 5.7 Flex & Follow enabled on an audio region in the Region Inspector

   You can also enable Flex & Follow in the Cell Inspector in the Live Loops Grid.

The selected audio region(s) will now automatically follow tempo changes in your project and conform to the project tempo map.

   By default, audio regions imported from the Loop Browser will have FLEX & FOLLOW enabled automatically.

Smart Tempo

If an audio file doesn't contain tempo information, the file can be analyzed using Smart Tempo. This feature uses the Flex algorithm to analyze and create tempo information that fits a performance. Smart Tempo is also useful if a recorded performance doesn't conform to the embedded tempo information.

To analyze an audio file using Smart Tempo, follow these steps:

1.   Select an audio region in the Tracks Area.

2.   Open the Editor by double-clicking the region or pressing the **E** key.

3.   Select the Smart Tempo tab and click **ANALYZE** to analyze the region. (If a region already has tempo information, the button will display **EDIT**.)

Once an audio region has been analyzed, you can preview the result, make changes or edits to the analysis, and decide how the region will apply to the project, including enabling **FLEX & FOLLOW**.

Project Tempo Modes

The Project Tempo mode determines how Logic Pro will handle the tempo of recorded and imported audio and MIDI. Depending on the mode, audio regions will follow the project tempo or vice versa. You can choose the mode by clicking on the LCD Tempo display in the control bar. (See Figure 5.8.)

Figure 5.8 Project Tempo modes pop-up menu in the LCD Display

The available Project Tempo modes include:

- **Keep Project Tempo.** This mode maintains the project tempo when recording and importing audio. This behavior is how most other DAWs handle tempo by default.

- **Adapt Project Tempo.** This mode adapts the project tempo to the tempo of recorded or imported audio. This mode is good for recording without a metronome or importing audio that you want the project to follow.

- **Automatic.** In this mode, Logic Pro will decide which behavior is best depending on whether there is a tempo reference present. If the metronome is active or regions are present, the mode will keep that tempo; when no tempo is present, the mode will adapt to incoming material.

Other Methods of Importing Audio Files

Audio files can be imported using menu commands or using the Finder, rather than using the built-in Browser in Logic Pro.

Importing with a Menu Command

Logic Pro gives you the option of locating and importing audio from the **FILE** menu. This can be useful if you know the disk location of the audio files you want to import, such as when you've downloaded files from an online resource or when you are importing shared files from a USB drive.

To import audio using the File menu:

1. Select the Audio track on which you'd like to insert the audio file:

    - In the Tracks Area, position the playhead where you want to insert the audio region.

    - In the Live Loops Grid, select the cell in which you would like to place the audio cell.

2. Select **FILE > IMPORT > AUDIO FILE** or press **SHIFT+COMMAND+I**.

3. Navigate the file browser to the location of the audio file.

4. Double-click on the file to import it.

Importing from the Finder

You can also import audio files by drag-and-drop from a Finder window on your computer.

To import files from the Finder:

1. Locate and select the files in a Finder window.

2. Drag the files from the Finder window into the Logic Pro Main Window. The results will depend on the number of files imported and number of available Audio tracks:

   • When importing a single audio file, it will be added to a track at the location where it is dropped (on an existing audio track, on a newly created audio track, or in a cell).

   • When importing multiple audio files, a dialog box will appear, allowing you to choose whether to create new tracks, use existing tracks, or place all files on the same track.

Importing Video

When you are scoring and/or performing sound design for visual media, it helps to bring the video directly into your project. This way, you can edit your composition to align with cuts and "hit points" in the video.

To import video into your project, do one of the following:

▪ Choose **FILE > MOVIE > OPEN MOVIE** and select a movie file.

▪ From a Finder window, drag a movie file into the Tracks Area.

▪ From the Browsers, navigate to the proper directory and drag a movie file into the Tracks Area.

Logic Pro supports video files in Apple QuickTime (MOV and MP4) format only. Every version of macOS comes with QuickTime installed.

When you import a video file, the **OPEN MOVIE** dialog box will display (Figure 5.9), giving you options to open the dedicated movie window and to extract the audio from the movie upon importing.

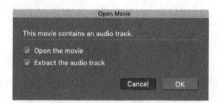

Figure 5.9 Open Movie dialog box

Depending on whether the movie file matches your project settings, you may be prompted with the following dialog boxes:

- **Frame Rate.** If the movie has a different frame rate than the project, a dialog box will ask which frame rate to use. For best synchronization results, use the same frame rate as the movie by selecting the option in blue.

Figure 5.10 Movie frame rate dialog box

- **Sample Rate.** If the movie has a different sample rate than the project, a dialog box will ask which sample rate to use. For best results, use the same sample rate as the movie by selecting the option in blue.

Figure 5.11 Movie sample rate dialog box

 The standard sample rate used for most video projects is 48kHz.

The first frame of the movie will be placed at the start of your project, unless otherwise specified during import.

Movie Track Display

If you select **OPEN THE MOVIE** during import, the movie will open in a dedicated window. If you don't select this option (or if you close the movie window), the movie will display at the top of the Inspector, giving you a compact view. To open the movie window, **DOUBLE-CLICK** the movie area in the Inspector. The movie area will close, and the floating movie window will open. In addition, a global Movie track will be created showing single frames on the timeline. Resizing the track will affect the number of visible frames.

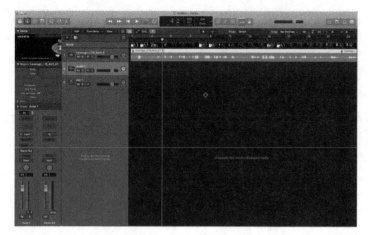

Figure 5.12 An imported video file and associated Audio track in the Main Window

The movie window can also be resized as needed to fit comfortably within the available display space on your screen.

To resize the movie window, do one of the following:

■ Click and drag the lower right-hand corner of the movie window to resize it.

■ Click the button in the upper right-hand corner of the movie window to expand to fit the screen. Click the button again to return to the previous size.

■ **CONTROL-CLICK** the movie and choose an option from the pop-up menu.

Working with Movie Tracks

The global Movie track displays movie frames as thumbnails, and the contents can be moved using the Pointer tool. This allows you to offset the movie to any start point.

If you select **EXTRACT THE AUDIO TRACK** in the Open Movie dialog box (Figure 5.9), the movie's audio file will be added to the project's Audio Files folder, and a new track will be created in the project containing the audio file as a region in the Tracks Area. This allows easy playback control or editing of the movie's audio. If you decide not to extract the audio upon import of the movie, the movie will still play back its audio, but the audio file will not be added to the Audio Files folder and no track with the audio region will be created. As a result, you will no control or metering for the volume of the movie.

 You can also add a movie's audio to your project by selecting FILE > MOVIE > IMPORT AUDIO FROM MOVIE.

The movie's Audio track takes its name from the imported video file. Audio tracks can subsequently be renamed, in the same manner as other tracks in your project.

See the "Naming Tracks" section in Chapter 4 for details on renaming tracks.

The movie and its audio will be synchronized as long as the SMPTE position remains locked. If either component is moved, the other will move to the same position, ensuring they always play back correctly. If you decide to unlock the SMPTE position, the movie and its Audio track will be freely movable.

To lock or unlock the SMPTE position, **CONTROL-CLICK** the movie's audio region and select an option from the **SMPTE LOCK** category of the pop-up menu.

 SMPTE timecode is a standard developed by the Society of Motion Picture and Television Engineers organization. This ensures consistent and accurate synchronization of video frames with timecode.

Only one video file can be associated with a Logic Pro project at a time. If you want to import a different movie into a project, repeat the preceding steps. The new movie will replace the original in the project.

You can remove a movie file by selecting **FILE > MOVIE > REMOVE MOVIE**.

Configuring the Position of a Movie File

If you're scoring a piece of video, it can be helpful to reposition the beginning of the movie to a preferred start position in your project. The movie can be repositioned using the mouse pointer.

To reposition the movie with more precision, do the following:

1. Choose **FILE > PROJECT SETTINGS > SYNCHRONIZATION**.

2. Set the **BAR POSITION** to the desired starting location.

 If you reposition the movie using the mouse pointer and later change the synchronization in the project settings, you the movie may not align with the set position. This may be due to a change or offset in the SMPTE timecode found in the STARTS AT SMPTE setting of the same menu.

 If no SMPTE timecode has been indicated in the movie file, the default is 01:00:00:00.00.

Review/Discussion Questions

1. What audio file formats can be imported to Logic Pro without requiring conversion? (See "Supported Audio File Formats" beginning on page 102.)

2. Name some of the other common audio file formats that Logic Pro supports. (See "Supported Audio File Formats" beginning on page 102.)

3. What automatically happens when you import a compressed audio file such as MP3 and AAC into a Logic Pro project? (See "Supported Audio File Formats" beginning on page 102.)

4. What video file format does Logic Pro support? (See "Supported Video File Formats" beginning on page 104.)

5. What are three methods you can use to import an audio or video file into a Logic Pro project? (See "Import Methods" beginning on page 104.)

6. How can you show and hide the Loop Browser? (See "Showing the Loop Browser" beginning on page 105.)

7. Once you've located an audio file in a browser, how can you import it into your project? (See "Importing Audio from the Browsers" beginning on page 108.)

8. How can you simultaneously import multiple audio files with each file being placed on its own new Audio track? (See "Batch Import in the Tracks Area" beginning on page 109.)

9. How can you show and hide the floating movie window once you have inserted a video file on a track? How can you re-size it? (See "Movie Track Display" beginning on page 115.)

10. How would you go about importing a movie file to Logic Pro while simultaneously importing the audio embedded in the file? (See "Working with Movie Tracks" beginning on page 116.)

11. How many movie files can be associated with a Logic Pro project at once? (See "Working with Movie Tracks" beginning on page 116.)

 To review additional material from this chapter and prepare for certification, see the Logic Pro 101 Study Guide module available through the Elements|ED online learning platform at ElementsED.com.

Importing Audio

🎧 Activity

In this exercise tutorial, you will use the Browsers to import audio files into the project you created in the previous exercise. You will import two fragments of a musical idea: a chord progression and a bass line, both created with synths. You can choose to place these audio files on tracks using either the Tracks Area or the Live Loops Grid, depending on how you prefer to work.

🕐 Duration

This exercise should take approximately 15 to 20 minutes to complete.

◈ Goals/Targets

- Locate files using the All Files Browser
- Import audio regions to tracks in the Tracks Area or Live Loops Grid

---

Media Files

To complete this exercise, you will need to use various audio files included in the **Media Files 2021-Logic101** folder. You should have downloaded the media files in Exercise 4.

If needed, you can re-download the media files by going to www.halleonard.com/mylibrary and entering your access code (printed on the opening page of this book). From there, click the **Download** link for the **Media Files 2021-Logic101** listing in your **My Library** page. The Media Files folder will begin transferring to your Downloads folder.

Getting Started

You will start by opening the project you saved at the end of Exercise 4. If that file is not available, you can use the Ex04 Sample file in the 01 Completed Exercises folder within the Media Files 2021-Logic101 folder.

Open the project and save it as Exercise 5:

1. Open the project file that you created in Exercise 4 (**Storage Drive/Folder > Exercise04-XXX.logicx**).

ⓘ **If your Exercise 4 project is not available, you can use the Exercise 4 Sample file (Media Files 2021-Logic101 > 01 Completed Exercises > Ex04 Sample.logicx).**

2. Choose **FILE > SAVE AS** and name the project *Exercise05-XXX*, keeping the file in the same drive location. (Move the project to your selected save location, if working from the sample file.)

3. Make sure the **ORGANIZE MY PROJECT AS A:** option still has **FOLDER** selected; then click **SAVE**.

The opened project will have four tracks—two Audio tracks and two MIDI tracks. These are the tracks you created in Exercise 4.

Locate Audio Files in the All Files Browser

In this exercise, you will use Logic's built-in Browsers to locate and import files. To get started, you will navigate to the **Exercise Media** folder in the All Files Browser.

Navigate to the exercise media folder:

1. Click the **BROWSERS** button or press **F** and select the **ALL FILES** tab to show the All Files Browser.

2. Navigate to the **Media Files 2021-Logic101 > 02 Exercise Media** location.

3. Open the **02 Exercise Media** folder in the Browser to display the audio files it contains.

Figure 5.13 The Exercise Media folder within the All Files Browser

The audio files in this folder are all in WAV format. Notice that the file names include a loose genre identifier, a descriptor (**Bass** or **Chords**), a key (**C major** or **A minor**), and a tempo. In the next section, you will select a chord progression and the matching bass part to use for this exercise. For example, if you select the pop chord progression in C major at 120 BPM, you should also use the pop bass in C major at 120 BPM. This way, you will combine two distinct instruments that work together.

Preview the chord progression and bass audio files:

1.   Click through the various audio files to listen to the different options for the project. As discussed in Chapter 5, you can click an audio file to preview it.

2.   Make note of the chord progression and corresponding bass part that you like the most. In the next section, you will place the files on audio tracks and start assembling a musical pattern in your project.

Importing Audio to Tracks

With the audio files for this exercise available through the Browsers, importing them to Audio tracks will be quick and easy. This is a good time to decide whether you want to work in the Tracks Area or the Live Loops Grid. If you prefer working in a traditional, timeline-based fashion, use the Tracks Area. If you'd like to use Logic's features for auditioning different combinations of sounds and creating flexible arrangements, you can try the Live Loops Grid instead.

Tracks Area (Option 1)

Complete this section to work in the Tracks Area. Alternatively, you can skip forward to Option 2 below.

Import the audio files to tracks in the Tracks Area:

1.   Set the project tempo so that it matches the tempo of the audio files you will be using.

2.   Drag and drop your selected chord progression file to Bar 5 of the **Chords** Audio track.

3.   Double-click the name in the Region Inspector to highlight the name.

4.   Rename the audio region to something simple and descriptive, such as **Chords**.

5.   Select the **Chords** region and press **COMMAND+R** to create a second copy of the region on the track, immediately after the original.

6.   Repeat the command two more times, for a total of four identical regions, to create a longer, 16-bar song segment.

7.   Drag and drop the corresponding bass part to the **Bass** track, this time starting at Bar 13.

8.   With the region selected, double-click the name in the Region Inspector to highlight the name.

9.   Rename the region to something simple and descriptive, such as **Bass**.

10. Duplicate the **Bass** region once, so it plays from the middle to the end of the 16-bar segment.

You've now created a 16-bar segment, with a chord progression spanning the whole duration and the bass part starting after 8 bars. Your composition should look similar to Figure 5.14 below.

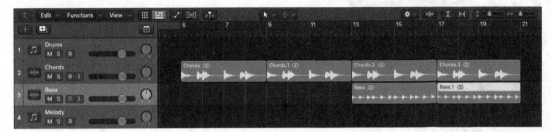

Figure 5.14 A project with chord and bass parts completed in the Tracks Area

Review your work:

1. Position the playhead at the start of the region beginning at bar 5.

2. Press the **SPACEBAR** to play back the project and confirm your results.

3. Press the **SPACEBAR** a second time when finished to stop playback.

Live Loops Grid (Option 2)

Complete this section to work in the Live Loops Grid. (If you've completed Option 1 above, you can skip forward to the next section.)

Import the audio files to tracks in the Live Loops Grid:

1. Set the project tempo so that it matches the tempo of the audio files you will be using.

2. Drag and drop your selected chord progression file onto the first and second cells of the **Chords** Audio track. This will place the region on both Scene 1 and Scene 2.

 Instead of dragging the audio file from the Browser a second time, you can press and hold OPTION while a dragging the region from cell 1 to duplicate it on cell 2.

3. Select the two regions and rename them in the Cell Inspector by double-clicking **2 SELECTED**.

4. Rename the regions to something simple and descriptive, such as **Chords**.

5. Drag the bass file onto the second cell of the **Bass** Audio track; this region should be on Scene 2 only.

6. Rename the region to something simple and descriptive, such as **Bass**.

At this point, you will have a basic, two-scene project. (See Figure 5.15.)

You can alternate playback between the chord progression in isolation (Scene 1) and the combination of the chord progression and the corresponding bass part (Scene 2).

Figure 5.15 A project with chord and bass parts added in the Live Loops Grid

Review your work:

1.   Click the **SCENE** trigger for Scene 1. The chord region will launch and begin playing. Left unchanged, the region will repeat when it reaches the end.

2.   When the region is just a couple beats away from repeating, press the **SCENE** trigger for Scene 2 to queue up the next scene. When the first Scene ends, the second Scene will launch, containing both the chord progression and the corresponding bass part.

3.   When finished, click the **SPACEBAR** or **GRID STOP** button on the Divider column to stop playback.

Finishing Up

To complete this exercise, you will save your work and close the project. You will be reusing this project in the next exercise, so it is important to save the work you've done.

Save your work and close the project:

1.   Choose **FILE > SAVE** to save the project.

2.   Choose **FILE > CLOSE PROJECT** (or click the red button on the top left) to close the project.

3.   If desired, you can press **COMMAND+Q** to quit Logic Pro.

(i)   Remember you can close a Logic Pro project by closing the Main Window as long as there are no other active windows associated with the project.

Chapter 6

Making Your First MIDI Recording

This chapter covers the basics of recording and working with MIDI data in Logic Pro. It describes how to set up and record onto MIDI-compatible tracks, how to use virtual instrument plug-ins, and how to select different views for the MIDI data on your tracks.

⊕ Learning Targets for This Chapter

- Understand the basics of the MIDI protocol

- Identify the two types of MIDI-compatible tracks that Logic provides

- Prepare a system to record MIDI data

- Set up a virtual instrument to play MIDI data recorded on a Software Instrument track

- Examine virtual instruments included with Logic

 Key topics from this chapter are illustrated in the Logic Pro 101 Study Guide module available through the Elements|ED online learning platform. Sign up at ElementsED.com.

Recording and editing MIDI data is similar to working with audio; many of the tools, modes, and menu functions work in a similar fashion. However, MIDI data is fundamentally different from audio; therefore, some of the processes and operations you use to work with this data will be different. This chapter introduces features in Logic Pro that are designed for recording and editing MIDI data.

MIDI Basics

MIDI, or *Musical Instrument Digital Interface*, is a protocol for connecting electronic instruments, performance controllers, and computers so they can communicate with one another. MIDI data is different from data stored in an audio file in that MIDI data does not represent sound waves; instead, it represents information about a performance, such as the pitch, duration, and intensity of the notes in the performance.

MIDI devices transmit performance data via MIDI messages, which are composed of 8-bit numbers (or *bytes*) and include information such as *note* or *pitch number* (indicating an individual note in a scale) and *velocity* (typically affecting an individual note's volume). Up to 16 separate channels of MIDI information can be sent over a traditional MIDI cable, allowing that single cable path to control multiple MIDI devices or to control a single device that is capable of multi-channel (or *multi-timbral*) operation.

The Format of a Traditional MIDI Message

The most significant bit in a MIDI message byte is reserved to distinguish between status bytes and data bytes. The remaining seven bits represent the unique data of the message byte, encompassing a range of values from 0 to 126. The maximum length for a standard MIDI 1.0 message is three bytes, consisting of one status byte and one or more data bytes.

Status Byte	Data Byte 1	Data Byte 2
1tttnnnn	0xxxxxxx	0xxxxxxx

Where:

t is used to specify the type of status message being sent
n is used to specify the associated MIDI Channel Number
x is used to specify the associated data value, such as a note number (pitch) or velocity value

---

 In January 2020, the MIDI Manufacturers Association adopted the MIDI 2.0 specification. This update increases velocity resolution. It also introduces a new Universal MIDI Packet that uses at least 32 bits (four bytes) per message.

Many other kinds of information can be conveyed via MIDI messages, such as pan and general MIDI volume information for instruments that support these, as well as program change events, or commands that tell MIDI instruments which of their available sounds, or *patches*, to use.

A *MIDI sequencer* allows you to store, edit, and play back MIDI information that can be used to control MIDI-compatible devices, such as synthesizers, sound modules, and drum machines. These don't have to be external hardware devices—today many synthesizers, samplers, and other sound modules are available as virtual instrument plug-ins, enabling you to add devices directly to tracks from within your DAW.

MIDI in Logic Pro

Logic Pro includes an integrated MIDI sequencer (or editor) that lets you program, record, import, and edit MIDI data in much the same way that you work with imported audio (see Chapter 5) or recorded audio (see Chapter 7). MIDI data is stored in MIDI regions and can be edited in the Piano Roll Editor or Step Sequencer, regardless of whether you're working in the Tracks Area or Live Loops Grid.

Creating MIDI-Compatible Tracks

If your project does not already contain them, you will have to create one or more MIDI-compatible tracks for your MIDI recording. The type of track you use will depend on your preferences and the MIDI devices you plan to use.

As you learned in Chapter 4, Logic Pro provides a two types of tracks for working with MIDI data: Software Instrument tracks and External MIDI tracks.

- A *Software Instrument track* stores MIDI performance data inside of MIDI regions. Software Instrument tracks route that MIDI data through a virtual instrument plug-in that emulates a hardware synthesizer or sample player. While MIDI data on its own doesn't generate any sound, playing the recorded performance through one of these plug-ins creates an audio output for the track.

- An *External MIDI track* is similar to a Software Instrument track in that it stores MIDI data inside MIDI regions. The difference is that on an External MIDI track, data must be routed out of Logic to a separate hardware device connected to your computer to generate sound. The MIDI data can be used to trigger sounds on an external keyboard synthesizer, sampler, drum machine, or other sound module. You can record the audio outputs from these external devices onto Audio tracks to get the sounds back into Logic, or route them as live inputs through an Auxiliary channel strip.

Some considerations for selecting a track type for your MIDI composition include whether you will be using a virtual instrument with the track (see "Using Virtual Instruments" later in this chapter) and the complexity of your setup. For basic MIDI recording with virtual instruments, you will probably find Software Instrument tracks to be easier to use, due to the simplified manner in which they allow you to route audio from your MIDI devices through your project.

To add MIDI-compatible tracks, do the following:

1. Chose **TRACK > NEW TRACKS** or press **COMMAND+OPTION+N** to open the New Tracks dialog box.

2. Specify the number of desired tracks in the Track Total field.

3.   Select either **EXTERNAL MIDI TRACK** or **SOFTWARE INSTRUMENT TRACK** in the New Tracks dialog box.

4.   For Software Instrument tracks, select a specific instrument plug-in from the drop-down menu in the details section.

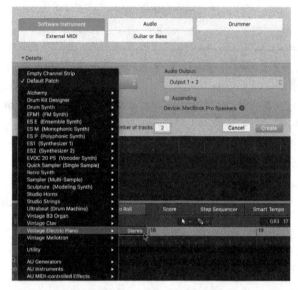

Figure 6.1   Selecting a Software Instrument plug-in in the New Tracks dialog box

5.   Click **CREATE**. The new track will be added to your project.

 When you create a new Software Instrument track using the shortcut COMMAND+OPTION+S, the new track will use whatever is selected in the *Instrument* drop-down menu. If you'd like to configure your own settings, select the *Empty Channel Strip* option.

You can create MIDI regions by recording a performance to a MIDI track or by manually programming in the MIDI notes. Both methods are covered later in this chapter.

 For a detailed breakdown of track types and associated keyboard shortcuts, see Chapter 4 of this book.

MIDI Versus Audio Region Operation

Audio and MIDI regions can and often do co-exist in a Logic Project. However, they're very different, and it is worth understanding the differences in how audio and MIDI regions behave. We've already established one key difference in that MIDI regions don't inherently produce sound; the other key difference is how MIDI regions behave when you make changes to the tempo of your Project.

Audio and MIDI regions respond differently to changes in tempo because their source material is different: audio regions contain samples whereas MIDI regions contain performance data.

Figure 6.2 A blend of MIDI and audio regions in the Main Window

MIDI Operation

MIDI regions easily conform to changes in the project tempo in Logic, as the MIDI data is flexible. MIDI events are recorded relative to particular bar and beat locations (such as Bar 16, Beat 1), and their locations in time adjust based on the project tempo:

- If the tempo increases, the MIDI data will play back faster, and individual events will occur earlier in time.

- If the tempo decreases, the MIDI data will play back more slowly, and the same events will occur later in time.

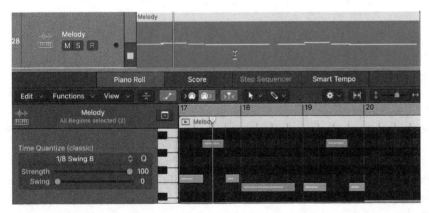

Figure 6.3 A MIDI region displayed in the Main Window (top) and in the Piano Roll Editor (bottom)

Standard Audio Operation

Audio regions, on the other hand, are generally absolute, meaning they will continue to play back at their original speed and location after changing the project tempo—though the audio regions' positions relative to the project's bars and beats will change. This behavior can be desirable for non-rhythmic audio, such as spoken words or ambient textures, but it can cause rhythmic audio like drum loops to fall out of sync in the context of a song.

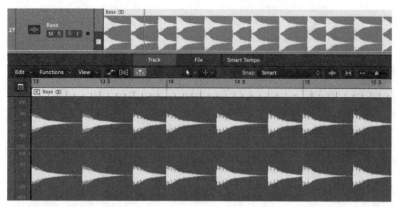

Figure 6.4 An audio region displayed in the Main Window (top) and Audio Track Editor (bottom)

Audio Warping

With Flex Time Warp algorithms, Logic is capable of time-warping audio regions while streaming them from disk so as to synchronize them with the project tempo. This happens without affecting the pitch, which can be changed independently. As such, even if you mix and match audio files from various sources with MIDI data, your project can remain flexible with respect to tempo changes.

 Flex Time and Flex pitch are covered in Chapter 7 of this book.

Sample-Based Operation

In sample-based operation, recorded information is tied to fixed points in time relative to the beginning of the project. Audio data is stored as individual audio samples in a file. In Logic, audio regions are represented on sample-based tracks by default. Audio regions that reside on a sample-based track are located at particular sample locations on the Timeline.

You can think of these sample-based locations as *absolute locations* in time, measured by the number of samples that have elapsed since the beginning of the project. Sample-based audio regions are not affected by the project tempo and will not move from their sample locations if the project tempo changes—though the audio regions' positions relative to the project' bars and beats will change.

Tick-Based Operation

In tick-based operation, recorded information is tied to specific Bar|Beat locations in an arrangement. When you record MIDI data, Logic uses tick-based timing to determine the locations of your MIDI events.

MIDI events are recorded relative to particular bar and beat locations (such as Bar 16, Beat 1), and their locations in time adjust based on the project tempo—if the tempo increases, the MIDI data will play back faster, and individual events will occur earlier in time; if the tempo decreases, the MIDI data will play back more slowly, and the same events will occur later in time.

Logic subdivides the bars and beats in your project into divisions and ticks, with divisions set to 1/16 notes by default, and 240 ticks comprising a division. With four 1/16 note divisions in a beat, each quarter note is comprised of 960 ticks. Timing can thus be specified with a precision (or resolution) of up to 1/960th of a quarter note when measuring in bars and beats.

You can think of tick-based locations as *relative locations* in time, measured by the number of bars, beats, and ticks that have elapsed since the beginning of the project. A tick-based event maintains its rhythmic location relative to other tick-based events in the song, regardless of the project tempo—but a tempo change will cause the event to occur earlier or later in *absolute* time, thereby changing its location relative to any sample-based audio in the project.

Setting the Base Meter and Tempo

Before you begin recording MIDI data, you should determine the required meter and tempo for the performance and make any necessary changes in Logic to match. The following sections describe how to set the meter and tempo for your composition.

Viewing Global Tracks

Logic Pro includes various timeline displays known as *global tracks*. Global tracks allow you to control various parameters for your Logic project. From these timeline displays, you can add events to change your tempo, time signature, and key signature; you can also add location markers.

To show or hide the global tracks, click the **GLOBAL TRACKS** button, or press the **G** key. Global tracks can be displayed in the Main Window above the tracks area, and in the Audio Editor or Piano Roll Editor. You can further configure which global tracks are shown or hidden by pressing **OPTION+G** or by right-clicking on an active global track.

Figure 6.5 The Global Tracks button enabled (left), and Global Tracks Configuration (right)

Setting the Project Tempo & Time Signature

When you open a new session in Logic, the tempo defaults to 120 beats per minute (BPM). If you intend to record with the click and you are working with a different tempo, make sure to set the tempo accordingly.

Entering a Base Tempo Value

If you know the tempo you'd like to use, you can enter it directly into the LCD. You can click and drag vertically on the Tempo Display to increase/decrease your projects tempo. Alternatively, you can double click the Tempo Display to type in a value.

Figure 6.6 The Tempo Display section of the LCD in Logic's Main Window

Adding Tempo Changes

Tempo changes, which can occur anywhere within a Logic Pro project, are added and displayed using the global tracks in the Main Window.

To add tempo change, do the following:

1. In the Main Window, click on the **GLOBAL TRACKS** button to display the project's Tempo track.

2. Using the Pencil or the Pointer tool, click a location on the Tempo track to create a tempo point, then drag vertically up or down to create a tempo change.

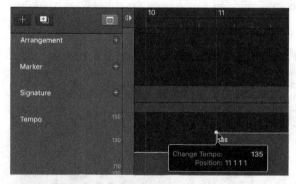

Figure 6.7 Dragging an existing tempo point with the Pointer tool to create a tempo change

Figure 6.8 Inserting a new tempo change while clicking and dragging with the Pencil tool

Setting the Base Time Signature

When you create a new Logic project, the time signature defaults to 4/4. Just like with Tempo, you can change the base time signature settings for your project by clicking into Time Signature Display portion of the LCD. (See Figure 6.9.) You'll then make a selection from the resulting list of Time Signatures.

If you are working with an odd time signature, you can click *Custom* to manually configure time signature numerator and denominator.

Figure 6.9 The Time Signature Display in the LCD (left) and list of time signatures (right)

To change a project's time signature, do the following:

1.   Position the playhead where you'd like to insert a time signature change.

2.   With the Signature track displayed in the global tracks, click on the **ADD SIGNATURE** button. The Time Signature dialog box will open.

Figure 6.10 The Add Signature button on the Signature track, and the Time Signature dialog box

> (i) You can also click on the SIGNATURE track with the Pencil tool to insert a time signature change.

3.   (Optional) Choose a note value that corresponds to the desired click timing. This may be desirable for meters such as 6/8 to play a click based on something other than the default quarter-note value.

4.   Click **OK** to insert the new Time Signature change at the start of the closest bar.

Figure 6.11 A time signature change shown on the Signature track

Preparing to Record MIDI

With MIDI-compatible tracks added to your project and the meter and tempo configured as desired, you will next need to prepare your MIDI device and software for recording. The general processes you will use to prepare for recording MIDI are as follows:

1.   Configure the metronome to aid in making a well-timed recording, if desired.

2.   Connect a MIDI device, if available

> (i)   In the absence of a dedicated MIDI device, you can record MIDI using your computer keyboard, or manually program MIDI using your mouse and keyboard.

3.   Check the track inputs/outputs.

4.   Record-enable the track(s).

Enabling the Metronome

When you're recording parts for a song or other composition that is based on a specific tempo (or tempos) with established bar and beat divisions, you might want to perform along with a metronome-based tick. The metronome can help you synchronize your performance to the composition while you're recording—whether recording MIDI data or audio—and that will ultimately help align the recorded parts to musical divisions.

Having your recorded parts in alignment with the Logic project's tempo makes it easy for you to make selections according to the musical grid, and perform such tasks as copying and pasting entire song sections as you work on your arrangements.

To enable or disable the metronome, click the **METRONOME** button in the control bar along the top of Logic's Main Window, or press the **K** key. When you click the **PLAY** button in the control bar, launch a cell from the Live Loops Grid, or begin recording, the metronome will play a tick sound at each beat.

Logic Pro provides various metronome options, which you can access by right-clicking the **METRONOME** button.

Figure 6.12 Right-clicking on the Metronome button to reveal additional metronome settings

Options available in the Metronome settings menu include the following:

- **SIMPLE MODE**—In this mode, whenever the metronome button is toggled on, you will hear a metronome click. The other options will be greyed out while this mode is active.

- **CLICK WHILE RECORDING**—This mode engages the metronome click while you're recording, giving you the option to not hear the metronome while playing material back. In this mode, the metronome during a record pass, regardless of whether it's toggled on or not.

- **ONLY DURING COUNT-IN**—This option turns off the metronome when the Count-In is not active. the metronome will sound only during the count-in prior to recording. (Note that Click While Recording must also be enabled for this to work.)

- **CLICK WHILE PLAYING**—In this mode, the metronome will sound whenever you're playing back material. Toggling this option on/off has the same effect as toggling the metronome on/off.

You can adjust further controls, including the volume level and tone of the metronome, by going into your project's Metronome Settings. You can do this from the right-click menu on the metronome, or by selecting **FILE > PROJECT SETTINGS > METRONOME**. You can also adjust the pitch of the bar and beat clicks, as well as their velocity.

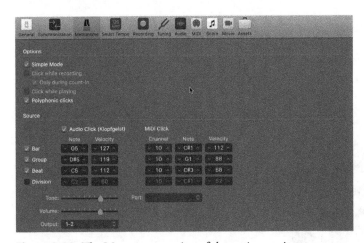

Figure 6.13 The Metronome section of the project settings

Connecting a MIDI Device

Recording MIDI data typically involves connecting a keyboard, a drum machine, or some other MIDI device as an input to your Logic system. Before starting to record, you should verify that the MIDI device you will use for input (also called a *MIDI controller*) is connected to your system through an input on your MIDI interface or a USB port on your computer, if applicable. You might also need to connect a MIDI output from your interface as a return to this device or as an input to a separate MIDI device, such as a synthesizer, for monitoring and playback purposes.

Example: Using MIDI Cables

For basic recording, you can connect a MIDI cable from the MIDI Out port on the back of a keyboard to the MIDI In port on many audio interfaces. (Not all audio interfaces include MIDI ports, so look for this feature when shopping for an interface, if it is something you'll need. Some audio interfaces provide this functionality via a breakout cable.)

For monitoring and playback purposes, you can also connect the MIDI Out port of the audio interface (if available) to the MIDI In port on the keyboard (assuming the keyboard has onboard sound capabilities) or to a separate synthesizer unit or sound module.

 Connecting a MIDI device to Logic with a USB cable provides both MIDI input and MIDI output for the device.

Checking MIDI Routing

Once your MIDI device is connected, you will need to configure the routing for your External MIDI tracks and Software Instrument tracks.

MIDI Channel Selector

The MIDI channel pop-up selector is available in the track inspector settings for External MIDI and Software Instrument tracks. This setting lets you choose which channel from your MIDI device will be routed to the track and determines which incoming MIDI data gets recorded onto the track.

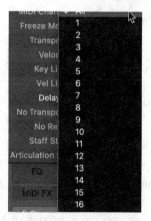

Figure 6.14 The MIDI channel pop-up menu in the track Inspector on a Software Instrument track

MIDI Destination Selector

The MIDI Destination selector for an External MIDI track determines which device or port is used for monitoring and playing back MIDI data from the track. Similarly, recorded MIDI signals can be routed to an audio sound source for playback purposes. You use the MIDI Destination selector in the New Tracks dialog box to configure the device or port and the MIDI channel that the signal is routed to for both of these purposes.

 When using MIDI Thru, you might need to disable Local Control on your MIDI keyboard controller. Otherwise, your keyboard could receive double MIDI notes, which can lead to stuck notes.

After creating the track, you can change these settings in the Inspector under Port. Ports carry MIDI data out a physical output to devices outside of Logic. The MIDI channel selector is underneath that.

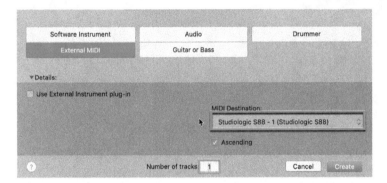

Figure 6.15 Routing MIDI to a hardware device using an External MIDI track

To set the MIDI Output, do one of the following:

- While creating a new External MIDI track, click on the **MIDI DESTINATION** selector in the new tracks dialog box.

- Select the instrument or port and channel you wish to route the output to for MIDI playback. This is set in the Track Inspector. (Note that this process is typically not required when using a virtual instrument on a Software Instrument track.)

Figure 6.16 Adjusting physical MIDI outputs via the Port tab in the Track Inspector

Using the Computer Keyboard for MIDI

To use your computer keyboard as a MIDI input device, select WINDOW > MUSICAL TYPING or press COMMAND+K. This will allow your computer keyboard to function as a MIDI device, as described below.

When active, the Computer MIDI Keyboard uses the top and middle rows of alphabetic keys on the QWERTY keypad to play the black and white notes on a piano keyboard, as indicated in Figure 6.18. The octave targeted by the computer keys can be adjusted up or down using the Z and X keys. You can adjust the velocity that will be used for the played notes using the C and V keys. Each key press will shift the velocity value up or down in 5-unit intervals. Pressing 1 or 2 will activate pitch bend down and up, respectively. Pressing 3 through 8 will provide varying amounts of modulation.

Finally, the TAB key functions as a sustain pedal input in this mode.

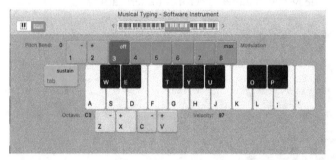

Figure 6.17 Musical Typing with the QUERTY keyboard in Logic Pro

Record-Enabling MIDI-Compatible Tracks

The process you use to enable recording on a Logic External MIDI track or Software Instrument track is the same as you use for an Audio track: Simply click the track's RECORD ENABLE button in the Main Window. The Record Enable button will turn solid red when a MIDI-compatible track is record-ready.

Using Virtual Instruments

Virtual instruments are the software equivalents of outboard synthesizers or sound modules. Many virtual instruments plug-ins are available for Logic. Several categories of virtual instruments are included with Logic, including synthesizers like Alchemy, EFM1, ES1, ES P, and Retro Synth; emulations of vintage instruments like a B3 Organ, Clavinet, and Electric Piano (which has several Fender Rhodes and Wurlitzer emulations); and models of orchestral instruments in the form of Studio Horns and Studio Strings.

Placing a Virtual Instrument on a Software Instrument Track

An Instrument plug-in can be placed directly on a Software Instrument track, allowing the instrument to be triggered by the MIDI data on the track during playback or by MIDI data passing through the track, for live input monitoring.

To add a virtual instrument to a Software Instrument track in Logic, do the following:

1. Display the track inspector, if not already shown, by clicking the Inspector button in the control bar.

2. Click on the Instrument slot to display the list of available instruments.

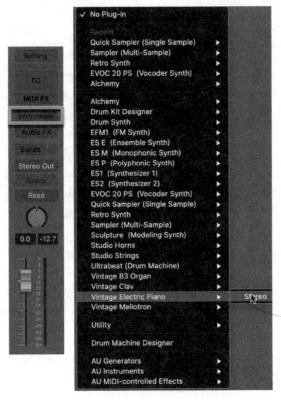

Figure 6.18 Selecting the Vintage Electric Piano instrument plug-in from the inspector tab

> (i) Logic shows the five most recently used virtual instruments on the top of the instruments list. Any third-party virtual instrument plug-ins that you have will be located in the AU Instruments sub-menu near the bottom of the list.

3. Select a Virtual Instrument plug-in to use on the track, such as **Vintage B3 Organ**, **Studio Horns**, or **Drum Kit Designer**. The track's MIDI Output will automatically be assigned to the virtual instrument plug-in, and the instrument's user interface will open.

4. Set the track's **VOLUME FADER** to the desired output level.

5. Record-enable the track and play notes on your MIDI controller. The meters on the Software Instrument track will register the instrument's audio output.

If the MIDI meter does not register a signal, verify that the MIDI output has been assigned with the MIDI Output selector in the Track Inspector.

As mentioned earlier in this chapter, many different virtual instruments are included with Logic. With most of these instruments, you have a couple different options for loading patches to create with them. You can place a virtual instrument plug-in on a Software Instrument track, which doesn't add any other plug-ins or routing. Within the plug-in are presets that showcase various configurations for that instrument.

Additionally, you can load Channel strip presets from the Library menu. These channel strips typically have several effect plug-ins loaded, and sometimes add some sends to one or more Auxiliary channel strips for parallel processing. We'll examine these options below.

Using the Vintage Electric Piano

Let's look at some of the settings in the Vintage Electric Piano plug-in, shown in Figure 6.19. When you initially load the plug-in using an instrument slot, it opens to the **Factory Default** setting. You'll immediately see several knobs. There are a few different sections to be aware of in this plug-in.

In the top left (highlighted in blue in Figure 6.19) you'll see a **MODEL** pop-up menu. This menu has a vast array of different Fender, Rhodes, and Wurlitzer modeled keyboard instruments.

Below that, you'll see an effect section (highlighted in red in Figure 6.19), which has five different effects with 2 to 3 parameters each. Each of these sections also has an independent on/off switch, which is helpful if you want to hear what each one is doing.

Lastly, you'll see the overall Volume knob and Bass Boost control. Selecting a different model will not change any of the effect settings or the Volume and Bass Boost you've configured.

Figure 6.19 The Vintage Electric Piano interface with the Model pop-up selector (blue) and FX section (red) highlighted

Using the Plug-In Presets/Patches

To select a different patch setting (or plug-in preset), you can click the **SETTINGS** pop-up menu in the plug-in window (where it shows Factory Default) and try out some other options. Each patch contains a preset configuration that will have custom settings not only for the model of keyboard emulation, but also for the volume and effects settings.

 If you want to preserve your settings in the effects section, you can select different options using the Model pop-up menu rather than the Settings menu.

Figure 6.20 The Settings pop-up menu in the Vintage Electric Piano plug-in

Using Channel Strip Presets/Patches

As an alternative, you can use the channel strip presets and patches in the Library tab. You can access this by clicking the **LIBRARY** button in the Main Window, or by pressing the **Y** key.

In the left-most column, you'll see a list of different instruments with presets designed. As you make selections, you will see a list of channel strip presets. These differ from presets in the Settings menu, in that they typically create a plug-in chain with several effects, and sometimes add additional routing to one or more Auxiliary channel strips with other effects on them.

In Figure 6.21, after selecting a channel strip preset, we have not only added two additional plug-ins on our Software Instrument track, but we've also created two different Auxiliary channel strips with multiple plug-ins on them.

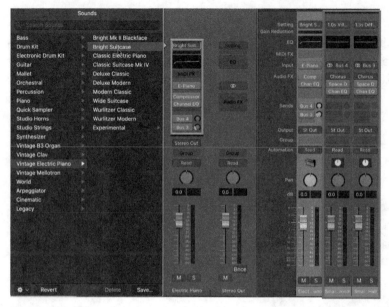

Figure 6.21 Selecting a channel strip preset can add extra plug-ins and routing (red), as well as additional Aux tracks, with multiple plug-ins (blue)

Using Drummer Tracks

Many musical arrangements start from the drums and build up from there. But it can be extremely time consuming to program drums and get everything sounding right.

Drummer tracks are a great way to get up and running quickly with a solid foundation. When you create a Drummer track, you select from a set of virtual drummers, each within a different genre. You can quickly modify their performance using the Drummer Editor and see those changes represented inside of the Drummer regions. Each virtual Drummer uses a unique drum kit. These can be built using either *Drum Kit Designer*, for emulations of acoustic drum kits, or *Drum Machine Designer*, for sounds from different sampled or synthesized drums.

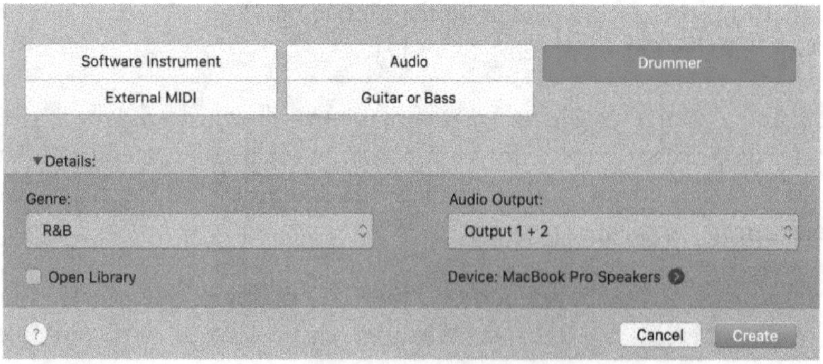

Figure 6.22 The Drummer track settings in the new track dialog box

To create a Drummer track, you can select **DRUMMER** in the New Tracks dialog box (see Figure 6.22, above). You can then select a Genre to narrow down your sound, and you can optionally enable a checkbox to open up the Library pane.

 For details on the Library, see "Using the Library" later in this chapter.

Once the track is created, an 8-bar Drummer region is automatically created on the track. At the bottom of the Main Window, you'll find the Drummer Editor. If this is not displayed, you can click on the Editors button in the control bar, or press the **E** key.

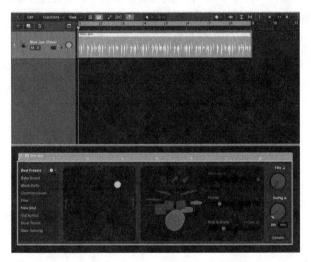

Figure 6.23 A Drummer region (blue), and the Drummer Editor (red) in the Main Window

Using the Drummer Editor

The Drummer Editor is where you can modify the sound of your drummer. On the left is a collection of beat presets, each of which contains 8-bar loops unique to that virtual drummer. These can each be modified.

By dragging the ball in the middle of the X-Y panel, you can alter the drummer region. Dragging horizontally changes the pattern from simple to complex, and dragging vertically changes the volume of the groove from soft to loud (vertical drag).

On the right are three sliders (Percussion, Hi-Hat, and Kick & Snare in Figure 6.23, above). Dragging these sliders will vary the groove on that portion of the kit. Clicking on a greyed-out section of the kit will switch the instrumentation of the groove slightly. For example, clicking on the Cymbals or Toms will activate those in place of the Hi-Hat. Clicking on a drum lit up yellow will de-activate that portion of the groove.

Lastly, you'll have two knobs on the far right. Adjusting the **FILL** knob will alter the frequency and length of fills thrown into the base groove. Adjusting the **SWING** knob will introduce swing into a groove's performance, with more swing added the further you rotate to the right.

If you'd like to get a bit further under the hood, you can click on the **DETAILS** button in the lower right corner of the Drummer Editor. This gives you access to additional controls, which vary depending on the drummer or genre you have selected.

Using the Library

If you'd like to browse other drummers and drum sets, you can open up the Library. Here you can choose a new drummer and get brief descriptions of their individual playing style. By default, making a selection will change out your virtual drum kit and swap out the Drummer region.

Figure 6.24 Browsing virtual Drummers and Drum Kit presets in the Library

Using the Drum Kit Designer

In addition to altering the playing style for your Drummer track, you can also tweak the sound of the individual drum kit parts in the *Drum Machine Designer* or *Drum Kit Designer* plug-ins. Let's take a brief look at some of the options in Drum Kit Designer.

To get started, simply click on one of the drum kit pieces, such as the kick drum. The selected piece will become highlighted.

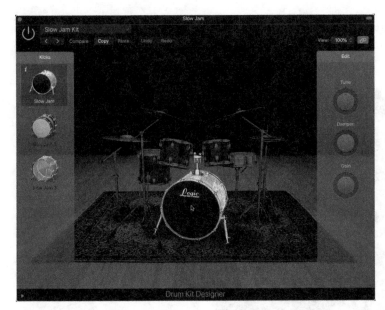

Figure 6.25 Selecting the Kick Drum inside of Drum Kit Designer

After selecting a kit piece, you're presented with some settings that you can adjust. In the case of the Kick and Snare drums, you're given a few options to choose from, based on the selected drum kit. You can replace the drum with an alternate that may better suite your composition. To swap kick and snare drums, make a selection from the options shown on the left.

On the right side, you're given options to adjust the tuning, the amount of dampening, and the gain of each drum kit piece. For the toms, you can either adjust for all three toms together or make changes for each individual tom. This gives you a huge amount of flexibility.

So, if you've found your perfect drummer and groove, but the kit doesn't sound quite right, try adjusting some of the drum's sounds.

Using the Quick Sampler

In addition to all the other virtual instruments, Logic Pro also has some very deep samplers. With Quick Sampler, you can import an audio region to serve as the sample, modulate the sample's pitch and sonic envelope, and loop a section of the sample to change its length. This lets you quickly turn a one-shot sound into a playable instrument.

 When you're sampling, be mindful of copyright issues with the sources you're using. If you don't have permission to use a sample of someone else's work, you can quickly get yourself in trouble.

Logic comes with a plethora of royalty-free loops. You're absolutely free to use those with Quick Sampler. You can also record a single sustained instrumental note, vocal pitch, or sung phrase and transform that into a playable instrument. You can also import a drumbeat and slice it up into individual drum hits.

Figure 6.26 Logic's Quick Sampler with a vocal region loaded

You'll notice a few different modes in which Quick Sampler can operate: Classic, One Shot, Slice, and Recorder:

- **CLASSIC** mode—The sample will play back while you're sending MIDI note data. As you switch MIDI notes, the sample will transpose chromatically, playing faster at higher pitches and slower at lower pitches. You can use the yellow loop start and end markers to define a range to loop while a MIDI note is being held.

- **ONE SHOT** mode—The sample will play from the start marker until the end marker (indicated by the blue arrows at the bottom of the waveform display). One Shot samples will play the full duration regardless of how long you hold down the MIDI note that's triggering the sample.

- **SLICE** mode—The region you drop into Quick Sampler is divided into sections, each triggered by a separate MIDI note. You can adjust the divisions by clicking and dragging the slice markers.

- **RECORDER** mode—Samples are recorded directly into Quick Sampler, creating a new sound to manipulate in real time. You can select an input in the lower left corner, and then click the big record button in the center of the waveform display to capture a sample.

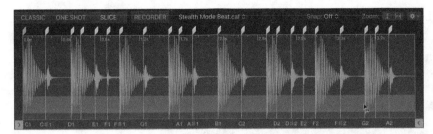

Figure 6.27 Quick Sampler in Slice Mode; underneath each slice is the note value that triggers its playback

You can also drag and drop any audio region to the blank space in the track header area, and you'll see a list of options. From here you can choose to load the audio into an instance of Quick Sampler. (See Figure 6.28.) Also keep in mind that Quick Sampler has presets to help get you started quickly.

Figure 6.28 An Apple audio loop being dragged to create a new track using Quick Sampler

Recording MIDI

With a MIDI controller selected, the MIDI signal routed to a MIDI-compatible track, and the track record-enabled, you are ready to begin recording.

Live Loops Grid

To record to a MIDI-compatible track in the Live Loops Grid, do the following:

1. Display the Live Loops Grid.

2. In the Cell Inspector, optionally adjust the attributes, such as where a loop starts, the overall loop length, and the Rec-Length setting.

(i) You can set the Rec-Length Auto (bars) to follow along and end the recording at the nearest bar, or record based on the *Cell Length* value.

3.   Click the **CELL RECORD** button on the cell where you'd like to record to immediately start recording.

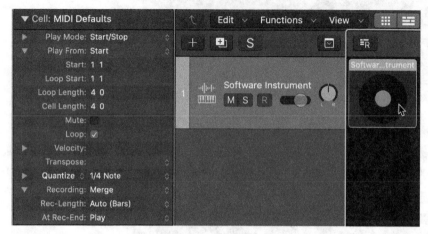

Figure 6.29 Recording onto a cell in the Live Loops Grid (mouse pointer shown over the Cell Record button)

> (i)   If the Count In button is enabled, the Cell Record button will flash during the count-in, after which recording will begin.

4.   When you have finished recording, press the **SPACEBAR** to stop the transport.

To play back the track through a connected virtual instrument or outboard device, do the following:

1.   In the Transport window, click the **GO TO BEGINNING** button.

2.   Click **PLAY** in the Transport window to begin playback.

3.   Alternatively you can click play on an individual cell, or launch a Scene containing that cell.

The Tracks Area

To record to a MIDI-compatible track in the Tracks Area, do the following:

1.   Arm at least one Software Instrument track for recording.

2.   Position the playhead or specify the cycle area for recording.

> 📕   Details on setting a cycle area are discussed in Chapter 3 of this book.

3.   Click the **RECORD** button in the transport at the top of the Main Window, or press the **R** key.

4.   When you have finished recording, click **STOP**.

Creating a MIDI Performance Manually

Sometimes, you might want or need to create a MIDI performance manually (by programming notes using the mouse and keyboard). This requires that you create a MIDI region and draw in notes in the Piano Roll Editor or Step Sequencer. The good news is this largely functions the same way regardless of whether you're working in the Live Loops Grid or the Tracks Area.

To create a blank MIDI region in the Live Loops Grid or Tracks Area, do the following:

1. Select the Pencil tool.

2. Click into a blank area within the Tracks Area or into a blank cell in the Live Loops Grid.

 You can also right-click an empty space in the Tracks Area or Live Loops Grid and select CREATE MIDI REGION from the pop-up menu.

3. In the Tracks Area, trim the blank region to the desired length. If you're working in the Live Loops Grid, adjust the Cell Length in the Inspector view.

The next section covers the Piano Roll Editor in detail, including its features for creating and editing notes.

Creating and Editing MIDI Performances

Logic's Piano Roll Editor allows you to both create new MIDI performances and edit existing ones. To access the Piano Roll Editor, select a MIDI region (if the editor is already open), or double-click a MIDI region (if editor is currently closed). This will not only open the editor, but will set the view inside to the location of the selected region.

 Click and drag the divider between the Editor and the Tracks Area to expand the Piano Roll Editor, if necessary.

The Piano Roll Editor

The Piano Roll Editor shows individual MIDI notes in a piano-roll format, with note pitch shown on a vertical axis, and note position and duration shown on the horizontal axis. The notes displayed here can reside on any single External MIDI track or Software Instrument track. MIDI notes are represented as colored bars of different brightness and color depending on their respective velocities. A dedicated velocity slider is located on the bottom of the editor left-hand corner of the editor. (See Figure 6.30.)

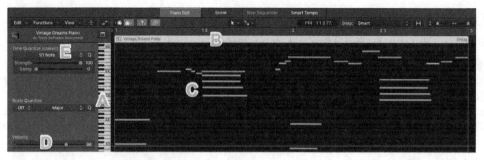

Figure 6.30 The Piano Roll Editor: (A) piano roll keyboard, (B) cycle area, (C) piano roll grid with MIDI notes, (D) Velocity slider, and (E) the Time Quantize menu

The visual nature of the Piano Roll Editor makes it easy to see musical performances as well as create, select, and edit notes. The following sections cover some editing functions that will allow you to create the exact performance you desire.

Creating MIDI Notes

During the production process, you may want to enter some MIDI notes by hand. For many producers, this is a faster way of entering MIDI data than playing a keyboard or other controller.

Inside of the Piano Roll Editor, you'll notice a different set of mouse tools are active. You still have the Pointer set to **LEFT-CLICK**, but instead of the Marquee tool, the Pencil tool is set to **COMMAND+CLICK**. The Pencil tool lets you quickly create and edit MIDI notes.

 You can audition pitches on the mini-keyboard by clicking on any key on the piano roll keyboard. The selected note will play through your connected virtual instrument or outboard device.

Selecting MIDI Notes

Whether you have recorded or manually created MIDI notes, you can make selections for editing multiple ways.

To make a selection of MIDI notes, do one of the following:

- Click an individual note in the piano roll editor.

- Starting from an empty space, click and drag in the Piano Roll Editor to draw a marquee around multiple notes.

- Using the Pointer tool, **SHIFT-CLICK** a note to add or remove it from a selection.

- With the cursor located in the Piano Roll Editor, or with any note selected, press **COMMAND+A** to select all notes currently displayed in the editor.

■ Click and drag vertically along the Piano Roll Keyboard to select all notes within a range of pitches.

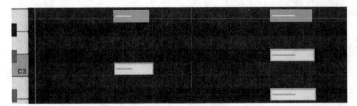

Figure 6.31 A multi-note selection in the Piano Roll Editor with the bottom three notes selected

Moving a Selection to a Different Note Value

Once you've made a selection of one or more MIDI notes, you can easily move the selection to a different note value (or pitch).

To move a selection from note to note, do one of the following:

■ Click and drag vertically to move the selection to a different pitch with the mouse.

■ Press **OPTION+UP/DOWN ARROW** to move pitches chromatically from the keyboard.

■ Press **OPTION+SHIFT+UP/DOWN ARROW** to move pitches up or down by an octave at a time.

 Hold Option while clicking and dragging a MIDI note to duplicate the note.

Editing Velocity

Velocity is MIDI data that represents how hard a key or pad is pressed when recording from a MIDI controller. This data is stored within the MIDI performance.

Velocity information can help you create more lifelike MIDI performances, as different velocity values can trigger different audio samples and different volume levels from virtual instruments.

Even if you don't record MIDI using a velocity-sensitive MIDI controller, you can manually edit velocity data for each note in a region. Velocity is represented both by the color and brightness of a note and by the velocity line displayed through the center of the pitch. The higher the velocity, the closer the line will be to extending through the entire note.

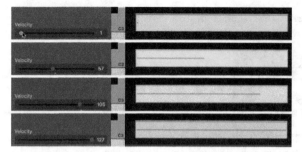

Figure 6.32 A selected MIDI note with velocity values ranging from 1 (top) to 127 (bottom)

To quickly adjust velocity for one or more notes:

1. Select one or more MIDI notes.

2. Click and drag the Velocity Slider in the lower left-hand side of the piano roll editor.

The velocity value will display next to the Velocity Slider, using a range from 1 to 127. When multiple notes are selected, the velocity of all notes will change relative to one another.

MIDI Quantization

Quantization allows you to align, or quantize, MIDI notes to a specified timing grid and/or scale. Quantizing to a strict musical grid creates a style of recording similar to working with a hardware sequencer or drum machine. While this may be desireable in some cases, Logic Pro's quantization feature also allows you to improve the accuracy of your MIDI performance without sacrificing its natural human quality.

We've already briefly touched on quantization for an entire region using the region inspector. Let's take a quick look at some options using the Piano Roll Editor. You can add time or pitch quantization to a selection of MIDI notes by making selections on the left side of the Piano Roll Editor.

In the time quantization pop-up, you can select a quantization grid value, or click the **QUANTIZE** button (labeled with a Q) to quantize using the current settings. In the same manner, you can transpose selected pitches, binding them to a scale, using the **Scale Quantize** function. Here you select the scale by first clicking in the **KEY** pop-up (where it shows **Off** by default), and then clicking the **SCALE MODE** pop-up (where it shows **Major** by default) to shift all notes to the closest scale tone. (See Figure 6.33.)

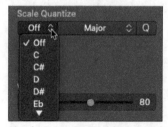 

Figure 6.33 Setting the key (left) and scale mode (right) in the Scale Quantize area located in the Piano Roll Editor

Review/Discussion Questions

1. What does the term MIDI stand for? How is MIDI data different from the data stored in an audio file? (See "MIDI Basics" beginning on page 126.)

2. How many channels of MIDI information can be sent over a single MIDI cable? (See "MIDI Basics" beginning on page 126.)

3. What two types of tracks does Logic provide for working with MIDI data? What is the difference between the two track types? (See "MIDI in Logic Pro" beginning on page 127.)

4. How many ticks are in a quarter note in Logic? (See "Tick-Based Operation" beginning on page 130.)

5. What is the default meter in Logic? How would you go about changing the meter? (See "Setting the Base Meter and Tempo" beginning on page 131.)

6. What is the default tempo in Logic? (See "Setting the Project Tempo & Time Signature" beginning on page 132.)

7. What physical connections can you use to connect a MIDI controller to your system for recording on a MIDI or Instrument track? (See "Connecting a MIDI Device" beginning on page 135.)

8. Give some examples of virtual instrument plug-ins that are installed as standard components of Logic. On which track types are virtual instrument plug-ins typically placed? (See "Using Virtual Instruments" beginning on page 138.)

9. What are some different ways you can modify a Virtual Drummer's sound with Drummer Tracks? (See "Using Drummer Tracks" beginning on page 142.)

10. What's the difference between loading a preset from within a virtual instrument plug-in and from the Library? (See "Using the Quick Sampler" beginning on page 145.)

11. What are some ways to slice a drum loops transients over MIDI notes in the Quick Sampler? (See "Using the Quick Sampler" beginning on page 145.)

12. Describe some of the features of the Piano Roll Editor in Logic Pro. (See "The Piano Roll Editor" beginning on page 149.)

13. What track types can display data in Piano Roll Editor? (See "The Piano Roll Editor" beginning on page 149.)

 To review additional material from this chapter and prepare for certification, see the Logic Pro 101 Study Guide module available through the Elements|ED online learning platform at ElementsED.com.

Working with MIDI

🎧 Activity

In this exercise, you will continue work on the project you started in Exercises 4 and 5. You will add character to the project by creating both a drum part and a melody part to accompany the chord progression and bass part.

This exercise provides three approaches: Option 1 lets you import existing MIDI clips to use for the new parts; Option 2 lets you record MIDI performances from a MIDI controller; and Option 3 lets you manually create MIDI performances using the Piano Roll Editor. Each of the three options is covered separately.

🕐 Duration

This exercise should take approximately 20 to 25 minutes to complete.

✛ Goals/Targets

- Configure the project
- Assign instruments to Software Instrument tracks
- Prepare the project for recording
- Record or manually create a MIDI performance

Media Files

To complete this exercise, you may need to use various media files included in the **Media Files 2019-Logic101** folder. You should have downloaded the media files in Exercise 4.

If needed, you can re-download the media files by going to www.halleonard.com/mylibrary and entering your access code (printed on the opening page of this book). From there, click the **Download** link for the **Media Files 2021-Logic101** listing in your **My Library** page. The Media Files folder will begin transferring to your Downloads folder.

Getting Started

You will start by opening the Logic Project you saved at the end of Exercise 5. If that file is not available, you can use the **Ex05 Sample** file in the **01 Completed Exercises** folder within the **Media Files 2021-Logic101** folder.

Open the project and save it as Exercise 6:

1. Do one of the following:

    - Open the project file that you created in Exercise 5 (**Exercise05-XXX.logicx**).

    - Alternatively, you can use the Ex05 Sample file (**Media Files 2021-Logic101 > 01 Completed Exercises > Ex05 Sample.logicx**).

2. Choose **FILE > SAVE AS** and name the project *Exercise06-XXX*, keeping the file in the same drive location. (Move the project to your selected save location, if working from the sample file.)

In Exercise 5, you created the foundation of a song segment using imported audio files. You had the choice of four bass and chord progression options, spanning several styles of music and several tempos. For this exercise, you'll continue with the example from Exercise 5, pop in Amin at 120bpm. If you need to double check what key and tempo your audio files are in, you can examine them in Logic's built in browser. This will clearly show the names, which include genre, key, and tempo of the files.

Figure 6.34 Audio files in current project with key/tempo information

From here, you will augment this song segment using the two Software Instrument tracks: **Drums** and **Melody**.

Configuring the Project

Before continuing, you will configure the project to ensure that the tempo is correct and that Quantization is enabled in the Inspector.

Configure the project:

1. Make sure the tempo of your project matches the tempo of your audio regions.

ⓘ   **As noted above, the tempo is listed on the file names of the audio files you selected in Exercise 5.**

2. Select Quantize in the Inspector and choose a value. This will automatically quantize your recorded MIDI regions to the specified value. Higher quantization values, such as 1/4 Note quantization, will have a more dramatic effect on your MIDI performance when you record from a MIDI controller.

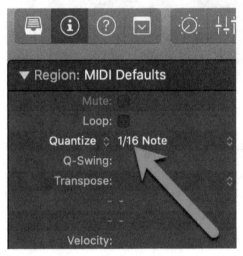

Figure 6.35   The Quantize grid value set in the Inspector

ⓘ   **Alternatively, you can leave Quantization disabled and quantize your MIDI regions after recording using the MIDI Note Editor.**

Assigning Instruments to MIDI Tracks

You will now assign instruments to both of the Software Instrument tracks in your project so that they can produce sound. The Drums track will use the Drum Kit Designer or Drum Machine Designer instrument, and the Melody track will use the Sampler instrument.

Assign a virtual instrument to each Software Instrument track:

1. Show the Library by clicking the Library button in the upper left corner of the Main Window, or by pressing the **Y** key.

2. Select the Drums Software Instrument track.

3.   In the Library, choose the **ELECTRONIC DRUM KIT** category.

4.   Audition the pre-created drum kits by clicking on each one to select one for use in your project.

Figure 6.36 Selecting a Drum Machine Designer preset in the Library for the Drums track

5.   Select the **Melody** Software Instrument track.

6.   In the Inspector, click on the **INSTRUMENTS** tab and select **SAMPLER (MULTI-SAMPLE) > STEREO**.

7.   Click on the Factory Default button at the top of the sampler window and scroll down to **Synthesizers > Synth Leads**. Once you're in this section of presets you can click on the left and right arrows to preview other sounds.

8.   Browse some options and make a selection for the main melody sound.

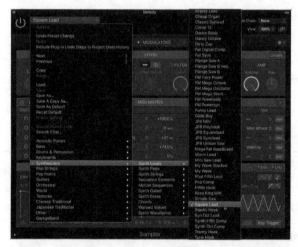

Figure 6.37 Selecting a Sampler preset in the Library for the Drums MIDI track

9.   Once you've found a sound you like that fits with your existing audio regions, close the Sampler window.

Importing MIDI Files (Option 1)

To use pre-created MIDI regions, you can simply import existing MIDI data into your project, using the steps outlined in this section. To record your own MIDI performances instead, proceed to Option 2.

Importing MIDI in the Live Loops Grid

In this section, you will import MIDI regions into the Live Loops Grid.

Import pre-created MIDI files in the Live Loops Grid:

1. Show the All Files Browser by clicking the **BROWSERS** button or pressing **F** and selecting the **ALL FILES** tab.

2. Navigate to the Media Files 2021-Logic101 > 02 Exercise Media > [MIDI Files] folder in the Browser to display the MIDI files it contains.

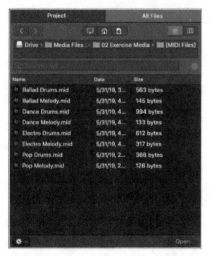

Figure 6.38 The MIDI files available in the 02 Exercise Media > [MIDI Files] folder

3. Drag and drop the corresponding drum part to the first cell of the Drums track.

4. Rename the MIDI cell to something simpler, such as Drums.

5. Hold **OPTION** while dragging the cell to create a duplicate in the second cell on the Drums track.

6. Edit the MIDI performance as desired by double-clicking the cells and using the Piano Roll Editor.

7. Repeat this process for the Melody Software Instrument track, selecting an appropriate melody file for your project.

Importing MIDI in the Tracks Area

In this section, you will import MIDI regions into the Tracks Area for your project.

Import pre-created MIDI files in the Tracks Area:

1.   Press **OPTION+V** as needed to toggle between the Tracks Area view and the Live Loops Grid.

2.   Show the All Files Browser by clicking the **BROWSERS** button or pressing **F** and selecting the **ALL FILES** tab.

3.   Navigate to the Media Files 2021-Logic101 > 02 Exercise Media > [MIDI Files] folder in the Browser to display the MIDI files it contains.

4.   Drag and drop the corresponding drum part to Bar 5 of the Drums track.

     A dialog box will appear prompting you to select an option for importing tempo and time signature information.

5.   Select **NO** in the dialog box, as you have already set the tempo of the project.

Figure 6.39 The Import Tempo dialog box

6.   Rename the imported region as Drums; then duplicate the Drums region across the Tracks Area by selecting it and pressing **COMMAND+R** for a total of 4 regions.

7.   Edit the MIDI performance as desired by double-clicking the regions and using the Piano Roll Editor.

8.   Repeat this process for the Melody Software Instrument track, selecting an appropriate melody file for your project.

Recording MIDI (Option 2)

This section will help you prepare to record a MIDI performance using a MIDI controller device or the computer keyboard. If you have imported the MIDI files under Option 1, you can skip this section.

Select a MIDI controller to use on each Software Instrument track:

1.   Make sure that the Inspector controls are visible by either selecting the **INSPECTOR** button or pressing the **I** key.

2. Locate the MIDI input ports for any connected hardware in **Logic Pro > Preferences > MIDI**.

3. Make sure the MIDI controller you'd like to use has a checkbox enabled.

Figure 6.40 In this example, a Native Instruments Komplete Kontrol keyboard is selected as a MIDI input device

4. Repeat this process for the **Melody** MIDI track.

5. Check that the MIDI outputs in the Track Inspector are set to **All** or a channel that you're routing to each specific track.

Figure 6.41 MIDI Output set to route all MIDI channels to the Drums track

(i) If you do not have a MIDI controller to use for recording, you can use the Musical Typing Window, or import MIDI data as described in Option 1.

Enable the metronome and count-in to aid in recording:

1. Enable the metronome, by selecting the **Metronome** button in the control bar.

2. Use the **Count In** button to give yourself a count-in before recording starts: click and hold the **Count In** button and select a count-in value of 1 or 2 Bars.

Recording in the Tracks Area (Option 2a)

Here, you will record a MIDI performance for both the Drums track and the Melody track, recording into the Tracks Area.

This option picks up where Exercise 5 (Option 1) left off. In this section, you will record MIDI regions onto tracks in the Main Window.

Record the MIDI drum and melody performance:

1. Make sure you can see the Tracks Area in your Main Window.

2. If needed, click the **TRACK ACTIVATION** button to switch over to working in the Tracks Area and re-activate your regions for playback. You'll see arrows pointing towards the Live Loop Grid, and regions greyed out in the Tracks Area if this is necessary.

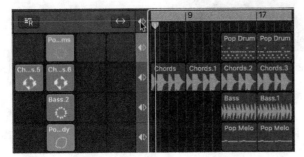

Figure 6.42 Clicking the Track Activation button

3. **RECORD ENABLE** the Drums Software Instrument track for recording.

4. Click the **RECORD** button (solid circle) in the Transport controls. This will initiate the count-in.

5. After the count-in completes, begin recording a 16-bar drum pattern.

   You can record an entire 16-bar region, or record a shorter region—such as 4 or 8 bars—and duplicate it to fill the required length.

6. Once you have completed the recording, press **SPACEBAR** to stop the recording.

7. Duplicate the region as needed to span 16 bars. (Select the region and press **COMMAND+R**.)

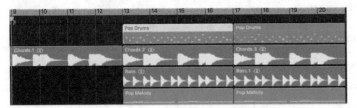

Figure 6.43 A 4-bar MIDI drum performance (green), duplicated to span a longer period

8. Repeat the above process to record a part on the Melody Software Instrument track. On this track, compose a simple melody to accompany the drums, bass, and chords.

ⓘ All of the provided audio regions for this exercise are in the keys of either C major or A minor. Try using the notes C, D, E, F, G, and A to construct your melody.

Recording a MIDI Performance in the Live Loops Grid (Option 2b)

Here, you will record a MIDI performance for both the Drums track and the Melody track, recording into the Live Loops Grid.

This option picks up where Exercise 5 (Option 2) left off.

Record the MIDI drum and melody performance:

1. Click the **LIVE LOOPS GRID** button as needed to display the Live Loops Grid in the Main Window.

2. Click the **RECORD** button in the second scene of the Drums track. This will start recording a new MIDI loop.

3. Begin recording your drum pattern.

    A good length is 4 bars, matching the audio region length in the project. However, you can record a cell of any length, and Logic will continue to loop the cell as you play Scene 2.

4. Once you have recorded your drum pattern, press **SPACEBAR** to stop the recording.

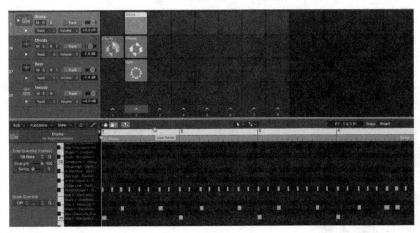

Figure 6.44 A 4-bar MIDI drum performance with the piano roll grid displayed

5. Launch Scene 2 by clicking the Scene Trigger button to listen to your MIDI performance along with the existing cells.

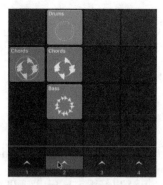

Figure 6.45 Listening to Scene 2 to audition the drum recording along with the bass and chord cells

6.   If you're not satisfied with the results, you can either delete the cell and try again, or edit and quantize the performance to improve the timing. You will have an opportunity to edit the MIDI performance later in this exercise.

7.   Once you are satisfied with your recording, copy the cell to the next scene of the **Drums** track by holding **OPTION** while dragging the cell to the empty cell on the right.

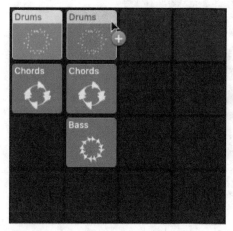

Figure 6.46 Duplicating a MIDI cell to an empty cell on the Drums track by Option-dragging

> (i) Alternatively, you could choose to have the drums only on Scene 2, allowing you to introduce the drums along with the bass.

8.   Repeat the above process on the **Melody** Software Instrument track. This time, you will record a simple melody to accompany the drums, bass, and chords.

> (i) All of the provided audio regions for this exercise are in the keys of either C major or A minor. Try using the notes C, D, E, F, G, and A to construct your melody.

Edit Your MIDI Performances

In this section, you have the opportunity to fine-tune your MIDI performances as needed.

Tweak your MIDI performances using the Piano Roll Editor:

1. Double-click a MIDI region you that would like to edit in the Piano Roll Editor.

2. Using editing features such as moving, trimming, and quantizing, tweak the MIDI performance to your liking.

> (i) To quantize your performance, select all of the notes in the Piano Roll Editor you want to affect. Next choose a value under TIME QUANTIZE (CLASSIC). You will see the MIDI notes adjusting as you make a selection.

Manually Creating a MIDI Performance (Option 3)

If you are unable to record a MIDI performance using a MIDI controller or your computer keyboard, you can instead create a MIDI performance manually using the Piano Roll Editor. (If you have completed the recording process in Option 1 or Option 2, you can skip this section.)

Creating a Performance in the Live Loops Grid (Option 3a)

In this section, you will create MIDI performances in cells in the Live Loops Grid.

Manually create a MIDI drum and melody performance in the Live Loops Grid:

1. Right-click the first cell on the Drums track and select **CREATE MIDI CELL** from the pop-up menu.

2. Double-click the newly created cell to open the Piano Roll Editor.

3. If desired, change the length of the cell by adjusting the Cell Length in the Cell Inspector.

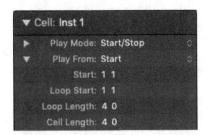

Figure 6.47 A cell in the Cell Inspector showing a Cell Length of 4 bars

4. Create notes for different drum sounds at different points in time. For instance, you might start by inserting a kick drum note on beats 1 and 3 of each measure and then add snare hits on beats 2 and 4.

5.   Optionally add hi-hats and other drums and experiment with other drums and timing patterns.

(i)   Hold COMMAND and click at the desired location in the Piano Roll Editor to add a new note with the Pencil tool.

6.   Once you are satisfied with your performance, copy the cell to the second cell of the **Drums** track by holding **OPTION** while dragging the cell to the empty cell slot.

(i)   Alternatively, you could choose to have the drums only on Scene 2, allowing you to introduce the drums along with the bass.

7.   Repeat the above process to create a part for the **Melody** Software Instrument track. On this track, compose a simple melody to accompany the drums, bass, and chords.

(i)   All of the provided audio clips for this exercise are in the key of either C major or A minor. Try using the notes C, D, E, F, G, and A to construct your melody.

Creating a Performance in the Tracks Area (Option 3b)

In this section, you will create MIDI regions and create a performance in the Tracks Area.

Manually create a MIDI drum and melody performance in the Tracks Area:

1.   Press **OPTION+V** as needed to toggle the display to the Tracks Area.

2.   Press the Track Activation button as needed to switch cell playback to region playback in the Tracks Area.

3.   Right-click an empty area within Bar 5 of the **Drums** track.

4.   Select **CREATE MIDI REGION** from the pop-up menu.

5.   Double-click the empty MIDI region to open it in the Piano Roll Editor.

6.   As listed in Option 3a, create notes for different drum sounds at different points in time. Start by inserting kick drum notes on beats 1 and 3 of each measure, then add snare hits on beats 2 and 4, and then add hi-hats, other drums, and pattern variations.

(i)   Hold Command and click at the desired location in the Piano Roll Editor to add a new note with the Pencil tool.

7.   Once you have created a drum pattern you like, you can move and repeat the region in the Tracks Area so that it plays at the times you desire.

To repeat the region, press **COMMAND+R**.

8. Repeat the above process on the **Melody** Software Instrument track. On this track, compose a simple melody to accompany the drums, bass, and chords.

 All of the provided audio clips for this exercise are in the key of either C major or A minor. Try using the notes C, D, E, F, G, and A to construct your melody.

Finishing Up

To complete this exercise, you will need to save your work and close the Logic Project. You will be reusing this project in Exercise 7, so it is important to save the work you've done.

Review your work in the Live Loops Grid:

1. Press **OPTION+V** as needed to toggle the display to the Live Loops Grid.

2. Press the **TRACK ACTIVATION** button as needed to switch region playback to the Live Loops Grid.

3. Click the **SCENE TRIGGER** button on Scene 1 to play back the cells in Scene 1.

4. Click the **SCENE TRIGGER** button on Scene 2 to play back the cells in Scene 2.

5. Repeat for any other Scenes that include cells.

6. Press the **SPACEBAR** to stop playback.

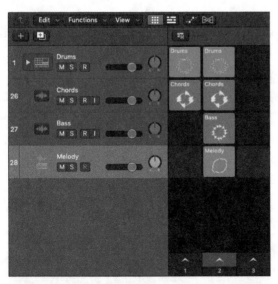

Figure 6.48 Example of the Live Loops Grid View after completing Exercise 6 with the Show/Hide Live Loops Grid button highlighted

Review your work in the Tracks Area:

1. Press **OPTION+V** as needed to toggle the display to the Tracks Area.

2. Press the **TRACK ACTIVATION** button as needed to switch from region playback to cell playback.

3. Press the **SPACEBAR** to play back the Logic Project and confirm your results.

4. Press the **SPACEBAR** a second time when finished.

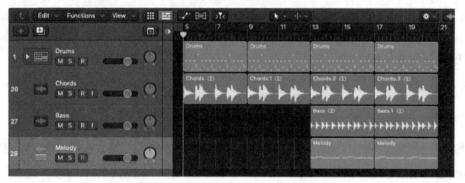

Figure 6.49 Example of the Tracks Area after completing Exercise 6 with the Show/Hide Tracks Area button highlighted

Save your work and close the project:

1. Choose **FILE > SAVE** to save the project.

2. Choose **FILE > CLOSE PROJECT** to close the project (or click the red button on the top left of the Main window).

3. If desired, press **COMMAND+Q** to quit Logic and close the project.

Chapter 7

Making Your First Audio Recording

This chapter covers the steps required to begin recording audio into a Logic Pro project. It also describes the types of audio regions your projects will include and covers processes for keeping your regions and audio files organized.

⊕ ## Learning Targets for This Chapter

- Configure the metronome and count-in to aid in recording audio

- Record audio onto tracks in your project from external and internal sources

- Record in both the Tracks Area and the Live Loops Grid

- Recognize the difference between audio regions and audio files

- Manage audio files after recording to minimize clutter and optimize your project

 Key topics from this chapter are illustrated in the Logic Pro 101 Study Guide module available through the Elements|ED online learning platform. Sign up for free at ElementsED.com.

Many Logic Pro projects require some amount of audio recording, whether the source is live instruments, vocals, or other tracks within the project. While the recording controls and processes in Logic Pro are intuitive in many respects, getting optimal results can be challenging if you are new to recording audio.

This chapter provides the background information on recording that you'll need to get started on the right foot. Whether your audio endeavors involve a simple setup in a home studio or an elaborate system in a professional environment, this information will help you take the first steps toward capturing quality audio recordings in Logic Pro.

Before Recording

Before you begin recording in a project, you should ensure that your system has enough storage space for your planned work. The amount of storage space consumed by audio files will vary, depending on the bit depth and sample rate of the project.

See the "Converting Audio to Digital Format" section in Chapter 1 for a detailed discussion of bit depth and sample rate.

Audio Storage Requirements

Logic Pro records all audio using sample rates ranging from 44.1 kHz to 192 kHz—the upper limit depends on the capabilities of your audio hardware, as discussed in Chapter 4—with bit depths between 16-bit and 24-bit. At a sample rate of 44.1 kHz, each track consumes approximately 5 megabytes (MB) of disk space per minute for 16-bit mono audio and 7.5 MB per minute for 24-bit mono audio.

With increasing bit depth and sample rates, drive space consumption increases correspondingly; recording at a sample rate of 88.2 kHz, therefore, consumes twice as much space as recording at 44.1 kHz. Similarly, recording in stereo consumes twice the space of recording in mono.

Table 4.1 in Chapter 4 shows approximate storage consumption at various data rates supported by Logic Pro.

Logic Pro audio files require a small amount of additional disk space to store associated metadata; this can add to the total file size.

Calculating File Sizes

The sample rate and bit depth of a recorded audio file are directly related to the resulting file size. In fact, you can calculate file sizes using these two parameters with the following equations:

Sample Rate x Bit Depth = Bits per Second

Sample Rate x Bit Depth x 60 = Bits per Minute

In the binary world of computers, 8 bits make a byte, 1,024 bytes make a kilobyte (KB), and 1,024 KB make a megabyte (MB). Therefore, the file size equation can be restated as follows:

(Sample Rate x Bit Depth x 60) / (8 bits per byte x 1,024 bytes per kilobyte x 1,024 kilobytes per megabyte) = Megabytes (MB) per Minute

Reducing terms gives us the following:

Sample Rate x Bit Depth / 139,810 = MB per Minute

So by way of example, recording audio at a sample rate of 44,100 samples per second with a bit depth of 24 bits per sample would generate files that consume space at the following rate:

44,100 x 24 / 139,810 = 7.57 MB per Minute

Verifying Available Drive Space

Now that you have an understanding of how much disk space is required to store recorded audio files at different sample rates and bit depths, you can estimate whether your system or storage drive has enough space available to allow you to complete your project. There are many ways to check the amount of available space on the storage drive where Logic Pro saves your audio files, but Logic Pro does not directly provide such information. Use the **GET INFORMATION** command or similar process in your operating system to determine the amount of free drive space on your record drive.

You can approximate the storage requirements for your recording project by multiplying the expected duration in minutes by the number of tracks in your project (count any stereo tracks as two mono tracks). Multiply the total as needed to account for the potential of recording multiple takes.

Then multiply this result by the number of megabytes per minute required by your sample rate. Verify that you have enough storage space remaining on your record drive to accommodate the planned recording.

Preparing to Record

Once you have created a Logic Pro project, added any required Audio tracks to record onto, and verified that you have adequate drive space available, you will need to prepare your hardware and Logic Pro project for recording. You might also want to enable and configure the metronome (sometimes called the click or tick) to use as a tempo reference while recording. Whether or not you use a metronome, the general processes you will use to prepare for recording audio are as follows:

1. Check the hardware connections, if you're using external instruments.

2. Route the input signal to be recorded to an Audio track.

3. Select the Audio track onto which you'd like to record, or record-enable multiple Audio tracks if recording on more than one track.

> (i) When a track is selected in Logic Pro, the R button will turn red, indicating it will be enabled when starting a record pass. If you need to record multiple tracks, manually arm each track before recording.

4. Set the track input level.

Enabling the Metronome

When you're working with a song or other composition that is based on a specific tempo (or tempo map) with established bar and beat divisions, it can help to perform along with a metronome. As discussed in Chapter 6, the metronome will help performers synchronize to the composition while tracking and will ultimately help align the recorded parts to the bars and beats in the project. Having your recorded parts in alignment with the tempo will help you to make selections according to the musical grid, and can simplify tasks such as copying and pasting an entire song section as you work on your arrangements.

To enable or disable the metronome, click the **METRONOME** button in the control bar or press the **K** key. When enabled, the metronome will create a click to the beat whenever you play back your project, play a cell from the Live Loops Grid view, or start a record pass.

Customizing the Metronome

As described in Chapter 6, Logic Pro includes several metronome options, which are available by clicking the down arrow icon on the **METRONOME** button or by opening the Metronome Settings window.

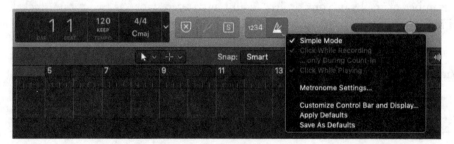

Figure 7.1 The Metronome button (purple) and associated settings dropdown menu

To recap, the available options for the Metronome include the following:

- **Simple Mode**—Metronome sounds only when the **METRONOME** button is engaged. When enabled, other options (grey) will be unavailable to adjust.

- **Click While Recording**—Metronome sounds during recording and not during playback, whether the **METRONOME** button is engaged or not.

- **Only During Count-In**—Metronome sounds during a count-in whether the **METRONOME** button is engaged or not. **CLICK WHILE RECORDING** must be selected to use this option.

- **Click While Playing**—Metronome sounds during playback.

- **Metronome Settings**—Opens the Metronome Settings within the Project Settings window.

- **Customize Control Bar and Display**—Opens a pop-up menu to customize Control Bar and Display settings.

- **Apply Defaults/Save As Defaults**—Lets you save the Metronome settings as default and apply default metronome settings.

The Metronome Settings window provides the same options as the Metronome pop-up menu, along with some additional settings. You can customize note and velocity settings of the metronome click, metronome tone and volume, output routing, and other options.

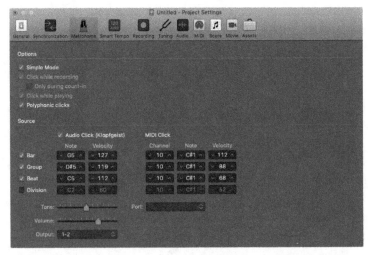

Figure 7.2 The Metronome Settings in the Project Settings window

Enabling the Count-In

Just like a drummer in a band counting to four to synchronize the start of a song, the Count-In can be used to help establish a feeling of the pulse when recording.

To enable or disable the Count-In, do one of the following:

■ Click the **COUNT-IN** button in the Control Bar.

■ Press **SHIFT+K**.

■ Select an option under **RECORD > COUNT-IN**.

When enabled, the Count-In will create a click to the beat for a period of time before recording whenever you start a record pass. The default Count-In is 4 beats, or 1 bar in the selected time signature (meter).

Customizing the Count-In

Logic Pro includes several Count-In options, which are available by clicking the down arrow icon on the **COUNT-IN** button or by opening the Recording Settings window.

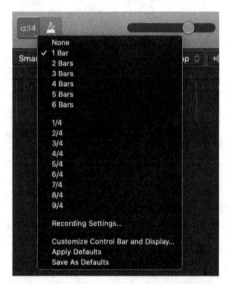

Figure 7.3 The Count-In button (purple) and associated settings dropdown menu

The available options for the Count-In include the following:

■ **None**—When selected, Count-In is disabled.

■ **Bars**—Lets you select a length of time between 1 and 6 Bars for the Count-In. Bars follow the project's time signature (meter) settings.

■ **Meter/Time Signature**—Lets you select a time signature (meter) for a 1-Bar Count-In.

■ **Recording Settings**—Opens the Recording Settings within the Project Settings with the same Count-In options as the pop-up menu.

- **Customize Control Bar and Display**—Opens the pop-up menu to customize the Control Bar and Display.

- **Apply Defaults/Save As Defaults**—Lets you save Count-In settings as default and apply default metronome settings.

Checking Hardware Connections

When recording audio from an external source, such as an instrument, microphone, or other sound source, you first need to connect the source to the system that is running Logic Pro. This is generally done through an audio interface, which is capable of converting incoming signals to digital audio and typically also lets you amplify the incoming signal using a preamp or gain control.

Most audio interfaces have inputs designated for different sound sources and input types. Before starting to record, you should verify that your sound source is connected to an appropriate input on the audio interface, and that the signal is being passed through the interface correctly.

For basic recording, it is simplest to use the lowest available inputs on your audio interface (for example, **INPUT 1** for a mono source or **INPUT 1-2** for a stereo pair).

If necessary, check the configuration of your audio interface and/or the **AUDIO PREFERENCES** window in Logic Pro to ensure that your audio device's hardware inputs will be available on Audio tracks.

 For details on configuring Audio Preferences in Logic Pro, see Chapter 4.

Selecting an Input Path

With your sound source connected to the inputs of your audio interface, you are now ready to configure an Audio track to receive a signal from your source and to pass the signal through the system for recording and monitoring purposes.

Each Audio track has an *Input* slot in the track's channel strip visible in the Inspector and Mixer. This slot allows you to route a signal from an input on your interface to the track for recording.

To set the incoming signal, do the following:

1. Open the Inspector by pressing **I** or open the Mixer by pressing **X**.

2. Locate the **INPUT** slot of the channel strip for the track you will record.

3. Verify that the input displayed on the **INPUT** slot matches the input that your sound source is plugged into on your audio interface. (See Figure 7.4.)

Figure 7.4 Input slot with Input 1 selected in the Inspector

4. If necessary, click the **INPUT** slot to make changes, selecting the correct input from the pop-up menu. (Note: Stereo tracks will have a pair of inputs routed to the track.)

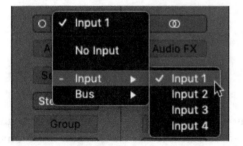
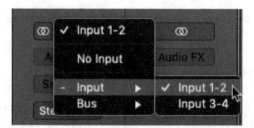

Figure 7.5 Input slot pop-up menu on a mono track (left) and stereo track (right)

 Make sure that the selection displayed on the Input slot matches the input number(s) that your sound source is plugged into on your audio interface. Otherwise you may record the wrong signal (or no signal) to the track.

5. If necessary, click the **CHANNEL MODE** button to switch between **MONO** and **STEREO** input routing.

Figure 7.6 Audio track channel mode set to mono (left) and stereo (right)

Setting Input Paths for Recording on Multiple Tracks

When recording to multiple tracks simultaneously, each track will need to have a unique input routed to it. For example, suppose you are recording a vocalist on Track 1 and an acoustic guitar accompaniment on Tracks 2 of your project. You might have the vocal microphone connected into Input 1 of your audio interface, and the guitar microphone connected into Input 2.

In the Logic Pro Inspector or Mixer display, you would set the Input for your first track to INPUT 1 (or the corresponding input name that receives signal from Input 1 on your interface). Similarly, you would set the Input for your second track to INPUT 2 (or the corresponding input path name that receives signal from Input 2 on the interface).

This setup will allow you to record and process the vocal signal on the first track separate from the guitar signal on the second track.

Record-Enabling Tracks

To set up an Audio track for recording, simply select the track. The **R** of the **RECORD ENABLE** button will turn red, meaning the track is ready to record. Alternately, you can click a track's **RECORD ENABLE** button in the Track header area, Inspector, or the Mixer display and window. The button will flash red when the track is record-enabled.

Figure 7.7 An Audio track selected and ready to record (left) and an Audio track with Record Enable button engaged (right)

 To record-enable multiple Audio tracks, click the RECORD ENABLE buttons on additional tracks. To record-enable all tracks or a contiguous range of tracks, click the RECORD ENABLE button at one end of the desired group and drag to the other end. Repeat the process to turn off RECORD ENABLE or OPTION-CLICK any record-enabled track.

Input Monitoring

In order to hear your sound source through Logic Pro when not in record, you need to enable **INPUT MONITORING**. To enable input monitoring, click a track's **INPUT MONITORING** button in the Track header area, the Inspector, or the Mixer display and window.

Figure 7.8 Input Monitoring button (orange) enabled

With Input Monitoring enabled, you can monitor your input signal continuously—regardless of whether the track is armed for recording or the project is playing. This mode can be useful to allow the talent to rehearse a part while listening to playback from other tracks in the project.

When Input Monitoring is disabled, you will not hear the sound source through Logic Pro. This might be useful if you are recording an acoustic instrument and want to exclusively hear the recorded sound during playback, rather hearing sound from the instrument microphone.

Logic uses Auto Input Monitoring by default. When enabled, input monitoring happens during recording only, automatically switching to track input during playback. Auto Input Monitoring can be enabled and disabled from the **RECORD** menu.

Figure 7.9 Auto Input Monitoring enabled in the drop-down menu

Controlling Input Level and Pan

Adjusting input levels and panning is essential to a smooth recording process.

Input Level

As a general rule, input levels should be adjusted to obtain a strong, clean signal while avoiding clipping. You do not, however, need to record at the highest possible level. Recording too hot can leave little room for subsequent gain-based processing (such as EQ) and can lead to digital clipping, which is always detrimental to audio quality.

For best results, aim for a peak input level around −6 dBFS or lower, and ensure that the track meter never turns red. To do this, adjust the level of your analog source while monitoring the volume meter of your track within Logic Pro.

 Meters in the Logic Pro mixer measure loudness in decibels relative to full-scale audio (dBFS), with full scale represented by 0 at the top of the meter. Digital clipping occurs whenever a signal exceeds 0 dBFS at an input or output.

The Logic Pro channel strip meter has Peak Level display that turns red when the track's output clips. Use this indicator to help set record levels. When the Peak Level exceeds 0.00, the button will highlight in red and display the overage value.

Adjusting the input level will typically require you to change the source volume, adjust the microphone placement, or modify the incoming signal strength using a mixer or preamplifier. Note that although a track's Volume Fader can be used to increase or decrease playback levels, the Volume Fader *does not* affect record levels.

Many audio interfaces provide preamplifier gains for their inputs. For all other I/O devices, record levels are set entirely from the source or pre-I/O signal processing.

 Some audio interfaces allow the option to adjust the input gain from within Logic Pro using the Input Gain field and knob located at the top of the channel strip.

Pan Position

Setting the pan affects the stereo placement of a signal for monitoring and playback purposes only; it has no effect on how the audio files are recorded.

To set the pan position of a signal, change the position of the **PANNING** knob in the Track header area, the Inspector, or the Mixer display and window.

Pan Controls on Mono Tracks

Mono tracks will have a single pan/balance control that allows you to position the track's output as desired in the stereo spectrum. Panning a signal hard left will cause it to play out of the left speaker only, panning to center will cause the signal to play at equal volume out of both speakers, and panning hard right will cause the signal to play out of the right speaker only.

Figure 7.10 Mono channels panned hard left, center, and hard right (from left to right)

Pan Controls on Stereo Tracks

Stereo tracks will have a few panning options: Balance, Stereo Pan, and Binaural Pan. In this course, we focus primarily on Balance pan knobs and Stereo pan knobs. You can switch between these panning options by Control-clicking on the pan knob and making a selection from the pop-up menu.

- **Binaural**—Binaural panning simulates spatial information like the elevation and distance of a sound. This kind of processing is best suited for headphone playback.

- **Balance**—Balance panning is the default mode for stereo channel strips. It processes the relative left and right channels together, allowing you to position the entire track within the stereo field.

- **Stereo Pan**—The Stereo Pan knob allows you to position the left and right signals independently within the stereo field.

Figure 7.11 Stereo Pan Knob with left and right white handles for adjustment

When using the stereo pan knob, you can adjust the stereo spread by moving one channel independent of the other. To narrow the stereo field for the right channel only, drag the white handle of the right side closer to center position. To invert the left and right channels, **COMMAND-CLICK** inside the pan knob or ring. The ring color will switch from green to orange. Command-click a second time to reset the channels.

You can position the stereo spread by dragging the center of the pan knob vertically. To reset these values to their starting positions, **OPTION-CLICK** anywhere in the pan knob or ring.

Recording and Managing Audio

With your sound source routed to one or more tracks and the desired tracks record-enabled, you are ready to begin recording audio.

Depending on whether you are working in the Tracks Area or Live Loops Grid, the recording process will vary.

Recording in the Tracks Area

The Tracks Area gives you a linear, timeline-based view of your recording progress. It is best suited for recording to multiple tracks simultaneously.

To begin recording audio in the Tracks Area, do the following:

1. Select an Audio track to enable recording or record-enable multiple Audio tracks for recording.

2. Position the playhead where you want the recording to begin.

3. Click the **RECORD** button in the control bar or press the **R** key. Both the **RECORD** button (red) and **PLAY** button (green) will engage.

Figure 7.12 Transport controls in the control bar with a recording pass initiated

4. When you have finished your record take, click the **STOP** button in the Transport window (or press the **SPACEBAR**).

Recording in the Live Loops Grid

The Live Loops Grid allows you to create individual regions and launch other cells while recording.

To begin recording audio in Live Loops Grid, do the following:

1. Record-enable an Audio track. Once armed, a record button will display when the mouse is hovered over a cell.

Figure 7.13 An armed Audio track in the Live Loops Grid

2. Click the **CELL RECORD** button on one of the cells to record a new region to that cell.

3. A region will be created, and the cell will flash red while numbers show the count-in. The region will stop flashing after the count-in, and the cell will remain red for the duration of the recording.

Figure 7.14 A cell during the count-in before recording (left) and during recording (right) in the Live Loops Grid

4. To stop recording, do one of the following:

   • To stop recording and stop playback, click the **STOP** button in the Transport window (or press the **SPACEBAR**).

   • To stop recording and continue seamless playback, click the **PLAY** button displayed on the region that is recording. Recording will stop at the end of a completed bar, the region will turn blue, and the newly recorded region will begin playback.

When a recording is stopped in the Live Loops Grid, Logic Pro automatically sets the region length to the nearest bar, so the length of the recording is an exact duration in full bars (such as 4 bars). This behavior can be changed or adjusted with the Cell Recording settings, as desired.

Cell Recording Length Settings

When recording in the Live Loops Grid, you might want to configure the Cell Recording settings to make the process more convenient for aligning recording takes with your project. Logic Pro will automatically begin recording from the start of a measure and trim the end of the recorded audio, based on the Rec-Length setting (the default is set to Bars).

   The Rec-Length setting is available in the Cell Inspector.

The available Rec-Length options include the following:

- **Cell Length:** The length of recording is determined by the Cell Length value. The default is 4 Bars.

- **Automatic (Bars):** The length of recording rounds up or down to the nearest full bar when you click the cell to end recording.

- **Automatic (Beats):** The length of recording is set to the nearest beat when you click to end recording.

Depending on your preferences or needs, you might prefer another choice other than the default behavior. For example, choosing the **CELL LENGTH** option will automatically stop recording after reaching the end of a cell. This is particularly useful when a performance requires both hands, or when it is difficult to manage recording operations in the project simultaneously with performing.

Organizing after Recording

Once you've completed a successful record pass, it is recommended that you complete a few steps to preserve and organize the audio file(s) that were created in the process.

Disarm the Record Tracks and Adjust Playback Settings

Unlike some other DAWs, Logic Pro makes it possible to play back your project while tracks are still record-enabled without inadvertently overwriting previously recorded material. While this feature can be convenient to quickly verify results after a record pass, it is generally recommended that you disarm tracks during playback and editing of your project.

After disarming the track(s) to which you recorded, you can proceed to dial in basic mixing controls, such as the track volume and panning.

To disarm tracks and adjust the playback settings, do the following:

1. Click the **RECORD ENABLE** button on the Audio track to disarm it.

 If you armed a track by selecting it to enable recording, there is no need to click the RECORD ENABLE button to disarm. When recording has stopped, the track's RECORD ENABLE button will change back to showing a red R.

2. Click **PLAY** in the control bar (Tracks Area) or on the recorded cell slot (Live Loops Grid) to hear your performance.

3. Adjust the playback level and panning as necessary.

Organize Audio Files and Regions

Each time you record audio into Logic Pro, you create a single audio file. This single audio file is the original, unedited, continuous audio recording. This file is referenced by one or more regions within the project, but it is stored externally. Organizing audio files involves maintaining information both within the project and in the project folder.

 When you record audio into a Logic Pro project, the audio files are stored in the project's Audio Files folder by default.

As you begin to edit your recording, you will likely end up creating multiple regions that reference the original audio file. These regions are simply electronic pointers within the project to the audio file—they do not store audio information directly, but instead are used to display, edit, and play back audio information contained within the referenced file. Regions can range in duration from a single sample to many minutes.

Working with Regions

Audio regions represent pieces of audio data that can be moved or edited within the Logic Pro project. They are block–like containers that can be positioned along the horizontal timeline in the Tracks Area and in dedicated cells in the Live Loops Grid. Regions are created during normal editing and can refer to any type of supported audio file.

For instance, after a file has been recorded to disk, a corresponding region will display in the Tracks Area that points to the recorded audio file. You can copy, paste, split, trim, duplicate, fade, and perform other editing functions on the region within the project without affecting the original audio file on disk.

Figure 7.15 A region referencing recorded audio, selected in the Tracks Area

Naming Audio Files and Regions

During recording and editing, Logic Pro assigns default names to audio files and regions. You can change these names from within the project, if needed, to make them more meaningful or to help with project organization.

Default Naming Conventions

When you record audio on a track, Logic Pro names the resulting file according to the track name. It also appends a number sign and a take ID to the file name. (The take ID is a sequential number based on the number of times you've recorded on that track).

Here is an example of a file name generated after recording on a new Audio track for the first time:

Guitar#01   Where *Guitar* is the mono track name and *#01* is the take number

Similarly, Logic Pro automatically assigns names to regions that have been created within a project after recording. Regions are named by default according to the track name, with a period appended followed by a sequential number for each new region that is created. When you copy or duplicate existing regions, the copies continue appending new numbers sequentially so no two regions will share a name.

 If a new audio track is left with the default name, like *Audio 1*, file names will be labeled using the project name. If the project isn't saved, the project and files will be named *Untitled*. For example, a track with the default name *Audio 1* in an unsaved project will create an audio file labeled *Untitled#01*.

Here is an example of a name Logic Pro will automatically generate for an edited or duplicated region:

Guitar#01.1   Where *Guitar#01* is the name of the audio track on which the
                          region was created and *.1* is the region number

 If there is only one region referencing an audio file, it will be named without an appended region ID. Once a second region is created for the same file, the region ID labeling sequence begins.

Changing Region and Cell Names

You can change the name that Logic Pro has applied to a region or cell at any time.

To rename, select a region in the Tracks Area or a cell in the Live Loops Grid and do one of the following:

- Right-click the region or cell and select **NAME AND COLOR > RENAME REGION** or **RENAME CELL** from the pop-up menu; then enter a new name for the region and press **ENTER**.

- Press **SHIFT+N**, enter a new name, and press **ENTER**.

- In the Inspector, double-click the name field of the selected region(s) or cell(s) and enter a new name.

You can apply the same name to multiple regions or cells by first selecting all the items you'd like to rename simultaneously and then performing one of the above actions.

Changing File Names

You can also change the names that Logic Pro has applied to audio files on disk, assuming the files aren't in use by another process.

To rename an audio file, do the following:

1. Click the **BROWSER** button in the control bar or press the **F** key to open the Project Audio Browser.

2. Navigate to the **PROJECT** tab, if not already displayed.

3. Locate the audio file you'd like to rename.

4. Double-click the file and enter a new name.

5. Press **ENTER** when finished.

All regions pointing to that audio file within the project will now point to the newly renamed version.

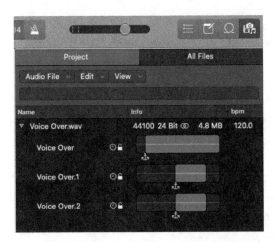

Figure 7.16 Audio file (selected) and regions listed in the Project Audio Browser

 Audio files are listed with their file extension appended to their name in the Project Audio Browser; audio regions are shown nested within the parent file they reference with no file extension.

 Renaming an audio file may prevent other projects or programs that reference the file from being able to locate it. Use the renaming feature with caution for files in loop libraries and sample collections.

Renaming or moving audio files from the Finder will disrupt the connection between the files and the associated Logic Pro project. If this happens, Logic Pro will prompt you to locate the missing files.

Removing Audio from a Project versus Deleting Audio Files

Logic Pro makes an important distinction between removing regions or cells from a project and deleting the associated files from disk:

- When you remove a region or cell from a project, the parent audio file remains on the storage drive and can be used in other regions or cells elsewhere in the project or in other projects.

- When you delete an audio file from disk, any regions or cells referring to that file will no longer be able to locate it and will not produce any sound.

Removing Audio Regions or Cells

Regions or cells can be removed from your project at any time.

To remove audio regions or cells from your project:

1. Select one or more regions on tracks in the Tracks Area, in cells in Live Loops Grid, or listed in the Project Audio Browser.

2. Do one of the following:

   - Press the **DELETE** key.

   - Right-click the selection in the workspace and choose **EDIT > DELETE** from the pop-up menu.

   - Choose **EDIT > DELETE** from the menu of the Project Audio Browser.

Removing audio regions or cells from a project does not delete the underlying audio files, so this action will have essentially no effect on the drive space used for the project.

In the event that you remove the only audio region in the project (the first region that was created, when no other sequentially created regions exist), Logic Pro will ask whether to keep the original audio file or delete it.

Figure 7.17 A region referencing recorded audio, selected in the Tracks Area

Deleting Audio Files

As you work on a project, you may accumulate unwanted audio files from test recordings or unusable takes. You might want to delete these unneeded audio files to clean up your project and free up drive space.

 Deleting files from disk will permanently remove them from your system. This can affect other Logic Pro projects that reference the same audio files.

To remove or delete audio files associated with the current project from your drive, do the following:

1. Open the Project Audio Browser by clicking the **BROWSER** button in the control bar or pressing the **F** key. Navigate to the Project Audio Browser tab, if not already displayed.

2. Select the audio file (or files) you'd like to delete. (Audio files are listed with their file extension appended to their names.)

3. Press **DELETE**, or select **EDIT > DELETE** from the menu.

As when you remove an audio region that is the only associated region for an audio file, when you attempt to delete a file that is in use, you will be presented with a confirmation message. (See Figure 7.16 above.)

Finding Unused Audio Files

Another option is to use the **SELECT UNUSED** function of the Project Audio Browser to isolate audio files that are contained within the current project but not used by the project.

 Using this process doesn't guarantee that the identified files are not used by a *different* Logic Pro project. Use caution when deleting files with this method.

To search for and delete unused audio files, do the following:

1. Open the Project Audio Browser by clicking the **BROWSER** button in the control bar or by pressing the **F** key.

2. Navigate to the **PROJECT** tab if not already displayed.

3. Choose **EDIT > SELECT UNUSED** from the menu, or press **SHIFT+U**.

 This SELECT UNUSED function also targets unused audio regions in the search. Results may only include unused audio regions only and no audio files.

4. Press **DELETE**, or select **EDIT > DELETE** from the menu.

Review/Discussion Questions

1. Aside from the length of the recording and the number of channels (mono or stereo) being recorded, what two factors ultimately determine the amount of disk space consumed by an audio recording? (See "Audio Storage Requirements" beginning on page 170.)

2. How can you enable the metronome in a Logic project? What are some of the metronome settings you can customize? (See "Enabling the Metronome" beginning on page 172.)

3. How can you select the sound source being routed to a record-enabled track? (See "Selecting an Input Path" beginning on page 175.)

4. How can you record-enable an Audio track for recording in the Tracks Area and Live Loops Grid? (See "Record-Enabling Tracks" beginning on page 177.)

5. How can you adjust the input level going to a record-enabled track? Can you use the Volume Fader to achieve a strong signal going to disk? (See "Input Level" beginning on page 178.)

6. What ways can you stop an audio recording take in the Tracks Area and Live Loops Grid? (See "Recording and Managing Audio" beginning on page 180.)

7. Where are recorded audio files stored for Logic Pro project? (See "Organize Audio Files and Regions" beginning on page 183.)

8. How do audio regions differ from audio files? (See "Organize Audio Files and Regions" beginning on page 183.)

9. How can you rename a recorded audio file from within Logic Pro? (See "Naming Audio Files and Regions" beginning on page 184.)

10. How would you go about removing audio files that are associated with your project but unused in the current project? (See "Deleting Audio Files" beginning on page 187.)

11. Which Logic Pro view or display can be used to locate unused audio files? (See "Finding Unused Audio Files" beginning on page 187.)

12. Why should you use caution when deleting unused audio files from a project? (See "Finding Unused Audio Files" beginning on page 187.)

To review additional material from this chapter and prepare for certification, see the Logic Pro 101 Study Guide module available through the Elements|ED online learning platform at ElementsED.com.

Recording Audio

🎧 Activity

In this exercise, you will be recording a new part to accompany the tracks you have set up in previous exercises. You have two options available to complete this exercise.

Option 1: Live Recording. For this option, you will first need to connect an external sound source, such as a microphone, guitar, or other instrument, to your audio interface. If you do not have an audio interface, you may be able to connect a microphone directly to a computer input or USB port, or use the computer's built-in microphone, if available. Don't worry too much about the quality of the recording—at this time, the goal is to understand how to route a signal into an Audio track and capture a recording.

 This exercise does not include instructions for routing audio from a USB microphone into Logic Pro.

 Refer to the section in Chapter 2 called "Accessing Connected Audio Devices" for basic setup information for audio interfaces and USB microphones. Consult the documentation that came with your device for additional details.

Option 2: Bus Recording. If the above live recording options are not available or are impractical, you can instead record from an existing bus in the starter project (included in the download media) by routing the bus to the input of a new audio track.

🕐 Duration

This exercise should take approximately 20 to 30 minutes to complete.

⊕ Goals/Targets

- Configure a project for audio recording

- Record an external audio source or record internally

Getting Started

You will start by opening the project you completed in Exercise 6. If that file is not available, you can use the Ex06 Sample file in the **01 Completed Exercises** folder within the **Media Files 2021-Logic101** folder.

 To re-download the media files, go to **www.halleonard.com/mylibrary** and enter the access code printed on the opening page of this book. Then click the DOWNLOAD link for the Media Files 2021-Logic101 listing in your **My Library** page.

Open the project and save it as Exercise 7:

1. Do one of the following:

    • Open the project file that you created in Exercise 6 (**Exercise06-XXX.logicx**).

    • Alternatively, you can use the Ex06 Sample file (**Media Files 2021-Logic101 > 01 Completed Exercises > Ex06 Sample > Ex06 Sample.logicx**).

2. Choose **FILE > SAVE AS** and name the project *Exercise07-XXX*, keeping the file in the same drive location. (Move the project to your selected save location, if working from the sample file.) Make sure **ORGANIZE MY PROJECT AS A:** still has the **FOLDER** radio button chosen and press **SAVE**.

3. Create a new Audio track to use as a record track: choose **TRACK > NEW AUDIO TRACK**, or use the keyboard shortcut **OPTION+COMMAND+A**.

Live Recording (Option 1)

Before getting too much further, think about what you plan to record. Since we have already created the foundation of a song segment, you can either record another layer to accompany the four existing tracks, or record a new part to replace one of the existing tracks. Remember that this musical idea is rooted in the key of C Major, so the notes C, D, E, F, G, A, and B will sound most natural.

Configure the Project

If you plan to capture a live recording from an external sound source, you will need to route its signal to the input of your new Audio track.

Route the external signal to the input of the new Audio track:

1. From the Inspector or Mixer, locate the **INPUT** slot of the new track you created.

2. Select the appropriate **INPUT SOURCE**. (Note: Stereo sources will have a pair of inputs routed to the track.)

3. Check that **AUTO INPUT MONITORING** is enabled by navigating to **RECORD > AUTO INPUT MONITORING** in the menu bar and confirming it has a check mark.

In Auto Input mode, the incoming signal will pass through to the output while you are tracking so you can hear what is being recorded. During playback, Logic will monitor from the track content, making it easy to listen to what you've recorded.

Figure 7.18 Audio Input Monitoring enabled in the Record drop-down menu

 If you are using your computer's built-in audio for recording and playback, enabling the Auto Input Monitoring mode may lead to feedback. In this case, disable Auto Input Monitoring or lower the track volume.

4.   Verify that the input displayed on the **INPUT** slot matches the input that your sound source is connected to on your audio interface.

5.   If necessary, click the **INPUT** slot to make changes.

Check Levels

Once you have your sound source routed to an Audio track, it's time to check the level of the signal to ensure you're receiving a strong signal, but not exceeding 0 dBFS and introducing digital clipping.

Monitor the incoming signal and check the level:

1.   Record-enable the Audio track for recording.

2.   Test the input level from your external sound source by playing the connected instrument, speaking or singing into a connected microphone, or otherwise activating the incoming signal.

3.   Adjust the strength of the incoming signal, as needed.

 Remember, the track's Volume fader does not affect the strength of the input signal. If your input signal is too strong or too weak, you need to adjust the instrument volume, microphone position, or gain control on your audio interface.

Be careful not to push the meter past 0 dBFS and into the red zone, as this could lead to irreversible clipping in the recorded audio file.

Record Your Performance

Once you've tweaked your sound source and arrived at a good input level, it's time to record the part to your Audio track. If you plan to replace one of the existing tracks with your recording, you might want to disable/mute the track before recording.

 To mute a track, click the M button on the track in the Track header area, or on channel strip in the Inspector or Mixer.

Record in the Tracks Area

In this section, you will record audio to a track in the Tracks Area.

Record the performance to an Audio track in the Tracks Area:

1. First, name the record track appropriately; for example, Guitar or Vocal.

2. Click the **METRONOME** button or press **K** to enable the metronome.

3. Click the **COUNT-IN** button or press **SHIFT-K** to enable the count-in.

4. Click the down arrow on the bottom-right of the Count-In button and select a 2-bar count-in. (Feel free to select a different count-in duration, if desired.)

Figure 7.19 Setting the Count-In to 2 Bars

5. Position the playhead where you would like the recording to begin.

6. Click the **RECORD** button or press **R** to initiate recording. (See Figure 7.20.)

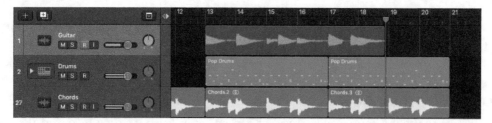

Figure 7.20 Recording audio on the Guitar track in the Tracks Area

7.   After completing the record pass, press **SPACEBAR** to stop the recording.

8.   Repeat this process, if necessary, until you are satisfied with the results. If you don't want to delete a recorded take but want to perform the part again, simply record a new take over the existing region.

Record in the Live Loops Grid

In this section, you will record audio to a track using the Live Loops Grid.

Record the performance to an Audio track in the Live Loops Grid:

1.   Verify that the record track has been named appropriately; for example, Guitar or Vocal.

2.   Click the **METRONOME** button to enable the metronome.

3.   Click the **COUNT-IN** button or press **SHIFT-K** to enable the count-in.

4.   Click the down arrow on the bottom-right of the Count-In button and select a 2-bar count-in (or other duration of your choice).

5.   Click the **RECORD** button on an empty cell, or with a cell selected, press **OPTION+R**. If you want to play along with the project, you can manually launch other regions by right-clicking them and selecting **QUEUE CELL PLAYBACK** or press **OPTION+RETURN** before performing the recorded part.

Figure 7.21 A red Cell Record button indicates that a track is currently recording.

6.   As the recording begins the fourth bar, click the **PLAY** button on the cell. This will conclude the record pass, and start cell playback of the newly recorded audio region.

Logic Pro automatically sets the region length to full bars, so stopping the recording will guarantee that the length of the recording is an exact amount in full bars (such as 4 bars).

To set an exact length for your recording pass, change the REC-LENGTH setting: From the Cell Inspector of the track, choose REC-LENGTH > CELL LENGTH. Set the CELL LENGTH to the desired value. Common lengths include 4, 8, and 16. With this method, the recording will stop automatically at the end of the specified length.

7. Repeat this process, if necessary, until you are satisfied with the results. You can either delete a record take from the selected cell, or move on to another cell for subsequent recordings. When you settle on a take, move that cell to the scene containing the other elements of the song.

Internal Recording (Option 2)

To complete this part of the exercise, you will use the Melody track that you created Exercise 6 as the source of the recording and route using a bus.

Configure the Project

To get started, you'll create a send using an available bus. Then you will route that bus to the input of your Audio track for recording.

Route the Send of an existing track through an available bus:

1. Select the Melody track.

2. From the Inspector or Mixer, locate the Send Slot of the Melody track.

3. From within the **SEND** sub-menu, select an available bus, such as **BUS 2**. This will allow internal routing of the sound source.

Figure 7.22 Selecting Bus 2 from the Send sub-menu

4. Click and drag the **SEND** knob or **OPTION-CLICK** on the knob to set it to **0.0**. This will set the output level of the send. (Send knobs default to **-INFINITY**, effectively outputting no signal.)

Figure 7.23 The Send knob set to 0.0

5. Arm the Melody Recording track for recording.

Route the bus of the existing Melody track to the input of the new audio track:

1. Name the audio track **Melody Recording**.

2. From the Inspector or Mixer, locate the **INPUT** slot of the **Melody Recording** track.

3. From the **INPUT** slot sub-menu, select the same bus you configured in the previous steps. If set up correctly, the previously configured bus will show the routed track name next to its bus number. (For example, **BUS 2 ← MELODY**.) This will now route the internal sound source to the track's input.

Figure 7.24 Selecting the configured Bus for the track's input

4. Click the **CHANNEL MODE** button to switch the input to stereo.

Figure 7.25 Audio track input set to stereo for Bus 2

5. Check that **AUTO INPUT MONITORING** is enabled by navigating to **RECORD > AUTO INPUT MONITORING** in the menu bar and confirming that it has a check mark.

6. Record-enable the **Melody Recording** track.

Record the Audio to the New Track

Now that you've routed the existing track to your new Audio track, you're ready to record.

Record in the Tracks Area

Record the existing track to your new Audio track in the Tracks Area:

1. In the Tracks Area, position the playhead where you want to begin recording from the **Melody** track.

Figure 7.26 Placing the playhead in the Tracks Area

2. Click the **RECORD** button or press the **R** key. Recording will begin on the track.

3. After completing the record pass, press **SPACEBAR** to stop the recording.

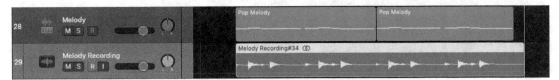

Figure 7.27 The completed record pass in the Tracks Area

Record in the Live Loops Grid

Record the existing track to your new Audio track in the Live Loops Grid:

1. From the Cell Inspector of the Melody Recording track, choose **REC-LENGTH > CELL LENGTH**. Double check that the **CELL LENGTH** is set to **4**.

Figure 7.28 Settings in the Cell Inspector

2. Right-click one of the regions of the Melody track and selecting **QUEUE CELL PLAYBACK** or press **OPTION+RETURN** to queue the cell for playback.

3. Click the **RECORD** button on an empty cell, or with a cell selected, press **OPTION+R**. Recording will begin for the cell.

Figure 7.29 A red cell region with updating waveform information indicates that a track is currently recording.

4. Recording will stop on its own after 4 complete bars. The newly recorded cell will begin playing back.

Figure 7.30 The recorded cell region is exactly four bars long and begins playing back.

After completing the internal recording, you can mute the Melody track by clicking the **MUTE** button on the track or pressing **M**, as it is essentially a duplicate of the audio recording you just created.

Finishing Up

To complete this exercise, disarm your record track(s) so that you don't overwrite any of your takes. After that, you can review your work and save the project.

Review your work in the Tracks Area:

1. Position the playhead at the start of the regions.

2. Press the **SPACEBAR** to play back the project and confirm your results.

3. Press the **SPACEBAR** a second time when finished.

Review your work in the Live Loops Grid:

1. Click the **PLAY** button on Scene 2 to play back the project and confirm your results.

2. Press the **SPACEBAR** or the **GRID STOP** button on the Divider Column to stop playback when finished.

Save your work and close the project when finished:

1. Choose **FILE > SAVE** to save the project.

2. Choose **FILE > CLOSE PROJECT** (or click the red button on the top left) to close the project.

3. If desired, press **COMMAND+Q** to quit Logic Pro.

ⓘ   Remember that you can also close a Logic Pro session by closing the Main Window as long as there are no other active project windows.

Chapter 8

Selecting and Navigating

This chapter covers various selection and navigation techniques that are available in Logic Pro. It includes descriptions of how to use counters and rulers, how to modify your project view (including setting track sizes and zoom displays), and how to create and use markers to quickly navigate your project.

⊕ Learning Targets for This Chapter

- Mark and adjust selection start and end points

- Adjust track height and track order in a project

- Adjust the project view for different needs

- Use the Tab key to cycle through active key focus areas the Main Window

- Add, delete, and work with markers and arrangement markers

- Learn new methods to organize your project

Key topics from this chapter are illustrated in the Logic Pro 101 Study Guide module available through the Elements|ED online learning platform. Sign up at ElementsED.com.

Understanding selection and navigation techniques can dramatically improve your efficiency when working with Logic Pro. Whether you need to audition material you have just added or you need to edit a transition between regions, being able to quickly find and select the right material is key. The sections in this chapter introduce you to various processes that you can use to streamline your work in all phases of your project.

Working with Selections in the Tracks Area

Making selections allows you to quickly edit material on Audio, Drummer, and Software Instrument tracks. Being able to quickly make selections will allow you to perform editing tasks with ease and efficiency. Most of the selection techniques described here are performed in the Tracks Area.

 This chapter covers selections of regions and time on any kind of track. Selections within regions and automation selections are covered in greater detail in later chapters.

Selecting Regions and Time

As discussed earlier, you can make selections in two main ways in the Tracks Area: by selecting regions or by selecting a span of time.

Selecting Multiple Regions

Using the Pointer tool, you can click on any region to select it. To select multiple regions, hold *shift* and click to add or remove regions for your selection. You'll be able to tell which regions are selected by their highlighting. You'll see this reflected near the top of the region around the region's name—on selected regions this area will be outlined in a lighter color.

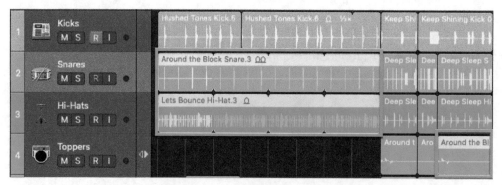

Figure 8.1 Making a selection of regions on multiple tracks with the Pointer tool (selected regions are highlighted)

Selecting Material on Adjacent Tracks

When you create a selection with the Marquee tool, you can click and drag vertically to select the same area across several adjacent tracks.

Figure 8.2 Making a selection across multiple tracks using the Marquee tool

Removing Tracks from a Selection

After making a selection with the Marquee or Marquee stripe, you may at times need to remove one or more tracks/regions. To do this with the Marquee tool selected, **SHIFT-CLICK** the selection on the track you'd like to remove with the Marquee tool.

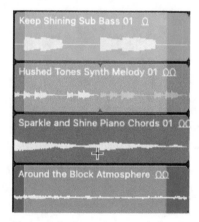

Figure 8.3 Removing a track from a multi-track marquee selection

Using the Arrow Keys

When you first select a track, Logic automatically selects (highlights) all regions on the track in the Tracks Area. Pressing the up and down arrow keys will change the track that is currently selected.

You can click the **LEFT** or **RIGHT ARROW** keys to change your selection, cycling through available regions on the track. This can be particularly helpful if you're using the Audio Tracks Editor, as using the Arrow keys will quickly change what's displayed in the editor. Try opening the editor and then pressing the Left/Right Arrow keys after selecting a track to see how your view changes.

Adjusting the View of Your Tracks

Logic Pro lets you customize many aspects of the tracks in your projects. For example, you can change the display size of individual tracks and change the order in which your tracks are displayed.

Adjusting Track Height

Logic Pro allows you to change the size of the track display in the Main Window by adjusting the track height. Track height can be adjusted on a track-by-track basis, allowing each track to be displayed at a different zoom height.

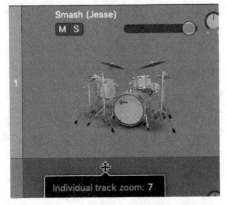

Figure 8.4 Adjusting individual track height

You can incrementally change the height of an individual track by clicking and dragging vertically on the bottom of the track header. Larger track heights are particularly useful for precision editing because they show more detail. Smaller track heights are useful for conserving screen space in large projects.

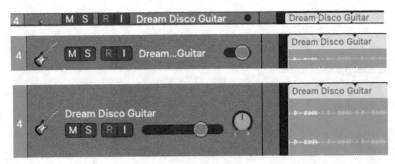

Figure 8.5 A Guitar track at different heights

 At small track sizes, the track display may do not show all of its controls. Notice in the top image of Figure 8.5, the volume slider and pan knob are not visible.

To incrementally resize the track height using the lower boundary of the track:

1. Position your pointer over the lower boundary at the head of a track; the cursor will change into a double-headed arrow. (See Figure 8.4, above.)

2. Click on the track boundary and drag up or down. The track height will change in increments.

Press and hold COMMAND to adjust the track height of all displayed tracks of the same type. For example you could resize all of the Audio tracks in your project.

Changing the Track Order

Logic Pro allows you to change the order of tracks in your project at any time to customize the onscreen layout. Changing the track order affects the display in both the Tracks Area and the Mixer, as well as the track layout on any connected control surface.

Arranging tracks in a logical order can simplify your navigation. This can be true even in relatively small projects. Consider arranging the tracks in your project such that related tracks are displayed together, instruments are displayed in a logical order, or commonly used tracks are presented at the top. The order can be rearranged as needed as you work your way through the editing process.

To change the project's track order, do the following:

■ In the Main Window, click within the track header and drag a track above or below other tracks in the project. You'll see the pointer turn into a small hand icon. (See Figure 8.6.)

Figure 8.6 Clicking on the Lead Vox track name and dragging the track to a new position (Main Window); before (left) and after (right)

Adjusting the Project View

Logic Pro also enables you to customize various aspects of your project display and behavior. You can change the Zoom settings for the current views and toggle the active key focus area to determine which section in the Main Window will respond to key commands and shortcuts.

Logic Pro's Audio Editor and Piano Roll Editor share many of the same settings you'll find in the Tracks Area. You'll see the Global Tracks button, Flex and automation controls, and various zoom buttons and sliders.

Using the Zoom Tool in the Logic Pro Editors

As discussed in Chapter 3, there are many ways to zoom in and out to view your material. Let's take a look at some of the zoom controls available in Logic's Audio Editor and Piano Roll Editor.

Figure 8.7 The Waveform Zoom, Horizontal Auto Zoom, and Horizontal Zoom Slider in the Audio Editor (upper right)

Zooming In and Out on a Range in the Tracks Area

To zoom in, centering on a certain point in a track, do the following:

1. If it is not already selected, click the **ZOOM** tool. The pointer will display a magnifying glass with a plus sign when positioned over a track.

Figure 8.8 The Zoom mouse tool

2. Click and drag to zoom in one level. The waveform will enlarge within the track display, with the zoom point centered horizontally in the Edit window.

3. To zoom in further, click and drag multiple times. Each successive click zooms in by one additional level.

To zoom back out, do the following:

1. After zooming with the left-click **ZOOM** tool, left-click to zoom back out.

2. Each successive click zooms out by one additional level, with the mouse position centered horizontally.

Zooming in the Audio Editor

Other zoom controls function just like in the Tracks Area.

In the Audio Editor, you can:

- Click and drag on the **HORIZONTAL ZOOM SLIDER** or press **COMMAND+LEFT/RIGHT ARROW** to zoom in and out horizontally with the Audio Editor or Piano Roll Editor highlighted.

- Click the **HORIZONTAL AUTO ZOOM** button to toggle zooming to fill the available space with the selected region. Click again to restore previous zoom settings.

- Click the **WAVEFORM ZOOM** button to toggle resizing waveforms to enlarge transients vertically. Click and hold to view a slider to manually configure the amount of zoom.

Zooming in the Piano Roll Editor

In the Piano Roll Editor, you have the same horizontal zoom options as described above for the Audio Editor. Additionally, you can zoom vertically, changing the number of displayed pitches on the Piano Roll Keyboard. To do this either click and drag on the **VERTICAL ZOOM SLIDER** or press **COMMAND+UP/DOWN ARROW** to zoom in and out.

Figure 8.9 Using the Vertical Zoom Slider to display different amounts of notes in the Piano Roll Editor

Using Toggle Zoom to Fit Selection

As discussed in Chapter 3, you can use the Toggle Zoom to Fit function to zoom in on a selected area, both vertically and horizontally. To activate Toggle Zoom to Fit, press the **Z** key. To return to the original zoom setting, press the **Z** key a second time.

This function works in the Tracks Area, the Audio Editor, and the Piano Roll Editor windows.

Identifying the Active Key Focus Area

Since the same zooming shortcuts can work in several areas, it is important to distinguish which area has the active key focus at any given time. The active key focus area will display a thin blue outline around its border. The Tracks Area, Live Loops Grid, Audio Editor, and Piano Roll Editor can each be set as the active key focus area; however, only one area can be active at a time. Only the active key focus area will respond to shortcuts for things like zooming.

Figure 8.10 The Main Window with the Tracks Area highlighted for shortcut use (indicated with a blue outline)

You can quickly cycle the active area by pressing **TAB**. The blue highlight/outline will move from the Live Loops Grid to the Tracks Area to the Audio or Piano Roll Editor, depending on what's currently displayed.

 Press SHIFT+TAB to move the active key focus area selection in the reverse direction.

Organizing Your Project

Logic Pro provides several ways to organize and arrange your project. Let's investigate some of best the tools available in the Global Tracks area for project management: marker locations, the Marker track, arrangement markers, and the Arrangement track.

Marker locations are shown on the Marker track. Markers can be added on this track to bookmark locations in your project for quick recall. The sections below describe how to add and delete marker locations, how to use the Marker List and other techniques to recall marker locations, and how to create selections using marker locations.

Arrangement markers are used on the Arrangement track and serve a different purpose. These define a project's structure and can be used to quickly reorganize the project. You can outline key sections in your project, then drag sections around and swap all the region information from within the selection. This gives you a way to easily drag a chorus later in the timeline, placing it after a bridge, for example.

Configuring Global Tracks

To get started, we'll need to display the Marker track and the Arrangement track. These are both located in the Global Tracks area. Global tracks include Signature (meter), Tempo, Arrangement, Marker, and various other track types. Using the Global Track controls, you can show only the global tracks you need for your project.

To show/hide different global tracks:

1. Click the **SHOW/HIDE GLOBAL TRACKS** button so that it becomes highlighted in blue.

2. Right-click on a shown global track (or next to the active **SHOW/HIDE GLOBAL TRACKS** button) and do one of the following:

    *   Select another global track type to display from the right-click menu.

    *   Select **CONFIGURE GLOBAL TRACKS** from the right-click menu. Then enable and disable the global tracks using the checkboxes, as desired.

You can also get to the **CONFIGURE GLOBAL TRACKS** check boxes (even when global tracks are not currently shown) using the keyboard shortcut **OPTION+G**.

 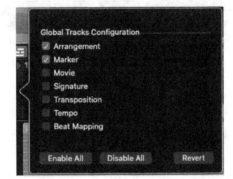

Figure 8.11 The Global tracks right-click menu (left) and the Configure Global Tracks checkboxes (right)

Using Markers for Locations and Selections

A marker in Logic Pro can identify an area or selection for quick recall. The start point stored with a marker location can be reestablished by moving the playhead to the start of the marker. The marker duration can also be used to establish a cycle area.

Creating a Marker

Markers can be added to a project at any time. Often you will set markers at specified points when playback is stopped. Other times, you might find it useful to add markers on the fly during playback or recording. For example, while tracking if you hear something that you may need to edit later, you can add a marker to designate the location. This lets you jump back to that exact spot whenever you need.

Markers appear as rectangular sections in on the Marker track. You can copy, move, and resize markers after they've been created.

Adding Markers at Specified Points

Markers can be used to map out the song structure or to identify song sections that you will commonly return to. Markers can be added while playback is stopped, by locating to the beginning of each song section and adding a marker at that point.

To create a marker at a specified point, do the following:

1. If needed, use the **SHOW/HIDE GLOBAL TRACKS** button to display the Marker track in the Main Window.

2. Place the playhead at the desired location on a track or in the Timeline.

3. Click the **CREATE MARKER** button (plus sign) at the head of the Marker track. A new marker will get placed at the playhead location.

Figure 8.12 Adding a new marker using the plus sign at the head of the Marker track

4. Double-click the marker to give it a descriptive name.

Adding Markers during Playback and Recording

Markers can be added during real-time playback and recording in much the same way as when playback is stopped. When added this way, the marker gets added at the playhead location at the time that the operation is initiated.

To create a marker during playback (or recording), do the following:

1. If it is not already displayed, click the **SHOW GLOBAL TRACKS** button or (press the **G** key).

2. Start playback (or record) from the desired starting position.

3. Click the **CREATE MARKER** button (plus sign) at the head of the Marker track. A new marker will be created at the location where you clicked the button.

(i)   You can also add a marker at the playhead location by pressing OPTION+'. This method also works while stopped and during playback.

The Marker List

The Marker List is located in the List Editors. It can be used to view all markers.

To access the Marker List in the Main Window, click the List Editors button, or press the **D** key, then click on the **MARKER** tab. The Marker List will open on the right side of the Main Window. (See Figure 8.13.)

Figure 8.13 The List Editors button active, showing the Marker List in the Main Window

Recalling a Marker Location

Logic Pro provides several options for recalling marker locations. You can use any of these techniques at any time; however, you will likely find the keyboard shortcuts to be the fastest in most cases.

To recall a marker location, do one of the following:

- Click the corresponding marker on the Marker ruler. (Hold **OPTION** while clicking to move the playhead to the start of the marker.)

- In the Marker List, click the entry for the desired marker location. (Hold **OPTION** to move the playhead while clicking on the marker name in the Marker List.)

- Press the shortcut **OPTION+/** to open the **GO TO MARKER** dialog box (Figure 8.14), and enter a marker number to jump to that location.

Figure 8.14 The Go to Marker dialog box

- Type a marker number [1] through [9] on the numeric keypad (numpad).

- Hold **CONTROL** while typing [0] through [9] on the numpad for markers 10 through 19, respectively.

The marker location will be instantly recalled, and the playhead will be positioned at the associated location on the timeline.

 Pressing the shortcuts OPTION+COMMA or OPTION+PERIOD will jump the playhead location backward or forward by one marker, respectively.

Deleting a Marker

Logic Pro also provides options for deleting any markers that you no longer need.

To delete a marker, do the following:

1. Display the Marker List from the List Editors.

2. Click on the entry that you want to delete.

3. Press **DELETE**.

You can also remove markers by selecting them on a Marker track and pressing Delete.

Changing Marker Lengths

Logic Pro provides a couple key methods for moving and changing lengths of markers in your project.

To change a marker's length in the Marker List, do the following:

1. Display the Marker List from the List Editors.

2. Click on the entry that you want to edit.

3. Click and drag in the **LENGTH** field, or double click and type a numerical value.

To change a marker position from the Marker List, do the following:

1. Display the Marker List from the List Editors.

2. Click on the entry that you want to move.

3. Click and drag in the **POSITION** field, or double click and type a numerical value.

L	Position	Marker Name	Length
	7 1 1 1	Marker 1	0 0 0 1
	13 1 1 1	Marker 2	0 0 0 1
	15 1 1 1.	Marker 3	0 0 0 1

Figure 8.15 Moving a marker's position in the Marker List area

You can also modify markers with the mouse. When you place your mouse cursor near the center of a marker, the Move icon will appear (< >) allowing you to reposition the marker by clicking and dragging. When you position the mouse near the edge of a marker, a Trim icon will appear (<]>) allowing you to adjust the marker's length.

Figure 8.16 The Move icon (left) and the Trim icon (right) on the Marker track

Creating a Selection Using Markers

You can easily select between two previously created markers. This can be handy for quickly selecting song sections that you have marked, such as a verse, chorus, bridge, or guitar solo, for example.

To make a selection using markers, do the following:

1. Click a marker (either on the Marker track or in the Marker List) to select from the start of the marker to the end of the marker.

2. Hold **SHIFT** and click a second marker to add it to your selection. This will select the entire length of both markers.

If you set a Marker's start position to the start of a verse, you can quickly jump to that section using any of the methods discussed above. Remember that you can create a cycle area from any selection, including a selected marker, by pressing **COMMAND+U** while the Tracks Area has the active key focus.

Using Arrangement Markers

Arrangement markers help organize your project into sections that you can easily rearrange or reorder. Changing the order of arrangement markers will reorder of all the regions in the Tracks Area that occur within the marked sections.

By default, arrangement markers are 8 bars in length. When you add the first arrangement marker in the project, it is always placed at the beginning. Any additional arrangement markers that are added start at the end of the previous one.

Adding Arrangement Markers

Arrangement markers are commonly used to map out the song structure while composing or arranging a song. Arrangement markers can be added while playback is stopped. After adding arrangement markers, they can each be trimmed to the appropriate length.

To create an arrangement marker, do the following:

1. If it is not already displayed, use the **GLOBAL TRACKS** button to display the Arrangement track in the Main Window.

2. Click the **CREATE ARRANGEMENT MARKER** button (plus sign) at the head of the Arrangement track. A new 8-bar arrangement marker will be created.

Figure 8.17 Adding a new arrangement marker using the plus sign at the head of the Arrangement track

3. Click on the section name in the marker, as needed, to select a different song section name.

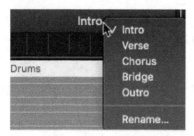

Figure 8.18 Selecting a different song section from the arrangement marker pop-up menu

4. To rename an arrangement marker, select **RENAME** from the markers pop-up menu, or double click anywhere except right on the name. Then type in a new name.

5. Click and drag near the right edge of the arrangement marker to adjust its length, as needed. This is commonly done to match the arrangement marker duration to the current song section.

Figure 8.19 Re-sizing an arrangement marker to match the verse length

Organizing your Project Media with Arrangement Markers

Once you have your song sections outlined with arrangement markers, you can easily try out alternate arrangements of the sections.

To change the order of sections in the Tracks Area, do the following:

1. Use the **GLOBAL TRACKS** button to display the Arrangement track in the Main Window, as needed.

2. Make sure your arrangement markers are lined up correctly with transitions in your project sections.

3. Click and drag one arrangement marker left or right to move the marker (and all associated media) to a different area in the project.

4. Play back your project to hear the newly re-arranged version. Pay close attention to new transitions between sections.

 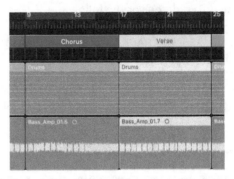

Figure 8.20 Moving an arrangement marker (left), and the resulting effect on regions in those sections (right)

As shown in Figure 8.20, swapping two arrangement marker positions not only moves the markers, but also affects all data on tracks and regions occurring over the marker's duration. As you move arrangement markers, the associated regions will be split on the marker boundaries, as needed, to facilitate the move.

Living in Color

By default, Logic Pro will color-code tracks and regions in your project by track type. However, track color bars are not necessarily active by default. As you work, you may find it helpful to display colors and to assign custom colors in order to visually organize your project.

Using the Color Palette

You can assign colors to channel strips, tracks, regions, markers and more by accessing the color palette. To open the color palette, select **VIEW > SHOW COLORS** from the main menus at the top of the application.

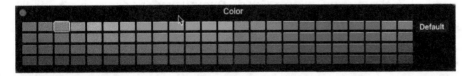

Figure 8.21 The color palette

With the color palette open, you can assign custom colors to selected items.

You can open the color palette from the keyboard by pressing OPTION+C.

Displaying and Changing Track and Region Colors

To display or change color indication to the left of tracks in the Main Window and on the bottom of channel strips in the mixer, do one of the following:

■ Select **TRACK > ASSIGN TRACK COLOR** to display the default colors, and then optionally select a color from the color palette.

■ Control-click the track header, choose **ASSIGN TRACK COLOR** from the menu to display the default colors, and then optionally select a color from the color palette.

■ Control-click the track header in the Mixer or Inspector channel strip and choose **ASSIGN CHANNEL STRIP COLOR** from the color palette.

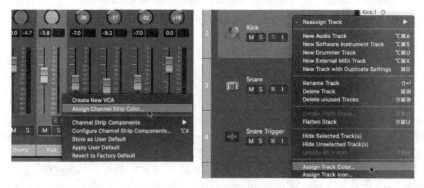

Figure 8.22 Assigning color from the Control-click menus for the mixer (left) and tracks area (right)

With a region selected, you have two options for changing its color:

■ Right-click the region and select **NAME AND COLOR > SHOW COLORS** then make a selection from the color palette.

■ Right-click the region and select **NAME AND COLOR > COLOR REGIONS BY TRACKS** to automatically color the selected regions to match track/channel strip colors.

Changing Marker Colors

To change color of a marker or arrangement marker, do the following:

1. Select the marker or arrangement marker you'd like to color.

2. Open the color palette (select **VIEW > SHOW COLORS** from the main menu or press **OPTION+C**).

3. Click on the color you'd like to use for the marker. The marker color will immediately change.

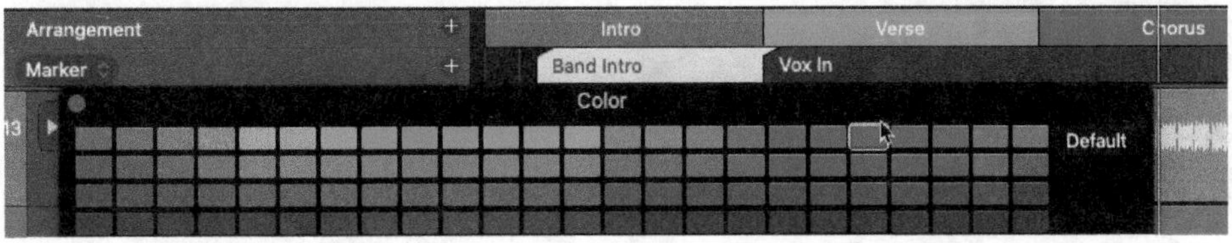

Figure 8.23 Color coding markers and arrangement markers using the color palette

Color Coding Notes in the Piano Roll Editor

As mentioned in Chapter 6, MIDI notes are colored in the piano roll editor according to their velocity, by default. You can change this setting so that notes are displayed based on Region color. This can be extremely beneficial when you have multiple regions selected from different tracks.

To change the color of notes in the Piano Roll Editor to match region color, do the following:

1. Select one or more regions on Software Instrument tracks in the Tracks Area.

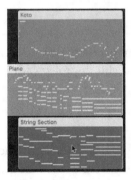

Figure 8.24 Three differently colored regions selected in the Main Window

2. Open the Piano Roll Editor. You can do this by pressing the **P** key.

3. Control-click on a blank spot in the Piano Roll Grid and select **REGION COLORS** from the drop-down menu.

Notes will now match the color of their corresponding regions in the Main Window. If you have multiple regions selected, you'll be able to view all their distinct colors from the Piano Roll Editor. This is extremely helpful when dealing with large orchestrated MIDI productions.

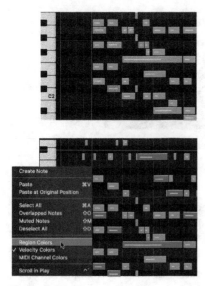

Figure 8.25 Notes colored by velocity (top) and by region color (bottom) in the piano roll editor

Submixing Workflows

Submixing is a technique whereby multiple tracks are summed to a common destination (typically an Auxiliary channel) to simplify certain mixing tasks. While submixing is most useful in projects with a large number of tracks, there are advantages to using submixes in smaller projects as well.

Simplifying the Mix

Submixing is frequently used to help simplify the mixing process. By submixing a group of related tracks, you can easily apply effects across the whole group. You can also automate the summed level of the group using a single fader.

Submixing for Multi-Track Drums

Submixing is an essential technique for working with drum recordings, which can typically span across multiple tracks. By routing all of the drums to a common Auxiliary channel strip destination, you can apply compression or limiting (or whatever effects you like) to the group using a single plug-in. You can also quickly set the volume level for the entire drum kit, while maintaining the relative levels between individual tracks, as set by their individual faders.

However, submixing isn't just for drums. It can be a great way to manage any related group of tracks, such as background vocals, guitars, and keyboards.

Using Track Stacks to Submix

Logic Pro offers a quick and convenient way to submix, using a feature called *track stacks*. This feature groups numerous tracks together into a collapsible display within the Tracks Area and Mixer window. The required signal routing to submix is handled automatically.

Submix workflows use a type of track stack called a Summing stack. Summing stacks combine the outputs from multiple tracks and route the summed output to a bus functioning as an audio subgroup. This subgroup is assigned to by a top-level Auxiliary track that is represented in both the Tracks Area and the mixer.

 Logic Pro provides two types of track stacks: Folder stacks and Summing stacks. This discussion focuses on Summing stacks.

By selecting the main track for a Summing stack, you can mute, solo, and adjust volume and send levels for the whole stack. You can also add plug-ins to the main track, which affect the sound of all the tracks within the stack.

In addition to all of the benefits to the mix process, Summing stacks also simplify organization of your project by letting you collapse all the tracks in the stack down into a single top-level main track.

Creating a Summing Stack

You can quickly create a Summing stack for selected tracks using either the Track menu or the associated keyboard shortcut.

To create a track stack for submixing, follow these steps:

1. Select the tracks you wish to submix.

2. Choose **TRACK > CREATE TRACK STACK**, or press **COMMAND+SHIFT+D**. The Track Stack dialog box will display.

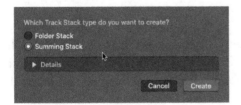

Figure 8.26 The Track Stack dialog box

 You can alternatively use the keyboard shortcut COMMAND+SHIFT+G to create a Summing stack directly, bypassing the Track Stack dialog box.

3.   In the dialog box, select the **Summing Stack** radio button and click **CREATE**. The Summing stack and the associated top-level Auxiliary track will be added to your project.

4.   Optionally, you can rename the main track with a descriptive name for your submix.

Showing and Hiding Tracks in a Summing Stack

Once you've created a Summing stack, you can expand or collapse the stack at any time by clicking on the track stack disclosure triangle. Expanding the stack will display all of the member tracks; collapsing it will hide the member tracks.

Figure 8.27 shows a main track, which in this example holds several keys tracks in a Summing stack.

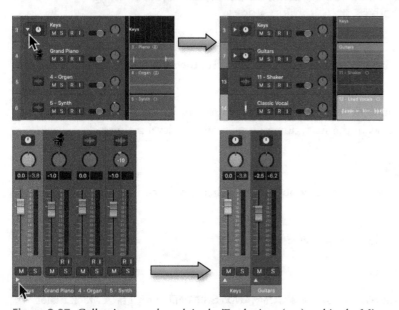

Figure 8.27 Collapsing a track stack in the Tracks Area (top) and in the Mixer window (bottom)

Benefits of Summing Stacks

You can easily insert plug-ins on the main track and have them apply to the whole submix. You can also adjust volume and panning on the main track to modify the submix level and position in the larger mix. Visually collapsing things you're not actively working on frees up space in the Main Window and in the mixer as well.

Review/Discussion Questions

1. How can you select multiple regions in the Tracks Area? (See "Working with Selections in the Tracks Area" beginning on page 200.)

2. How would you make the same selection with the Marquee tool on adjacent tracks? (See "Selecting Material on Adjacent Tracks" beginning on page 200.)

3. What modify key can you use with the Arrow keys to zoom in the Tracks Area? (See "Using the Arrow Keys" beginning on page 201.)

4. How can you adjust the track height for a track in your project? How can all tracks of a given type be set to the same height? (See "Adjusting Track Height" beginning on page 202.)

5. Describe how you would change the order of tracks in the Main Window in Logic Pro. (See "Changing the Track Order" beginning on page 203.)

6. How can you determine which area is active for keyboard shortcuts when you have multiple areas displayed in the Main Window? How can you toggle the active key focus area? (See "Identifying the Active Key Focus Area" beginning on page 205.)

7. What does the Toggle Zoom to Fit function do? How can you activate this setting? (See "Using Toggle Zoom to Fit Selection" beginning on page 205.)

8. What are markers used for in Logic Pro? (See "Using Markers for Locations and Selections" beginning on page 207.)

9. How can you add a marker at the current playhead location? Can you add markers on the fly during playback? (See "Adding Markers at Specified Points" and "Adding Markers during Playback and Recording" beginning on page 208.)

10. Describe at least two ways to recall a marker location on a marker track. (See "Recalling a Marker Location" beginning on page 209.)

11. What is the difference between a marker and an arrangement marker? When would you want to use arrangement markers instead of markers? (See "Using Arrangement Markers" beginning on page 211.)

12. Name some of the things that you can color-code in Logic Pro? How can you access the color palette to apply custom colors? (See "Living in Color" beginning on page 213.)

13. Why might you want to color-code MIDI notes in the Piano Roll Editor? (See "Color Coding Notes in the Piano Roll Editor" beginning on page 215.)

14. What is a track stack used for? How can you quickly create a track stack that can use audio effects? (See "Using Track Stacks to Submix" beginning on page 217.)

To review additional material from this chapter and prepare for certification, see the Logic Pro 101 Study Guide module available through the Elements|ED online learning platform at ElementsED.com.

Recording, Configuring, and Adding Markers to an Arrangement

🎧 Activity

In this exercise, you will extend and configure an arrangement using the techniques discussed in Chapter 8. You will make basic selections, add markers, duplicate a segment of an arrangement, and color-code everything.

🕐 Duration

This exercise should take approximately 30 to 45 minutes to complete.

◈ Goals/Targets

- Record from the Live Loops Grid to the Tracks Area

- Organize the tracks in the Tracks Area

- Add markers for different song sections

- Color-code the project

- Extend the arrangement in the Tracks Area

> ### Media Files
>
> To complete this exercise, you may need to use various media files included in the **Media Files 2021-Logic101** folder. You should have downloaded the media files in Exercise 4.
>
> If needed, you can re-download the media files by going to www.halleonard.com/mylibrary and entering your access code (printed on the opening page of this book). From there, click the **Download** link for the **Media Files 2021-Logic101** listing in your **My Library** page. The Media Files folder will begin transferring to your Downloads folder.

Getting Started

You will start by opening the project you completed in Exercise 7. If that project is not available, you can use the **Ex07 Sample** file in the **01 Completed Exercises** folder within the **Media Files 2021-Logic101** folder.

Open the project and save it as Exercise 8:

1. Do one of the following:

   - Open the project file that you created in Exercise 7 (**Exercise07-XXX.logicx**).

   - Alternatively, you can use the Ex07 Sample file (**Media Files 2021-Logic101 > 01 Completed Exercises > Ex07 Sample > Ex07 Sample.logicx**).

2. Choose **FILE > SAVE AS** and name the project *Exercise08-XXX*, keeping the file in the same drive location. (Move the project to your selected save location, if working from the sample file.)

Recording from the Live Loops Grid to the Tracks Area

Up until this point, you've had the option of completing exercises in either the Live Loops Grid or the Tracks Area. For this exercise, you will need to be working in the Tracks Area. If you have been working in the Live Loops Grid, you will first record your work into the Tracks Area. Logic Pro makes this process of translating your Live Loops Grid into the Tracks Area fairly simple.

If you have been working exclusively in the Tracks Area thus far, you can simply review these steps to familiarize yourself with the process, as it may be useful for you in the future.

Complete a Record Pass

Record from the Live Loops Grid into the Tracks Area:

1. Click the **STOP** button in the control bar twice to place the playhead at the project start: the beginning of Bar 1. This will ensure that your recording begins at the start of the Tracks Area.

2.   Click the **ENABLE PERFORMANCE RECORDING** button in the top left corner of the Live Loops Grid. The button will turn red, preparing the project for recording into the Tracks Area. However, recording will not begin until you launch a cell or scene.

Figure 8.28 The Enable Performance Recording button in the top-left corner of the Live Loops Grid

3.   Right-click the Scene Trigger button for Scene 1 at the bottom of the Live Loops Grid and select **QUEUE SCENE** from the pop-up menu.

4.   Press the **RECORD** button to trigger Scene 1 and start recording to the Tracks Area.

5.   Allow the scene to repeat twice.

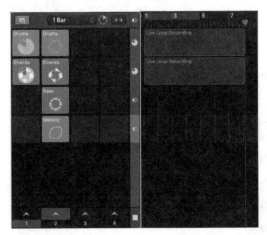

Figure 8.29 Active recording of Scene 1

6.   Roughly two beats before the second repetition ends, launch Scene 2 with the Scene Trigger button. The scene will begin playback at the end of the current cycle.

7.   Allow Scene 2 to repeat twice.

8.   After the second repetition of Scene 2, click the **STOP** button in the control bar or press the **SPACEBAR** to end the recording.

You've now recorded your scenes into the Tracks Area.

Clean Up the Recording

Next, you will verify your recorded results and clean up the ending of the arrangement, if necessary.

Switch to the Tracks Area and verify your results:

1.   Press **OPTION+V** to switch your view from the Live Loops Grid to the Tracks Area and see your recorded scenes. The recorded material will be displayed on tracks along a horizontal timeline.

> (i) You can also use the Show/Hide Live Loops Grid and Show/Hide Tracks Area buttons to go from one view to the other.

Figure 8.30 The Show/Hide Live Loops Grid button (left) and Show/Hide Tracks Area button (right)

2.   Click the **TRACK ACTIVATION** button at the top of the divider column to activate the tracks for playback in the Tracks Area.

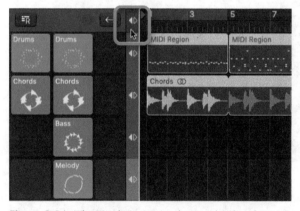

Figure 8.31 The Track Activation button (outlined in red)

3.   Trim the ends of regions as necessary. Your recording should be 16 bars in length; you can trim any regions that extend into Bar 17 so you have a clean ending to the arrangement. (See Figure 8.32.)

Figure 8.32 The Workspace after recording two scenes into the Tracks Area and cleaning up the tracks

Configuring the Project

In this part of the exercise, you will adjust the track order and track heights to your liking.

Change the track order according to your preferences:

- Click the name of any track that you wish to change and drag it up or down. You'll see the tracks shift their order as you drag.

Change the track heights to a size of your choosing:

1. Position your pointer over the lower boundary of any track you wish to resize in the Mixer area; the cursor will change into a double-headed arrow.

2. Click on the track boundary and drag up or down. The track height will change in increments.

Figure 8.33 Changing track height in the Tracks Area

Adding Markers

To start organizing this project, you will add three markers to the tracks area. You will use these to mark where different sections of the song occur.

Add markers at each change:

1. Place the playhead at the start of your project.

2. Configure Global Tracks for the project by pressing **OPTION+G**.

3. Make sure the Marker track is shown. You can hide the Arrangement, Signature, and Tempo tracks, as these wont be used in this exercise.

4. Next, click the **CREATE MARKER** button (plus sign) on the right side of the Marker track. **Marker 1** will be added at the start of the project.

5. Double-click on the new marker (anywhere other than on the current name) to rename the section. Rename this first marker **Intro**.

6. Add a second marker at Bar 9 of your arrangementby moving the playhead to Bar 9 and clicking the **CREATE MARKER** button.

7. Double-click on the new marker (anywhere other than on the current name) to rename the section. Rename this second marker **Drums**.

8. Move the playhead to the start of Bar 17 and add a third marker at this location. Rename this marker **Bass**.

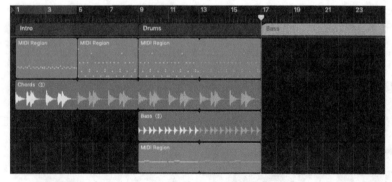

Figure 8.34 Exercise 8, after adding markers at each 8-bar increment

Organizing the Project

Next, you'll color-code your tracks, markers, and regions for better visualization of the project.

Start using the color palette:

1. Bring up the color palette by pressing **OPTION+C**.

2. Open up the Mixer by pressing **X**; then select the **Drums** track.

3. Click on the color you'd like to assign to the **Drums** track.

4. Repeat this process for the **Bass**, **Chords**, and **Melody** tracks. Each track should have a distinct color.

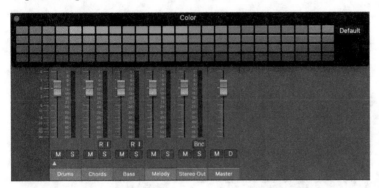

Figure 8.35 Changing track colors from the Mixer window

5. Control-click on a track nameplate in the Tracks Area and select **ASSIGN TRACK COLOR** from the menu to add color strips on the left side of each track. This will carry over the colors you selected in the Mixer window.

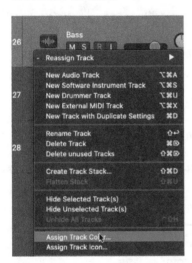

Figure 8.36 Assigning track colors in the Tracks Area

Next, you will add color-coding to your regions. You can color regions after selection using the color palette, or automatically match them to track color. Here, you'll match them to the track colors.

Match region colors to track colors:

1. Select all of the regions in the Tracks Area by pressing **COMMAND+A.**

2.   Control-click on one of the selected regions and select **NAME AND COLOR** > **COLOR REGIONS BY TRACKS** from the pop-up menu. The region displays will update to match the colors used on their respective tracks. (See Figure 8.37.)

 Alternatively, you can use the shortcut OPTION+SHIFT+C to color-code regions by their track colors.

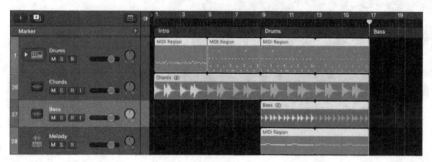

Figure 8.37 The Tracks Area after color-coding Tracks and Regions

Finally, you will color-code your markers. This process works just like color-coding channel strips in the Mixer.

Add marker colors:

1.   Select the Intro marker; then click on a red color in the color palette.

2.   Select the Drums marker; then click on a green color in the color palette.

3.   Select the Bass marker; then click on a blue color in the color palette.

Now your project will be much more organized visually, and you can get to work editing your arrangement.

Extending the Arrangement

In this part of the exercise, you will make a basic selection and use it to extend the duration of your existing 16-bar song segment. You can do this by moving some parts so they come in later.

Extend the arrangement:

1.   Start by moving the drums and bass regions so that they start playing after the Intro marker, under the second and third arrangement markers, respectively.

     • With the Pointer tool, select the regions on the Drums track and drag them to the right by 8 bars.

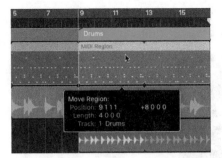 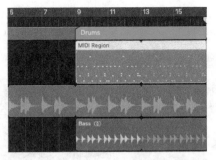

Figure 8.38 Moving the Drums regions so that they start at Bar 9, under the Drums arrangement marker

- Select the **Bass** region and drag it right so that it starts at Bar 17, under the Bass marker.

2. Using the Loop Pointer, extend regions on the **Chords** and **Melody** tracks so that they also play during Bars 17 through 24.

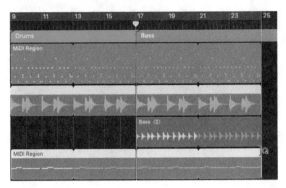

Figure 8.39 Looping the melody and chords regions to extend from Bar 17 through 24 of the arrangement

3. Next, split the drums in the bass section into a separate region.

- Create a marquee selection of the drum region from Bars 17 to Bar 24.

- Click within the selection with the Pointer tool to split the selection. You should now have two drum regions.

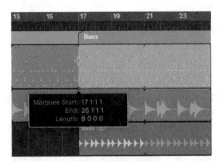 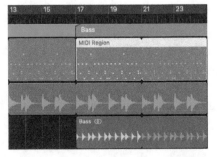

Figure 8.40 Creating a marquee selection (left); after separating the region with the pointer (right)

4.   Now, select the newly created second region and mute it: Control-click the region and select **PLAYBACK > MUTE ON/OFF** from the pop-up menu, or press the shortcut **CONTROL+M**.

Figure 8.41 Muting the second drum region

You'll now have three eight-bar segments, each with different levels of activity.

Finishing Up

Feel free to continue editing and extending the basic musical idea, as time allows. To complete the exercise, you will need to save your work and close the project.

Review your work:

1.   Place the playhead at the start of your arrangement.

2.   Press the **SPACEBAR** to play back the project and confirm your results.

3.   Press the **SPACEBAR** a second time when finished.

Save your work and close the project when finished:

1.   Choose **FILE > SAVE** to save the project.

2.   Choose **FILE > CLOSE PROJECT** (or click the red button on the top left) to close the project.

3.   If desired, press **COMMAND+Q** to quit Logic Pro.

Chapter 9

Editing Your Media

This chapter covers the basics of editing audio and MIDI data in Logic Pro. It provides details on playback options, grid functionality, Edit menu commands, and moving and trimming operations. It also introduces techniques for creating fades and for undoing edit actions.

✪ Learning Targets for This Chapter

- Set options for scrolling (follow behavior) and looping during playback
- Recognize the difference between fixed and Smart snap modes
- Configure Division and Nudge values
- Apply standard editing commands to regions
- Learn about Flex Time and Flex Pitch
- Understand the effects of Snap and the grid on moving and trimming operations
- Apply fade-in, fade-out, and crossfade effects to specific regions

Key topics from this chapter are illustrated in the Logic 101 Study Guide module available through the Elements|ED online learning platform. Sign up for a free account at ElementsED.com.

Any time you add audio or MIDI data to the tracks in your project, you are likely to need to do some editing. Whether you need to adjust timing, smooth out a transition, or improve a performance, editing techniques will play a large part in transforming a project from a basic recording to a polished final product. The processes described in this chapter will help you make that transformation.

Selecting Playback Options

To simplify navigation and workflow, Logic Pro provides various playback options to choose from while working on a project. Two settings you may want to explore include the scrolling options and cycle functionality.

Scrolling Options

Logic Pro provides two different scrolling options that affect how the contents of the workspace and editors are displayed during playback and recording. The available options are Catch mode and Scroll in Play.

Catch Mode

With Catch mode active, the visible section of the project will follow the playhead during playback and recording. You can toggle Catch mode on and off by clicking the **CATCH** button in the menu bar of the Tracks Area or an Editor, or by pressing the backtick key (`).

By default, Catch mode is automatically engaged when you roll the transport or move the playhead. To change this behavior, choose **PREFERENCES > GENERAL > CATCH** and turn off one or both of these options:

- **Catch when Starting Playback**—With this setting enabled, as soon as you start or pause playback, Catch mode will be engaged.

- **Catch when Moving Playhead**—With this setting enabled, Catch mode will be engaged whenever you position the playhead.

Scroll in Play

Catch mode can also be used in combination with the Scroll in Play setting. This lets you center the playhead and have it remain stationary as the workspace moves behind it during playback.

- **Scroll in Play**—You can toggle this setting from the View menu in the Tracks Area menu bar. Select **VIEW > SCROLL IN PLAY** or press **CONTROL+`**.

Figure 9.1 The Main Window menu bar with the Catch button shown enabled

 Note that Catch mode must also be enabled for Scroll in Play to function.

Looping a Selection with the Cycle Area Button

During editing, you will often want to listen to a selection repeatedly. The Cycle Area button allows you to repeat a selection in the Tracks Area continuously, looping from the end of the selection back to the start without interruption. This allows you to easily review the continuity of an edit or transition point.

Enabling the Cycle Area Button

To enable Cycle playback, press **C** or click the **CYCLE AREA** button in the control bar. When enabled, the cycle area will display as a yellow strip in the ruler. The cycle area itself can be set a few different ways.

Setting the Cycle Area

To set a cycle area, you can click and drag in the upper portion of the ruler. (This will enable the Cycle Area button, if not already enabled.)

To adjust the cycle length, you can either **SHIFT-CLICK** in the ruler, or drag the left/right locators to adjust their positions. You can also move the entire cycle area, while maintaining its length, by clicking in the center and dragging left or right.

If you have an existing selection made with other methods, you can quickly create a cycle area from the selection by pressing **COMMAND+U**.

 The COMMAND+U key command will set a cycle area length matching a selection. If your selection uses complete bars, or you want the cycle area to round to the next full bar, press U.

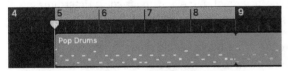

Figure 9.2 Cycle area in yellow for looped playback

Using the Grid, Division Value, and Snap Settings

The Tracks Area shows a visual grid to help with aligning audio and MIDI regions in your project. The size of the displayed grid increments depends on both your current zoom level within the Main Window and your current Division value. Your current Division value will set the resolution limit for the grid line display. The Division value can in turn affect the Snap behavior as you edit regions.

Musical Grid versus Time Grid

The horizontal ruler at the top of the Tracks Area displays the grid in bars and beats for projects using the musical grid, or in minutes and seconds for projects not using the musical grid (i.e., projects referencing absolute time values). Projects in Logic Pro use the musical grid by default.

To choose whether or not a project follows the musical grid, do the following:

1. Select **FILE > PROJECT SETTINGS > GENERAL** to open the General tab of Project Settings.

2. Next to Project Type, enable the check box for **USE MUSICAL GRID** to use bars and beats, or disable the check box to use time values in minutes and seconds.

Grid Line Displays and the Division Value

In addition to the grid shown in the ruler, grid lines are displayed in the Tracks Area by default. Grid lines can be shown or hidden by selecting **VIEW > BACKGROUND GRID LINES** from the Tracks Area menu.

The size of the displayed time increments is based on your zoom setting and the Division value. As you zoom in, more ruler increments and grid lines are shown; at high zoom settings, grid lines will be shown at each Division increment. As you zoom out, fewer ruler increments and grid lines are shown.

The Division value in Logic is used to represent beats or sub-beats within each bar in the musical grid, such as quarter notes, eighth notes, sixteenth notes, etc. Available settings range from 1/4 notes to 1/192 notes.

 In Logic, musical values are measured in Bars, Beats, Divisions, and Ticks. The default Division value is 16th notes.

What the Division Value Affects

The Division value does not determine the allowable size for a rhythmic event. Instead, it determines how that event is measured and represented in the LCD display.

For example, setting the Division value to 1/8 notes would mean that a single quarter note beat would be represented by two eighth-note Divisions. Setting the Division value to 1/16 notes would mean that a quarter note beat would be represented by four sixteenth-note Divisions.

The Division value is displayed below the time signature in the Custom LCD display.

To set the Division value, do the following:

1. Make sure the Custom LCD Display is selected and is showing the Division value.

2. Click on the Division value and select the desired increment from the pop-up menu.

Figure 9.3 The division value (/16) shown in the Custom LCD display below the 4/4 time signature display

Using the Snap Function

Any time you move or edit a region or parameter, the Snap setting determines the behavior of these actions. By default, the Snap function is turned on in Logic Pro. In most editing and arranging situations, this is preferred because it keeps musical elements aligned, relative to the bars and beats of the project. When moving or editing regions in this mode, regions will snap to positions according to the current Snap value.

Selecting the Snap Value

The current Snap value is displayed in the Snap pop-up menu in the Tracks Area menu bar. When you position your mouse over this menu area, a blue power button will display. Clicking this button will toggle the Snap function on/off.

Figure 9.4 The blue power button next to the Snap pop-up menu indicates that Snap is active.

When the Snap function is active, you can set the Snap value to an appropriate size.

To set the Snap value:

1. Click the Snap pop-up menu above the Tracks Area.

2. Select the desired snap size or snap behavior from the displayed menu.

Figure 9.5 The Snap pop-up menu in the Tracks Area menu bar

Snap Value Settings

By default, the Snap value is set to **SMART**. With this setting, movements and edit actions will snap to the nearest bar, beat, division, etc., depending on the current ruler division value and zoom level. As the name implies, the "smart" choice of a snap value varies dynamically depending on your conditions.

Disabling Snap allows you to move or arrange the parts of your project freely and to place material anywhere on the timeline. To disable Snap, turn off the blue power button on the Snap pop-up menu.

When dragging or resizing a region with Snap active, you can press and hold CONTROL to override the Snap function. Depending on zoom level, the grid will switch to ticks or samples.

You also have the option to select a specific, fixed snap value if you prefer. You can select Bars, Beats, Divisions, Ticks, Frames, Quarter Frames, and Samples. Each option represents successively smaller time divisions.

Two additional settings are worth noting in the Snap pop-up menu. When adjusting or editing regions, actions can snap to Absolute or Relative values.

- *Snap Regions to Absolute Value:* Edits will snap the region start to the nearest Snap grid division regardless of its original starting position.

- *Snap Regions to Relative Value:* Edits will maintain a region's existing offset from the Snap grid, causing regions to move in grid increments. This is the default behavior in Logic Pro.

ⓘ *Snap Region to Relative Value* is useful when moving a region whose starting point is not on the grid. The relative starting position will be preserved, maintaining the correct alignment with the bars and beats of the project.

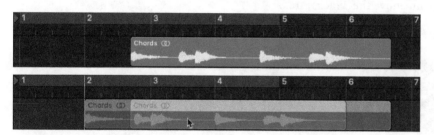

Figure 9.6 Moving a region earlier with Absolute Snap values (Before: top; After: bottom)

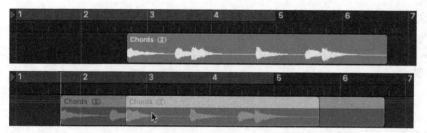

Figure 9.7 Moving a region earlier with Relative Snap values (Before: top; After: bottom)

Editing Regions

Logic Pro offers a variety of common editing commands—such as Copy and Paste—as well as application-specific commands—such as Split and Join—that affect regions.

As we've seen previously, Logic Pro supports audio regions and MIDI regions. The editing techniques described in this section apply to both types of regions, unless otherwise specified.

Basic Editing Commands

Like most commercial applications, Logic Pro offers standard Cut, Copy, Paste, and Delete commands. The Logic Pro Repeat command also offers functionality similar to that found in other media applications.

Logic Pro performs each of these editing functions nondestructively, meaning that the operations do not alter the original media files on disk.

Each of these commands can be performed on a single track or on multiple tracks simultaneously, depending on the selection or the Clipboard contents. Edits can apply to the following material:

- Part of a region or parts of multiple regions (selected with the Marquee tool)

- A whole region or multiple whole regions (selected with the Pointer tool)

Selections can cross multiple region boundaries, can include entire regions or partial regions, and can even include silence, if desired.

When you use any of these editing commands on audio selections within a region or regions, Logic Pro creates derivative regions and automatically lists them in the Project Audio Browser.

The Cut Command

Using the Cut command, you can remove selected material from its current position and place it on the Clipboard (in the computer's RAM) to be inserted elsewhere using the Paste command.

To cut a selection and place the material on the computer's Clipboard, do the following:

1. Make a selection of any length on a single track or multiple tracks.

2. Choose **EDIT > CUT**, or press **COMMAND+X**. The selected audio and/or MIDI data will be removed from the original location and copied to the Clipboard.

When you cut or delete a selection with drag mode set to Shuffle L or Shuffle R, all regions to the right or left will slide over by the amount of time removed so that no gap remains. This can throw off the timing of musical material.

Drag mode is discussed later in this chapter.

The Copy Command

The Copy command is much like the Cut command, but instead of removing the selected range, it leaves the original and places a copy of it on the Clipboard so that you can paste it elsewhere.

To copy a selection, do the following:

1. Make a selection of any length on a single track or multiple tracks.

2. Choose **EDIT > COPY**, or press **COMMAND+C**. The selected audio and/or MIDI data will be copied to the Clipboard.

 When you place a selection on the computer's Clipboard using a Cut or Copy command, you replace any material previously stored on the Clipboard.

The Paste Command

Using the Paste command, you can insert the contents of the Clipboard at a location that you have selected. You can paste data only after something has been cut or copied to the Clipboard.

To use the Paste command, do the following:

1. Select the desired paste destination using one of the following methods:

   • Place the playhead at the desired location and select the destination track.

   • Place Marquee start on the desired destination track or tracks at the location where you want the start of the paste to occur.

   • Make a selection of any length on the desired destination track or tracks, with the beginning of the selection at the location where you want the start of the paste to occur.

2. Choose **EDIT > PASTE**, or press **COMMAND+V**. The material on the Clipboard will be pasted in, beginning at the selected start point.

 If the Clipboard contains material from multiple tracks, the data will paste to their original tracks regardless of what track is selected.

 To paste data immediately after a selected region, press **CONTROL+END** (on a full-size keyboard) to place the playhead exactly at the region's end before using the Paste command.

The Delete Command

The Delete command allows you to remove any selected material without placing it on the Clipboard.

To delete a selection, do the following:

1.   Make a selection of any length on a single track or multiple tracks.

2.   Do one of the following:

     • Press the **DELETE** key.

     • Choose **EDIT > DELETE**.

     • Select the **ERASER TOOL** from the Tracks Area Tool menu and click within the selection.

The Repeat Command

The Repeat command makes a copy of any selected material and places it immediately after the end of the selection. This command provides a quick way to repeat a selection, extend a sound, or create a simple looping effect—it is faster and more convenient than copying and pasting data to achieve the same result.

To repeat audio or MIDI data, do the following:

1.   Make a selection of any length and content on one or more tracks.

2.   (Optional) Play the selection with Cycle enabled to ensure that it plays smoothly in succession. If the selection plays smoothly when it loops, you can repeat it without creating an audible edit point.

3.   (Optional) Adjust the selection as needed to create a smooth loop transition.

4.   Once you are satisfied with the selection, do one of the following:

     • Press **COMMAND+R** to repeat the selection one time.

     • Choose **EDIT > REPEAT > ONCE** to repeat the selection one time.

     • Choose **EDIT > REPEAT > MULTIPLE** and enter the number or copies you want in the resulting Repeat Regions/Events dialog box; then click **OK**.

5.   The selection will be duplicated, with the copies placed at the end of the selected area or region.

Special–Purpose Editing Commands

Logic Pro also includes editing commands that are specific to the needs of audio and MIDI production. The following sections introduce commands for separating regions and joining regions.

The Split Command

Splitting a region is the process of breaking a region in two or separating a selection as a new, independent region.

You can split a region for one of several purposes:

■   To divide a source region into two new regions on a track. (See Figure 9.8.)

■   To separate a selection from a parent region or from the material on either side. Use this process to create a region from a selection, creating new derivative regions on either side. (See Figure 9.9.)

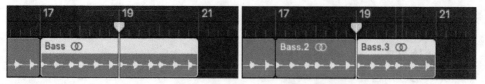

Figure 9.8 Splitting a region at the playhead: before (left) and after (right)

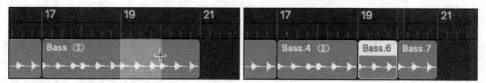

Figure 9.9 Splitting a selection as a new region: before (left) and after (right)

When you split regions, you create derivative regions from the material on either side of the selection. Logic Pro provides various different methods for splitting regions.

To split a region based on the playhead position, do the following:

1.   Select a region or multiple regions you want to split.

2.   Place the playhead at the location where you want a split to occur.

3.   Do one of the following:

    •   Choose **EDIT > SPLIT > SPLIT AT PLAYHEAD**.

    •   Press **COMMAND+T**.

    •   Right-click within the selection and choose **SPLIT > SPLIT AT PLAYHEAD** from the pop-up menu.

To split a region with the Scissors tool, do the following:

1.   Select the **SCISSORS TOOL** from the Tracks Area Tool menu.

2.   Click at the location on a region where you want a split to occur.

To split a region with the Marquee tool, do the following:

1.   Press and hold **COMMAND** to change the pointer to the Marquee tool.

2.   Click at the location on a region where you want a split to occur, or click and drag vertically over multiple regions on adjacent tracks to set a Marquee position.

3.   Click on the Marquee position to split at that location.

To separate a selection from a region, do the following:

1. Make a selection of any length within a region or across multiple regions using the Marquee tool.

2. Click on the selection to split at that location and create a new region or regions.

 Logic Pro will automatically rename the regions by appending a decimal and a number that ascends sequentially for each new region created.

The Join Command and Glue Tool

If you've separated a region and you later decide you do not want the separation, you can repair the region and restore the original unedited material using the Join command or Glue tool. These options restore the original content when used across separated regions, provided that the pieces are contiguous and their relative start and end points haven't changed since the separation.

 The Join command and Glue tool can operate on non-contiguous regions by rendering new audio files on disk and replacing the audio on the track.

To repair a separation between two or more contiguous regions, do the following:

1. Select the regions you wish to repair.

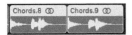

Figure 9.10 Selected regions for repair

2. Do one of the following:

    *   Choose **EDIT > BOUNCE AND JOIN > JOIN**.

    *   Press **COMMAND+J**.

    *   Right-click within the selection and choose **BOUNCE AND JOIN > JOIN** from the pop-up menu.

    *   Select the **GLUE TOOL** from the Tracks Area Tool menu; then click within the selection.

Figure 9.11 Selected region after separations are repaired with Glue Tool

Flex Time and Pitch

Flex Time is a Logic Pro feature that allows you to manipulate the timing of notes, beats, and other events in audio regions. A related feature, Flex Pitch, lets you manipulate the pitch of audio material. Flex operations are not enabled in Logic Pro by default. However, you can enable Flex processing on individual tracks at any time.

 Flex Time operations in Logic Pro are similar to Elastic Audio or Time Warping operations in other DAWs.

With Flex enabled, you have a number of options available to alter the timing and pitch of your regions.

Enabling Flex

Flex Time and Flex Pitch can be accessed in the Workspace of the Main Window and in the Audio Track Editor. You can use one of several methods to activate Flex.

To enable Flex in the Main Window, do the following:

1. To show Flex parameters, do one of the following:

    *   Choose **EDIT > SHOW FLEX PITCH/TIME** from the Tracks Area menu bar.

    *   Click the **SHOW/HIDE FLEX** button in the Tracks Area menu bar.

    *   Press **COMMAND+F** when the Tracks Area has the active key focus.

Figure 9.12 The Edit menu and Show/Hide Flex Pitch/Time button in the Tracks Area menu bar

    A Track Flex button and Flex pop-up menu will appear in the track header for each audio track.

2. On the target track, click the **TRACK FLEX** button in the track header to enable Flex for the track (or select multiple tracks and click the **TRACK FLEX** button on one track to enable Flex for all selected tracks).

To enable Flex in the Audio Track Editor, do the following:

1. Select the desired track.

2. Click the Editors button (or press the **E** key) to open the Audio Track Editor.

3. In the Audio Track Editor, click the **SHOW/HIDE FLEX** button.

Figure 9.13 The Show/Hide Flex button enabled in the Audio Track Editor

A dialog box will display prompting you to turn on Flex for the selected track, if not previously enabled for the track in the Tracks Area.

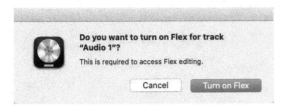

Figure 9.14 Prompt to turn on Flex for a track

4.   Select **Turn on Flex** to enable Flex on the track.

Flex Time

Once you've enabled Flex parameters on a track, you can begin to manipulate the timing of the audio on that track. Regions or portions of a region can be expanded or compressed to fit your editing needs. Logic Pro provides a number of options for editing the timing in audio regions.

One of your first considerations is to select the Flex algorithm to use on the track. After enabling Flex on a track, you can select the desired algorithm using the Flex pop-up menu underneath the Track Flex button at the head of the track or to the right of the Show/Hide Flex button in the Track Editor.

Figure 9.15 Flex pop-up menu to the right of the Show/Hide Flex button

The available Flex algorithms include the following (see Figure 9.16):

- **Monophonic**—This algorithm is ideally suited to monophonic material such as vocals or bass guitar when only single notes are played at a time.

- **Slicing**—This algorithm cuts audio into slices at transient markers. This is a good option for drums, percussion, and other material with clear breaks in audio. Slices are played at their original speed, so no expansion or compression occurs.

- **Rhythmic**—This algorithm is the best choice for material that includes rhythm guitars, keyboard parts, and other complex percussive elements.

- **Polyphonic**—This is an all-purpose algorithm that works well on complex material such as chords and mixes. Polyphonic is the most processor intensive of the algorithms.

- **Speed (FX)**—This algorithm links time and pitch changes to create tape-speed effects. Slowing audio by stretching results in lower pitch. Speeding up audio by compresssing results in higher pitch.

- **Tempophone (FX)**—This algorithm creates an effect similar to granular synthesis with sound artifacts.

Figure 9.16 The Flex options in Logic Pro

 When Flex is initially enabled on a track, Flex Time – Automatic is selected by default. In this mode, Logic Pro analyzes the audio and chooses a suitable algorithm based on the track content.

Flex Time Quantization

The fastest way to tighten the rhythm of an audio performance is to use standard Logic Pro quantize features. This uses the same settings found in the Region Inspector and Cell Inspector that are commonly used to alter MIDI performances. The Quantize settings can be used to edit audio data as long as the desired track or regions are selected.

What Is Quantization?

Quantization is the process of aligning musical events to an underlying rhythmic pattern. This process is commonly used to improve the timing of MIDI performances by moving individual MIDI notes closer to the selected grid resolution. This results in more precise timing and a tighter rhythmic feel.

Extreme quantization can make a performance sound "mechanical," which can be desirable for certain genres of music such as EDM. For a more "human" feel, you can apply a subtler amount of quantization and include a degree of strength, randomization, swing, or other characteristics.

To quantize audio:

1. Verify that Flex Time is enabled on the target track.

2. Select the audio regions or cells that you would like to quantize.

3. From the Quantize pop-up menu of the Region or Cell Inspector, select a quantization value. Once a value is selected, quantization will be applied to the selection.

Figure 9.17 Quantize value set to a quarter note in the Region Inspector

 You can change the quantization settings at any time by selecting a different quantize value. You can also disable quantization by selecting OFF in the menu.

Manually Edit Flex Markers

If you need to change the timing of your tracks without quantizing to a grid, you have the option of manually editing flex markers. When you enable the Show/Hide Flex button in the Track Editor, audio waveforms will show transient markers, and the pointer will turn into a Flex tool. With the pointer, you can convert transient markers into flex markers and add new flex markers anywhere within the region. Flex markers can be used to warp the audio by dragging with the pointer.

In this mode, the pointer provides two different behaviors within a region, depending on where it is positioned. Placing the pointer in the upper half of a region allows you to add a single flex marker with each click. Placing the pointer in the lower half of a region allows you to add a flex marker at the pointer position as well as at the transient markers on either side of the marker. This automatically delineates a range for warping, allowing you to correct the timing of a single note, for example, without affecting the notes on either side.

To add flex markers to change the timing of audio:

1. Verify that the Show/Hide Flex button is enabled for the target track in the Track Editor.

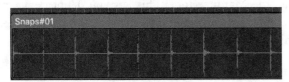

Figure 9.18 A region with Flex enabled showing transient markers

 The Flex Time function adds transient markers automatically at all transient locations and other significant rhythmic events within a region.

2. If no flex marker exists at the location that you'd like to stretch, create one by placing the pointer over the lower half of the region. The pointer will change into a flex tool that shows three flex markers.

Figure 9.19 The Flex tool showing three flex markers when positioned on the lower half of the region

 Flex markers anchor the audio at a given point on the timeline. Flex markers are recognizable in Flex view by a pentagon at the top and a solid white line.

3. Click on the transient marker. Three flex markers will be added in a row: one at the previous transient location, one at the pointer location, and one at the next transient location.

4. Use the pointer to reposition the flex marker in the center to adjust the timing of the underlying audio event relative to the events on either side.

Figure 9.20 A region with flex marker before time stretching (left) and after (right)

 When flex markers are adjusted to stretch time, the waveform color will change to reflect the adjustment. When audio is compressed, the waveform becomes white. When audio is expanded, the waveform becomes gray.

Flex Time and the Marquee Tool

Another option for editing time with Flex is to use the Marquee tool. This lets you delineate a range for warping based on the marquee selection. Alternatively, you can reposition the selected range rather than moving a single point within the range. Repositioning a selection helps to preserve the original audio within the range while still making time corrections.

 When defining a selection to reposition, you'll get best results by selecting audio that has clear separations between transients at the selection boundaries.

Similar to the workflow described above, changing the pointer position within the selection will produce different results. Clicking with the pointer positioned in the lower half of the marquee selection will add three flex markers: one at each of the borders of the marquee selection and one at the clicked position within the selection. As in the above workflow, this action delineates a range for warping, allowing you to correct the timing of a single point in the audio without affecting the performance on either side.

When positioned in the upper half of a marquee selection, the pointer will display a hand icon. Clicking with this icon will add four flex markers: one at each of the borders of the marquee selection and one at each of the transients on either side of the selection (before and after). This allows you to move the selection like a slice, relative to the markers on either side.

To move a marquee selection with Flex:

1. Verify that the Show/Hide Flex button is enabled for the target track in the Track Editor.

2. Make a selection with the Marquee tool.

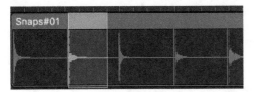

Figure 9.21 A marquee selection on a Flex-enabled region

3. Position the pointer over the upper half of the selection where the hand icon appears.

4. Click with the hand icon. Four flex markers will be created, delineating the boundaries of the marquee selection and anchoring the transients on either side of the selection.

5. Grab the marquee selection with the hand and drag to the desired location.

 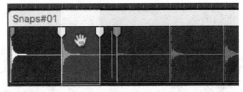

Figure 9.22 A marquee selection with flex markers before editing (left) and after (right)

Flex Pitch

Flex Pitch allows you to alter the melodic material of an audio file. Instead of displaying transient markers, audio content will have an overlay of MIDI notes. When Flex Pitch is enabled, you can adjust the individual notes on a piano roll, much like you would for a Software Instrument track. Notes can be moved vertically or horizontally, resized, split, and merged.

To enable Flex Pitch, do the following:

1. Enable the Track Flex button in the header area of a track in the Tracks Area of the Main Window, or enable the Show/Hide Flex button for a track in the Track Editor.

2. Click on the Flex pop-up menu, and select **Flex Pitch**. Logic will analyze the audio material for the track and display the detected notes as a MIDI overlay.

(i) Flex Pitch works best for monophonic, or melodic, content. It cannot process individual notes in a chord or other complex sonic material.

Flex Pitch Parameters

Each displayed note provides six parameters that can be adjusted, independent of the other notes. When you select a note or move the pointer over it, the six parameters, or "hotspots," will appear. (See Figure 9.23.)

From left to right, hotspots along the top of the note are as follows:

■ Pitch drift at the note start

■ Fine pitch

■ Pitch drift at the note end

The hotspots along the bottom of the note are as follows, from left to right:

■ Gain

■ Vibrato

■ Formant shift

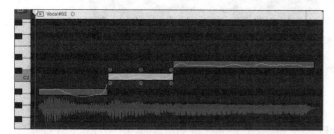

Figure 9.23 Flex Pitch "hotspots" on a selected note in the Audio Track Editor

Basic Pitch Adjustments

The fine pitch parameter (top center hotspot) allows you to fine tune a note's pitch. This is useful for when the notes of a performance are correct but are out of tune (sharp or flat). Fine pitch allows you to make subtle adjustments so that a performance will better harmonize with other parts.

The visual display helps indicate when a note is out of tune. When a note is in perfect pitch, it will display right on a piano roll lane. Notes that are sharp of flat will sit above or below their lane, respectively.

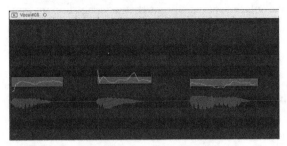

Figure 9.24 Flex Pitch shows whether notes are in perfect pitch (left), sharp (middle), or flat (right)

To fine-tune and modify pitches of a melody with Flex Pitch:

1. Verify that the Flex Pitch is enabled for the target track.

2. Position the pointer over the note you want to fine-tune. The six hotspots will display on the note.

3. Drag the top center hotspot up or down to set the Fine Pitch parameter to 0 (or other desired value).

 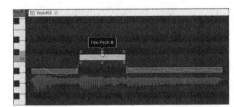

Figure 9.25 Using Fine Pitch parameter to adjust the sharp note (left) and make it perfect pitch (right)

4. Drag any notes played at the wrong pitch vertically up or down to select the desired pitch.

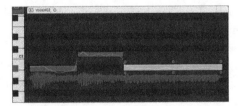

Figure 9.26 The third note selected for adjustment with Flex Pitch

Moving and Resizing Regions

The following sections describe techniques for moving and resizing/trimming regions and discuss the effects of the Snap setting on these operations. The Nudge function is also introduced, along with the process for setting the Nudge value.

Moving Regions

In Logic Pro, you can easily move regions within the Tracks Area view. You can drag a region to a different location within the same track or to a different track. You can place regions so that they overlap, line up end-to-end, or have space between them on a track. During playback, you will hear silence in any open areas.

Drag Modes

Drags modes allow you to control the results of moving, resizing, and editing regions in the Tracks Area. The Drag pop-up menu is located in the Tracks Area menu bar. By default, Drag is set to No Overlap.

Figure 9.27 The Drag pop-up menu in the Tracks Area menu bar

The following options are available from the Drag pop-up menu:

- **Overlap**. Region borders are preserved when dragging one region on top of another.

- **No Overlap**. When two regions overlap, the overlapping region is preserved and the underlying region is shortened.

- **X-Fade**. When two regions overlap, the overlapping area generates a crossfade.

- **Shuffle R** and **Shuffle L**. When moving, resizing, or deleting regions, material will align in the following ways:

  - Moving a region will align it adjacent to the nearest neighboring region, leaving no gap between the regions.

  - Resizing a region will shift it and other regions on the track in the direction of the selected shuffle option by the edited amount.

  - Deleting a region will cause other regions on the track to shift in the direction of the selected shuffle option by the amount of the deleted content.

Moving Regions with Snap Enabled

When the Snap function is enabled, moving and dragging operations are constrained by the current Snap setting, as configured in the Tracks Area menu bar.

To move a region with Snap enabled, do the following:

1. Verify that the Snap value is configured as desired. (See "Selecting the Snap Value" earlier in this chapter.)

2. Position the mouse pointer over the middle section of the region that you'd like to move.

3. Click and drag the region to the desired destination. A preview of the region will appear on the track, snapping to each successive snap point as you drag.

4. Release the mouse to position the region at the desired location.

 As you drag a region, the Help Tag pop-up will dynamically update to show you the precise position and length.

Moving Regions with Snap Disabled

With Snap disabled, you can move regions freely.

To move a region with Snap to Grid disabled, do the following:

1. Position the mouse pointer over the middle section of the region that you'd like to move.

2. Click on the region and drag it to the desired destination. A preview of the region will appear as you drag, moving smoothly across the Tracks Area.

3. Release the mouse to position the region at the desired location.

 You can temporarily disable Snap by holding CONTROL while dragging a region.

Moving Regions to Specific Locations

Moving regions with the mouse pointer is a practical approach to moving content, but at times you may find that you need to move regions to a specific location within the project. Two useful commands in Logic Pro are **MOVE TO PLAYHEAD POSITION** and **GO TO POSITION**. Both of these commands allow you to pick a location before moving regions.

To move and place a region to start at the playhead position, do the following:

1. Click on the desired region on a track.

2. Position the playhead at the location where you want to place the region.

3. Do one of the following:

    - **RIGHT-CLICK** the selected region(s) and select **MOVE > MOVE TO PLAYHEAD POSITION**.

    - Press the semicolon key (;).

To move and place a region at a specified location, do the following:

1. Click on the desired region on a track.

2. Do one of the following:

   • Select **NAVIGATE > GO TO > POSITION** from the main menu bar.

   • Press the forward slash key (/).

   The **GO TO POSITION** dialog box will appear.

Figure 9.28 The Go To Position dialog box

3. Enter a location in either musical grid format (Bars and Beats) or standard time (SMPTE timecode).

4. Press **OK**.

5. **RIGHT-CLICK** the selected region(s) and select **MOVE > MOVE TO PLAYHEAD POSITION** or press the semicolon key (;).

Resizing Regions

The resize function in Logic Pro allows you to easily trim regions within the Tracks Area view and/or the Editor display. You can shorten or lengthen regions as desired by trimming their edges at any time.

The Resize Pointer

By resizing the edge of a region, you can eliminate unwanted material or reveal additional material that precedes or follows the currently visible data. When you position your mouse pointer over the lower edges of a region, the pointer will change into the Resize Pointer, allowing you to adjust the length of a region.

To trim a region using the Resize Pointer, do the following:

1. If needed, zoom in on the region you want to resize in the Tracks Area or Editor.

2. Position the mouse pointer at the lower edge of the region near the start or end. The pointer will change to the Resize Pointer showing a left or right bracket shape.

Figure 9.29 The Resize Pointer, as displayed near the start (left) or end (right) of the region

3. Click and drag to resize the region in either direction.

4. Release the mouse button at the desired location to complete the trim.

The Loop Pointer

When you position your mouse pointer over the upper-right edge of a region, the pointer will change to the Loop Pointer. This tool allows you to create loops from a region by resizing.

To loop a region using the Loop Pointer, do the following:

1. If needed, zoom in on the region you want to resize in the Tracks Area or Editor.

2. Position the mouse pointer at the upper-right edge of the region. The pointer will change to the Loop Pointer, showing a right bracket shape with a looping arrow.

Figure 9.30 The Loop Pointer, as displayed near the end (right) of a looped region

3. Click and drag to create loops from the region.

4. Release the mouse button at the desired location.

Once you have looped a region, you can modify the length of the initial content while preserving the overall length of the looped area by resizing the original region.

To adjust the initial region length of a looped area, do the following:

1. If needed, zoom in on the region you want to resize in the Tracks Area or Editor.

2. Position the mouse pointer at the lower-right edge of the initial region that has been looped. The pointer will change to the Resize Pointer, showing a right bracket shape.

3. Click and drag to resize the region.

Figure 9.31 The Resize Pointer, as displayed near the end (right) of the initial region of the looped area

4. Click and drag to resize the region.

5. Release the mouse button at the desired location. The initial region will be resized, and the overall loop length will remain. (See Figure 9.32.)

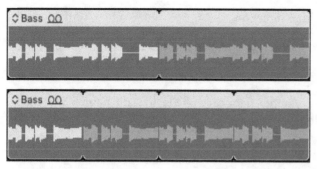

Figure 9.32 A 4-bar segment, before resizing (top: two 2-bar iterations) and after (bottom: four 1-bar iterations)

Cropping Regions

Logic Pro also makes it possible to trim a region to the boundaries of a Marquee selection or cycle area with the Crop command.

To use the Crop command, do the following:

1. Select the portion of a region you want to retain using one of these methods:

    *   Hold **COMMAND** and make a selection with the Marquee tool.

    *   Set the cycle area locators over the desired range and select the target region.

Figure 9.33 A selected area to crop using a Marquee selection (left) and cycle area (right)

2. To crop the region, do one of the following:

    *   Press **COMMAND+**.

    *   Choose **EDIT > TRIM > CROP REGIONS OUTSIDE MARQUEE SELECTION** (if using a Marquee selection).

    *   Choose **EDIT > TRIM > CROP OUTSIDE LOCATORS** (if using a cycle area).

Figure 9.34 Selection after cropping to the cycle area

Resizing Cells in the Live Loops Grid

The resize behavior in Logic Pro is similar when working with cells in the Live Loops Grid. Cells act like containers for region content, making it possible to have cells with content of different lengths. Regions in a cell can be resized, looped, and edited while the cell can remain at a fixed length. This behavior can be convenient when working with content that is not an exact number of bars and beats, resulting in a loop that may drift out of sync with the rest of the project.

When viewing a cell in the Editor, the cell content will have a Loop Range set above the ruler. The content length and Loop Range can be adjusted using the same tools discussed previously.

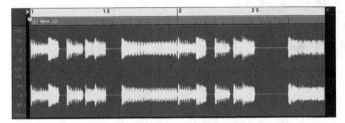

Figure 9.35 Editor showing a region within a cell

To resize the content within a cell, do the following:

1. Double-click on a cell to open it in the Editor.

2. If needed, zoom in on the region you want to resize.

3. Position the mouse pointer at the lower edge of the region near the start or end. The pointer will change to the Resize Pointer, showing a left or right bracket shape.

4. Click and drag to resize the region in either direction.

5. Release the mouse button at the desired location to complete the trim.

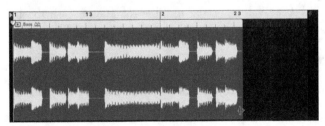

Figure 9.36 A resized region within a cell

To adjust the cell length, do the following:

1. Double-click on a cell to open it in the Editor.

2. If needed, zoom in on the content you want to adjust.

3. Position the mouse pointer at the edge of the loop range above the ruler. The pointer will change to the Resize Pointer, showing a left or right bracket shape. Depending on where you position the pointer, you can adjust the Loop Start locator, Loop End locator, or Cell End marker.

4. Click and drag to adjust the locator or marker in either direction.

5. Release the mouse button at the desired location to complete the trim.

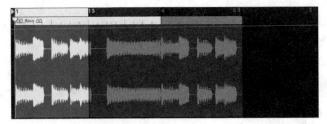

Figure 9.37 A cell with independent Loop End locator (Bar 1, Beat 3) and Cell End marker (Bar 2)

(i) Cell Length and Loop Range can be set independently. When cells are set to loop, they follow the Loop Range. When cells do not loop, they follow the Cell Length.

(i) Start and end points for cells, regions, and loop ranges can also be set and adjusted in the Cell Inspector.

Using the Nudge Function

Logic Pro allows you to adjust the placement of regions by nudging them forward or backward. The default nudge value is set to ticks and can be adjusted in the Toolbar.

Configuring the Nudge Value

The Nudge value can be based on bar and beat values, a set number of frames, an absolute time measurement (in milliseconds), or a single sample, as selected in the Nudge Value pop-up menu.

To configure the Nudge value, do the following:

1. Click the Toolbar button in the control bar or press **CONTROL+OPTION+COMMAND+T** to display the Toolbar.

Figure 9.38 The Nudge Value menu shown in the Toolbar below the control bar on the Main Window

2.   From the **NUDGE VALUE** pop-up menu, choose the desired Nudge increment.

Figure 9.39 The Nudge Value pop-up menu

Nudging Regions

To nudge a single region or multiple regions, do the following:

1.   Verify that the Nudge value has been set as desired. (See "Configuring the Nudge Value" above.)

2.   Select the region or regions you want to nudge.

3.   Press **OPTION+LEFT ARROW** key to move the region(s) earlier in the track or **OPTION+RIGHT ARROW** key to move the region(s) later in the track. The regions will move incrementally by the Nudge value. Optionally, you can use the Nudge Left/Right buttons in the Toolbar.

Creating Fade Effects

A *fade* is a steady volume ramp that you create on a region boundary. Fades have many different applications, from smoothing out an edit, to creating seamless region overlaps, to building volume fade-ins and fade-outs for music and sound effects. This section covers the process of creating simple fade-ins, fades-outs, and crossfades.

Applying Fade-Ins and Fade-Outs

Fade-in and fade-out effects can be created at the beginning or ending of any audio region, respectively, using the Fade tool.

To create a fade-in or fade-out, do the following:

1.   Select the Fade tool from the Left-click Tool menu.

You can temporarily change the Pointer tool to a Fade tool at any time by holding CONTROL+SHIFT when positioned over the edge of a region.

2. Position the Fade tool at the edge of the region near the start or end.

3. Click and drag over the region. A diagonal line graphic will appear denoting the fade location and duration.

4. Release the mouse at the desired location to apply the fade to that point.

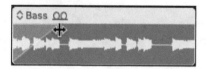

Figure 9.40 Creating a fade-in at the start of a region

 You can also apply and adjust fades using the Fade In and Fade Out values listed in the Region Inspector.

Optionally, you can make adjustments to any fade after it has been applied:

■ To adjust the length of a fade, click and drag with the Fade tool at the top inside edge of the fade; this lets you move the end point of a fade-in curve or the start point of a fade-out curve.

■ To adjust the shape of a fade curve, click and drag with the Fade tool anywhere along the diagonal fade line; the fade shape will change to a concave or convex parabolic curve as you drag left or right.

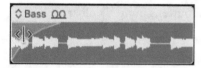

Figure 9.41 Adjusting the curve of a fade-in

Applying Crossfades

You can also create crossfades between any two adjacent audio regions. *Crossfading* is essentially the process of overlapping two audio sources and fading out the first source while simultaneously fading in the second source. Regions will need to contain overlapping audio in order to create a crossfade.

To create a crossfade between two adjacent regions, do the following:

1. Select or activate the Fade tool.

2. Click and drag across the boundary between two regions for the desired length of the crossfade. An X graphic will appear denoting the crossfade position and duration.

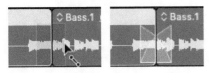

Figure 9.42 Dragging across regions with the Fade tool (left) and the resulting crossfade (right)

3. Release the mouse at the desired location to apply the crossfade at that location.

 Use caution when creating a crossfade over regions that have space between them. Logic Pro will apply the crossfade, but the audible result will include a gap of silence during the space between the regions.

Undoing Your Work

Editing tasks often involve performing a series of related steps to achieve a desired effect. Along the way, you might at times need to revert to an earlier point, either to start over or to do a before-and-after comparison. Fortunately, Logic Pro provides rich undo options that give you the flexibility to work without constraints.

Using Multi-Level Undo

Multi-level undo operations make it possible to return to earlier stages of work during the editing process. This lets you work and experiment with confidence, knowing that you can back out of changes if you are not satisfied with the results.

Logic Pro provides up to 200 steps of undoable operations. All commands that are undoable are stored sequentially in an undo queue and can be undone in reverse order.

Changing the Number of Undo Steps

The default settings in Logic Pro provide 100 undo steps. If available memory (RAM) for your system is running low, you can reduce this setting to free up memory. If RAM is not a concern, you can increase this setting to provide greater flexibility as you work.

 Large undo queues require more RAM and can affect performance under certain conditions, where the available RAM is insufficient.

To change the number of undo steps, do the following:

1. Choose **LOGIC PRO > PREFERENCES > GENERAL** and then click the **EDITING** tab. (See Figure 9.43.)

2. Set the desired undo size, from 1 to 200, in the Number of Undo Steps field.

3. Close the Preferences window when finished.

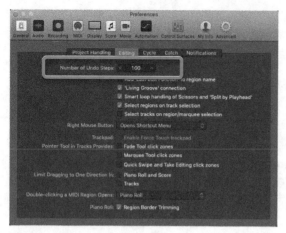

Figure 9.43 Undo Steps setting at the top of the Editing tab in the General Preferences window

Using the Undo and Redo Commands

To access the Undo command, choose **EDIT > UNDO** or press **COMMAND+Z**. The Undo command in the Edit menu lists the action that the command will undo.

Figure 9.44 The Undo command at the top of the Edit menu, showing the action that will be undone

To perform multiple undo operations, repeat the above process as needed, up to the limit set on the Editing tab in General Preferences.

If you undo an action that you want to reinstate, you can use the Redo command. To access the Redo command, choose **EDIT > REDO** or press **COMMAND+SHIFT+Z**. Like the Undo command, the Redo command lists the action that it will affect.

Using the Undo History

The Undo History command displays a list of recent actions (up to 200) that can be undone, as well as any actions that have recently been undone.

To show the Undo History, choose **EDIT > UNDO HISTORY**. A window will display, showing undoable operations as active text and operations that have already been undone as dimmed text.

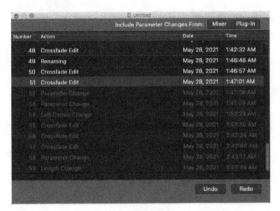

Figure 9.45 The Undo History in Logic Pro

The Undo History allows you to instantly return to any previous state from the actions listed. This list also shows the creation time of each action, enabling you to revert to the state of a project at a particular time.

The following actions can be performed using the Undo History:

- **Multiple simultaneous undos.** To undo multiple operations, click on the last operation that you want to keep in the list. All operations performed after that point will be undone; the undone operations will display as dimmed text.

  (i) Undoable actions are stored sequentially in the queue, with the most recent action at the front of the queue (bottom of the list). Actions must be undone in consecutive order; you cannot undo an individual action out of sequence.

- **Multiple simultaneous redos.** To redo multiple operations in the Undo History, click the last dimmed operation that you want to restore. The selected operation and all operations that precede it will be redone and will display in active text.

When the number of operations in the Undo History exceeds the limit set in Preferences, the oldest operations (at the top of the list) are removed.

To permanently clear the entire Undo History, choose **EDIT > DELETE UNDO HISTORY**. This operation will clear all undo steps from the list and cannot be undone.

Revert to Saved Version

If you need to undo changes that are no longer available in the Undo History, you can use the REVERT TO command to restore a previously saved version of your project. Reverting to a previous saved version has the same effect as closing the project without saving changes and then reopening the previously saved version.

To revert to the last saved version of your project, do the following:

1.   Choose FILE > REVERT TO > SAVED. A dialog box will display to confirm action.

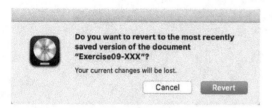

Figure 9.46 Confirmation dialog box for reverting a project

2.   Click REVERT to continue. The previously saved project will open.

Review/Discussion Questions

1. What scrolling behaviors are available in Logic Pro? (See "Scrolling Options" beginning on page 232.)

2. What does the Cycle Area button do? (See "Looping a Selection with the Cycle Area Button" beginning on page 233.)

3. What two Grid displays are provided in Logic Pro? What is the difference between them? (See "Musical Grid versus Time Grid" beginning on page 233.)

4. How can you configure the size of the increments shown by the grid lines? How can you display or hide the grid lines in the Main Window? (See "Grid Line Displays and the Division Value" beginning on page 234.)

5. What are the differences between Snap Regions to Relative Position and Snap Regions to Absolute Position? (See "Snap Value Settings" beginning on page 235.)

6. Name some common editing commands provided in Logic Pro. (See "Basic Editing Commands" beginning on page 237.)

7. What are some operations that the Split command can be used for? (See "The Split Command" beginning on page 239.)

8. How can you enable Flex on a track? How can you quantize audio using Flex Time? (See "Enabling Flex" and "Flex Time Quantization" beginning on page 242.)

9. When dragging a region, what key command allows you to temporarily disable the Snap function? (See "Moving Regions" beginning on page 250.)

10. What are two methods for moving regions to specific locations? (See "Moving Regions to Specific Locations" beginning on page 251.)

11. What is the Resize tool used for? What are some methods of resizing regions in the Tracks Area and the Live Loops Grid? (See "Resizing Regions" beginning on page 252.)

12. What is the Nudge value used for? What nudge values are available? (See "Using the Nudge Function" beginning on page 256.)

13. What keys are used to nudge a region earlier or later on a track? (See "Nudging Regions" beginning on page 257.)

14. How would you go about creating a fade-out at the end of a region? How would you go about creating a crossfade between two adjacent regions? (See "Applying Fade-Ins and Fade-Outs" and "Applying Crossfades" beginning on page 257.)

15. How many levels of operations can you undo in Logic Pro? Can this setting be changed? (See "Using Multi-Level Undo" beginning on page 259.)

16. How can you display the Undo History? What are some actions you can perform using the Undo History list? (See "Using the Undo History" beginning on page 261.)

 To review additional material from this chapter and prepare for certification, see the Logic Pro 101 Study Guide module available through the Elements|ED online learning platform at ElementsED.com.

Editing Audio

🎧 Activity

In this exercise, you will use the markers you created in Exercise 8 to add a noise effect. You will also shorten the music tracks to fit within a 45-second target length.

🕐 Duration

This exercise should take approximately 20 to 25 minutes to complete.

⊕ Goals/Targets

- Configure the Division value

- Use markers to add a noise sweep

- Position the noise sweep region using Nudge

- Extend the end of song to a specific length

- Apply a fade out at the end of a region

Media Files

To complete this exercise, you may need to use various media files included in the **Media Files 2021-Logic101** folder. You should have downloaded the media files in Exercise 4.

If needed, you can re-download the media files by going to www.halleonard.com/mylibrary and entering your access code (printed on the opening page of this book). From there, click the **Download** link for the **Media Files 2021-Logic101** listing in your **My Library** page. The Media Files folder will begin transferring to your Downloads folder.

Getting Started

You will start by opening the project you completed in Exercise 8. If that project is not available, you can use the **Ex08 Sample** file in the **01 Completed Exercises** folder within the **Media Files 2021-Logic101** folder.

Open the project and save it as Exercise 9:

1.   Open the project file that you completed in Exercise 8 (**Exercise08-XXX.logicx**).

     Alternatively, you can use the Ex08 Sample file (**Media Files 2021-Logic101 > 01 Completed Exercises > Ex08 Sample.logicx**).

2.   Choose **FILE > SAVE AS** and name the project *Exercise09-XXX*, keeping the file in the same drive location. (Move the project to your selected save location, if working from the sample file.) Make sure **ORGANIZE MY PROJECT AS A:** still has the Folder radio button chosen and click **SAVE**.

Adding a Noise Sweep

In this part of the exercise, you will use the markers you added earlier to create a transition using a noise sweep effect.

Configure the Division value:

1.   Make sure the Custom LCD Display is selected and showing the division value.

2.   Click on the division value and choose **/8** from the pop-up menu.

Figure 9.47 Setting the Division value to 1/8 notes

Place the noise effect:

1.   In the Browser, navigate to the **Media Files 2021-Logic101 > 02 Exercise Media** location and locate the **Noise_Sweep_120** file.

2. Drag the file onto an empty track lane in the Tracks Area so that the start of the region lines up with the **DRUMS** marker. Note that the region placement does not need to be exact.

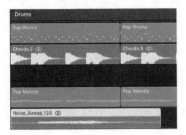

Figure 9.48 The Noise Sweep region placed at the Drums marker position

Nudge the noise sweep:

■   With the **Noise_Sweep_120** region selected, use **OPTION+LEFT ARROW** and **OPTION+RIGHT ARROW** to nudge the region so that it peaks near the Drums marker position.

> (i) Nudge the region by Division increments until the middle of the region is visually aligned with the Drums marker. Continue to nudge with smaller Division or nudge values, auditioning periodically, to align the region by ear at the best location.

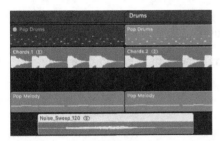

Figure 9.49 The Noise Sweep peaking near the Drums marker

Extending the Song

In this section of the exercise, you will extend the Drums, Bass, Chords, and Melody tracks so that the song is around 60 seconds in length.

Duplicate the regions:

1. Locate the final regions at the end of the song.

2. Select any 4-bar region (Pointer tool) or make a 4-bar selection (Marquee tool) in a looped area.

3. Choose **EDIT > REPEAT > ONCE** or press **COMMAND+R** to duplicate the region or selection. Repeat this command to make two copies.

If you have a song that you need to shorten, you can select a region and use the Resize Pointer to trim content, reducing the total duration.

Resize the Chords region:

1.   Place the pointer near the lower-right edge of the final Chords region. The pointer will display a Resize Pointer.

2.   While referring to the time displayed in the Custom LCD, click and drag to trim the end of the Chords region to around 1:00.

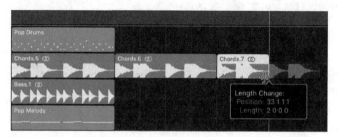

Figure 9.50 The Chords region trimmed to end around 1:00

Add a fade out to the end of the Chords region:

1.   Place the Fade tool near the right edge of the Chords region.

2.   Click and drag to the left to create a fade out. Try creating a fade out over approximately one bar.

Figure 9.51 The Chords region with a fade out

Finishing Up

Using the knowledge you have gained thus far, continue to edit and fine-tune this basic musical idea to your liking, as time allows. To complete this exercise, you will need to save your work and close the project.

Review your work:

1.   Position the playhead at the start of the regions.

2.   Press the **SPACEBAR** to play back the project and confirm your results.

3.   Press the **SPACEBAR** a second time when finished.

Save your work and close the project when finished:

1. Choose **FILE > SAVE** to save the project.

2. Choose **FILE > CLOSE PROJECT** to close the project. (You can also click the red button on the top left of the Main Window.)

3. If desired, press **COMMAND+Q** to quit Logic Pro.

 Remember that you can also close a Logic Pro session by closing the Main Window as long as there are no other active windows associated with the project.

Chapter 10

Mixing and Creating a Bounce

This chapter covers basic mixing techniques and processes as they are performed in a Logic Pro environment. It includes a discussion of mixer terminology, an examination of the Logic Mixer (including configuring inserts, sends, and returns), exploration of basic automation functions, and a review of using real-time plug-ins. The chapter also covers techniques for finishing your work, including creating a project back-up/archive and mixing down your project to a stereo file.

◈ Learning Targets for This Chapter

- Recognize common mixer terminology

- Understand how inserts and send-and-return paths are used to add signal processing to your tracks

- Configure inserts and sends in the Logic Pro Mixer

- Record and edit basic automation for your mix

- Add plug-ins to your tracks for internal effects processing and sound shaping

- Understand the Save A Copy As command and recognize situations in which you should use it

- Select appropriate options for your stereo mix when using the Bounce command

Key topics from this chapter are illustrated in the Logic Pro 101 Study Guide module available through the Elements|ED online learning platform. Sign up at ElementsED.com.

With all of your tracks recorded and edited, it's time to start thinking about how to create a good balance between the audio elements, adding emphasis where it's needed, and creating the subtle touches required for a professional-sounding result. Setting levels, adding signal processing, and creating dynamic automation are all parts of this process.

Once the mix sounds the way you want it, you will be ready to output the finished product as a stereo file. This chapter outlines the essential concepts and techniques required to complete all of these mixing tasks.

Basic Mixer Terminology

The fundamental job of any audio mixer is to route incoming and outgoing audio via the mixer's inputs and outputs. Additional signal routing and processing can be achieved using the mixer's inserts and send and return functions. These terms are defined in this section as they apply to general audio mixing; specific Logic Pro applications of these concepts are described in the section on "Working in the Mixer" later in this chapter.

Inputs

The term *input* refers to an audio signal traveling into an audio hardware device, such as a mixer or an audio interface. The inputs available in Logic Pro can vary depending on the system and the audio interface(s) in use.

Outputs

The term *output* refers to an audio signal traveling out of an audio hardware device. The outputs available in Logic Pro can also vary depending on the system and the audio hardware in use. Typically, all tracks will route to the main stereo outputs (left and right) by default.

Inserts

Most mixers have a feature known as a *channel insert*. An insert is an audio patch point that allows a signal processor to be placed directly into the signal path of the audio channel.

Logic Pro provides 15 Effects Slots per track for adding inserts, allowing you to process a track's signal through multiple software plug-ins and/or external effects loops in series.

Sends and Returns

The term *send* refers to a signal path carrying a mix output of one or more channels (or tracks) routed for parallel processing. The send may route to an external receiving device, such as a hardware effects unit, or to an internal processor, such as a software plug-in.

Send Configurations

Sends in Logic can be configured using three available options: Post Pan, Post Fader, and Pre Fader. Sends are Post Pan by default, meaning the panning applied to the source track will also determine the pan position for the send. Sends configured as Post Pan are also Post Fader. For any Post Fader send, the send *level* will also be affected by changes made to the volume fader on the source track. For sends set to Pre Fader, the send level *will not be* affected by the source track's volume fader level.

Send and Return Processing

When using a send for external processing, the signal is routed out of the mixer, through an external device where some type of processing is added, and then brought back into the mixer through a *return channel* (sometimes called an *auxiliary return*). When using a send for internal processing in Logic Pro, effects are added using a plug-in applied to the returned signal on the destination Auxiliary channel strip.

The return channel in the mixer provides level and pan controls, allowing precise control over how the reintroduced signal combines with other audio in the system.

Working in the Mixer

The Logic Pro mixing operations and functions are performed using the Mixer panel in the Main Window or in the standalone Mixer window. The Logic Mixer is similar to a standard mixing console. This area offers a variety of display options, many of which can also be customized.

To view the Mixer panel in the Main Window, choose **VIEW > SHOW MIXER** from the main menus at the top of the application. The Mixer controls will be displayed, docked at the bottom of the Main Window.

 Press X to toggle the Mixer panel display on/off from the keyboard.

Alternatively, you can display the Mixer window by choosing **WINDOW > OPEN MIXER** from the main menus. A new Mixer window will display.

 Press Command+2 to open a new Mixer window from the keyboard.

 It is possible to open several different Mixer windows. This can be useful to quickly switch between different arrangements of channel strips and views.

The Mixer panel and the Mixer window both provide access to the same controls and functionality. Some of the available parameters are shown in Figure 10.1 below.

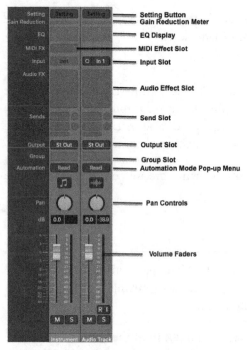

Figure 10.1 Mixer controls in Logic Pro

Showing and Hiding Mixer Parameters

You can show or hide any of the displayed parameters in the Mixer channel strips. To configure the display areas in the Mixer, click on the Mixer's **VIEW** menu and select **CHANNEL STRIP COMPONENTS**; then select or deselect individual options in the submenu to toggle their state on/off.

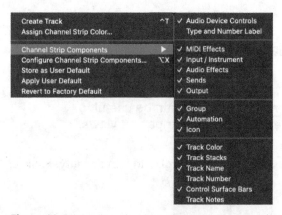

Figure 10.2 Toggling the channel strip components that are displayed in the Mixer

You can also use the Mixer's View menu to select **CONFIGURE CHANNEL STRIP COMPONENTS**. This will display an overlay window where you can enable/disable multiple parameter displays simultaneously.

Configuring the Mixer

Among the Mixer controls that you will use to create your mix are Volume Faders, Pan controls, Input and Output Slots, and Audio FX Slots and Send Slots.

 Input and Output Slots provide access to Audio Input and Output selectors, for channel strips that route audio.

Input and Output Slots

The Input and Output Slots route signals to and from your channels and tracks. The Mixer window displays the main Input and Output Slots for each channel in the project by default. Though much of your signal routing might have been set up during the recording and editing stages of your project, it is a good idea to double-check these settings when you begin mixing.

Input Routing

For channels that are playing back material already on the associated track, no input routing is necessary. Channels that are receiving live input from other sources will need to have their inputs set accordingly.

When configuring your mix, pay particular attention to the Input Slot settings for any Auxiliary channel strips used in your project. These channels are often used to route audio from a send or submix. Auxiliary channels may also be used to receive live audio from an external source.

Output Routing

Logic Pro enables you to route the output of each channel to any hardware output or bus. For the purposes of creating a stereo mix, you will generally use the main stereo outputs of your audio interface (default).

To set up a basic stereo mix, verify that the Output Slots for the channels in your project are set to the main outputs of your audio interface, as appropriate, so that the audio from each track is included in the stereo playback. This is typically done through an output path labeled **Output 1-2, Analog 1-2**, or similar.

Effects Slots and Send Slots

The Mixer window has independent areas for the channel inserts (Effects Slots) and sends (Send Slots). These areas expand vertically as inserts and sends are applied throughout your project.

Effects Slots are available in two general types—audio effects and MIDI effects:

- **Audio Effects.** The Audio Effects Slots allow you to access and view the audio plug-in positions. Logic Pro provides up to 15 Audio Effects Slots per channel.

- **MIDI Effects.** The MIDI Effect Slots allow you to access and view the MIDI plug-in positions. Logic Pro provides up to eight MIDI Effects Slots per channel.

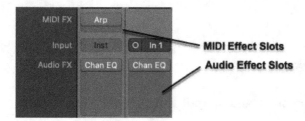

Figure 10.3 Empty Audio and MIDI Effect Slots in the Mixer underneath a single loaded plug-in

Send Slots allow you to access and view send positions. Logic Pro provides up to 12 Send Slots per channel.

Figure 10.4 Send Slots in the Logic Pro Mixer

 Clicking on an occupied Audio or MIDI Effects Slot will open the plug-in, allowing you to configure its settings.

Configuring Inserts

With Audio Effects Slots displayed in the Mixer, you can add a plug-in processor to any track. To add a plug-in, click on an empty Audio Effects Slot and choose a plug-in option from the pop-up menu. Plug-ins provide software-based signal processing.

Plug-ins route audio through a software add-on from within a track in the Mixer. Choose a plug-in to add a software signal processor, such as an EQ plug-in, directly into the signal path of the channel.

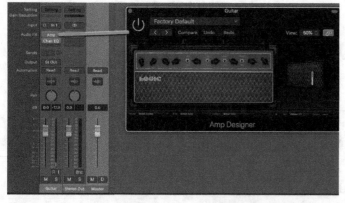

Figure 10.5 Amp Designer plug-in on the first Audio Effects Slot of a guitar track

Configuring Sends and Returns

Send Slots are used to route a channel's signal to a secondary path for parallel processing (internal or external) without interrupting the signal flow through the originating channel. To add the processed signal back into the mix, it is typically returned via an Auxiliary channel strip.

Sends to External Devices

To route a send to an external device, choose **OUTPUT** from the Send Slot and select the appropriate output path on your audio interface. Connect this output to the external device, and return the processed signal from the device to an available input on your audio interface. This signal is the return, which then must be routed to an Auxiliary channel strip to be represented in the mix.

Sends to Internal Plug-In Processors

To route a send to an internal processor, such as a plug-in on an Auxiliary channel strip, choose **BUS** from the Send Slot and select an appropriate bus for routing the signal. When you select an available Bus, Logic automatically creates an Auxiliary channel strip in the Mixer and routes the selected bus to its input.

Using Plug-In Processors

As you learned earlier, plug-ins are software add-ons for Logic Pro that provide added functionality such as effects processing or a virtual instrument sound source for a track.

Plug-In Channel Formats

Plug-ins may be available in mono, mono > stereo, stereo, and dual-mono formats. The plug-in formats available depend on the selected plug-in and the format of the source track (mono or stereo).

On stereo tracks, it is generally simplest to use stereo plug-ins, for linked processing between the left and right channels. If you want to process the left and right channels differently, you can use a dual-mono version instead.

- **Mono plug-ins.** Plug-ins in this format are available for use on mono tracks, applying a mono effect.

- **Mono > Stereo plug-ins.** Plug-ins in this format can generate stereo output from a mono track.

- **Stereo plug-ins.** Plug-ins in this format are designed for use on stereo tracks. Controls for the left and right channels are always linked together in stereo plug-ins.

- **Dual-mono plug-ins.** Plug-ins in this format can be used on stereo tracks and will process the left and right channels independently.

Plug-Ins Provided with Logic Pro

The sheer variety of plug-ins available can seem overwhelming when you're just getting started. Logic Pro comes with a large collection of professional effects that are capable of handling the most common production needs, as well as a number of specialty plug-ins.

Two of the most commonly used types of processing for Audio tracks are dynamics processors (such as compressors, limiters, and gates) and equalizers (such as graphic and parametric EQs). Popular plug-ins in these categories include the following:

- Channel EQ
- Compressor
- Limiter

Channel EQ

The Logic Pro Channel EQ is an 8-band equalizer plug-in for adjusting the frequency spectrum of audio material in Logic Pro.

To add the Channel EQ plug-in to a Logic Pro track, click on a blank **AUDIO FX** Slot and choose **EQ > CHANNEL EQ**. The Channel EQ window will open.

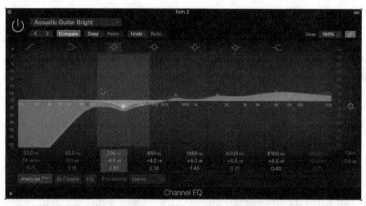

Figure 10.6 The Channel EQ 8-band equalizer plug-in window

Compressor

The Logic Pro Compressor plug-in provides a suite several emulations of different types of compressors inside one window. The Compressor plug-in can be used to control dynamic levels, using standard attack, release, threshold, and ratio controls. Different models of compressor can be selected by clicking on the buttons above the meter display. (See Figure 10.7.)

To add a Compressor plug-in to a track, click on a blank **AUDIO FX** Slot and choose **DYNAMICS > COMPRESSOR**. The Compressor window will open.

Figure 10.7 The Compressor plug-in window

Limiter

The Logic Pro Limiter is typically used on complete mixes, but can also be used on individual Audio and Software Instrument tracks to prevent levels from exceeding the specified Output Level value.

To add the Limiter plug-in to a track, click on an **AUDIO FX** Slot and choose **DYNAMICS > LIMITER**. The Limiter window will open.

Figure 10.8 The Limiter plug-in window

Applying Mix Automation

Automation can be used to apply dynamic changes to your mix throughout the project. For example, you can automate the Volume Fader levels on tracks to emphasize different instruments in different sections or automate the pan control on a track to create the effect of a sound sweeping from left to right.

Selecting an Automation Mode

Logic Pro provides six automation modes. The currently active automation mode on each track determines how automation will function for the track.

You can set the automation mode for each track independently, using the track's Automation Mode pop-up menu in the Mixer.

Figure 10.9 Automation Mode pop-up menu in the Mixer

The automation modes available in Logic Pro include the following:

- **Read mode** (default)—This mode plays back existing automation on the track but will not write any new automation. Use this mode when you want a track to play automation you have previously recorded for the track, if you do not want to record new changes as automation.

- **Latch mode**—This mode writes automation only on parameters that you change during the automation pass. Automation will retain, or latch onto, the last set value and will overwrite any existing automation after that point. Use this mode to write automation selectively for some track settings without locking in other settings.

- **Touch mode**—This mode writes automation only on parameters that you change, and only while you are actively modifying those parameters. Use this mode to change certain track settings in only specific areas of the track.

- **Write mode**—This mode writes automation for all parameters whenever the transport is rolling. Write mode ignores all previous automation, and will replace existing automation as the playhead passes over it.

- **Trim mode**—This mode offsets the value of existing automation (Volume, Pan, Send level) by adjusting it up or down by an amount you move the fader or a control. This mode works in combination with Touch/Latch modes.

- **Relative mode**—This mode adds a secondary automation curve which offsets an existing curve for a selected parameter. Both the initial primary curve and new secondary curve will be visible and can be edited. This mode works in combination with Touch, Latch, and Write automation modes.

To select an automation mode, do the following:

1. Click on the Automation Mode selector in the Inspector, Mixer or Main Window in either the Live Loops Grid or the Tracks Area.

2. Select the desired mode from the pop-up menu.

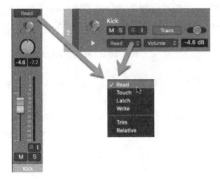

Figure 10.10 Selecting an automation mode: Mixer window (left) and Tracks Area in the Main Window (right)

To display current automation modes and see automation curves in the Main Window, you have to enable the **SHOW AUTOMATION** button just above track list in the Main Window or the Audio/Piano Roll Editor. Alternatively, you can press the **A** key to activate this function from the keyboard.

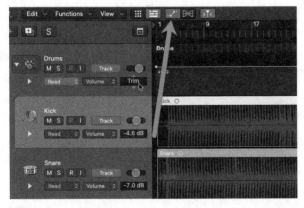

Figure 10.11 Enabling the Show Automation button in the Main Window

Writing Real-Time Automation

When writing real-time automation, you will commonly use Latch mode for basic settings on your initial automation passes. This can be useful when writing automation across long sections.

By way of example, you might use Latch mode to automate changes for different sections of a song, such as to increase the level of the lead vocals during the choruses and return to a lower level during the verses.

To automate basic settings, do the following:

1. Click on the **AUTOMATION MODE POP-UP MENU** to put the target track(s) into **LATCH** mode.

2. Begin playback. Automation will not be writing at this point.

3. When you want to make a change, adjust the volume, pan, or other settings on the target track(s). The changes will begin writing as new automation and will continue until you make the next change.

4. Continue playback through the project, adjusting the settings during each section as needed.

5. When finished, stop playback and return the track(s) to **READ** mode.

With your initial track settings and automation in place, you can use Touch mode to refine the mix in specific areas. This can be useful to touch up existing automation or to make dynamic changes that affect only small areas of the project.

 By way of example, you can use Touch mode to increase the send levels for reverb or delay at the ends of certain vocal lines, while automatically returning to previous levels in between the changes.

To add or modify automation in specific areas, do the following:

1. Use the **AUTOMATION MODE POP-UP MENU** to put the target track(s) into **TOUCH** mode.

2. Begin playback. Automation will not be writing at this point.

3. When you want to make a change, adjust the volume, pan, or other settings on the target track(s). New automation will be written and will continue while you hold the control in place.

4. Release the control to return the parameter to its previous setting.

5. Continue playback through the project, making additional changes in selected areas as needed.

6. When finished, stop playback and return the track(s) to **READ** mode.

Viewing Automation Curves

Each automatable parameter on a track has an associated automation curve. The automation curve can be displayed in the Tracks Area of the Main Window, allowing you to see a visual representation of the automation changes.

To display an automation curve, do the following:

1. Enable the **SHOW AUTOMATION** button, or press the **A** key. (See Figure 10.11 above.)

2. Select the type of automation that you want to display from the **AUTOMATION PARAMETER POP-UP MENU**. The automation curve will be displayed as a faint orange line, superimposed on the track.

(i)   Click anywhere on a track playlist to make the automation curve more prominent.

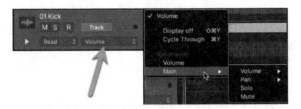

Figure 10.12 Selecting the Volume automation view (left); the Volume automation curve displayed (right)

As an alternative, you can display automation curves beneath a track using the **SUBTRACK DISCLOSURE TRIANGLE** at the head of the track. On Audio tracks the Volume automation curve will display by default. Additional automation subtracks can be added by clicking on the plus sign (**+**) within a displayed subtrack lane.

Figure 10.13 Clicking the Subtrack Disclosure Triangle (left); the Volume automation subtrack displayed (right)

Editing Automation Points

With an automation curve displayed, you can edit the automation using the automation points. Automation points are locations on the automation curve where the automation line changes slope or direction.

Using the Pointer Tool for Automation

You can edit the automation curve by adding, moving, or deleting automation points using the Pointer tool.

To edit automation with the Pointer tool, do any of the following:

■   Click on an automation curve to add a new automation point.

■   Click and drag an existing automation point to adjust its position.

■ **DOUBLE-CLICK** on an existing automation point to delete it.

Figure 10.14 Editing the Volume automation curve using the Pointer tool

Automation can also be edited using other Mouse tools, such as the Pencil tool.

Using the Pencil Tool for Automation

The Pencil tool can be quite useful for creating or modifying automation. This tool lets you draw automation changes on a displayed automation curve. This allows you to freely draw a variety of automation shapes.

To draw a freehand automation shape, do the following:

1. In the Main Window, press **T** to display the left-click tool menu; then select the Pencil tool.

Figure 10.15 Selecting the Pencil tool

2. Click and drag on an automation curve to draw a new shape or curve. A series of new automation points will be created, matching the shape you draw.

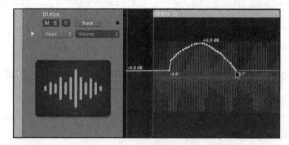

Figure 10.16 Drawing freeform automation with the Pencil tool

Backing Up Your Project

Once you've finished crafting your mix with automation and plug-in processing, you can safeguard your work by creating a backup copy. Creating backups is critical for archival and disaster-recovery purposes. The backup process will help protect against loss due to accidentally deleting or overwriting files, having a file become corrupt, encountering a virus, or having a drive fail.

Considerations for Backup and Archive Copies

Some of the best protection measures include creating multiple copies of your files, using a separate drive for backup copies, and storing copies in the cloud to protect against disasters such as fire or flood. The more valuable your projects, the more robust your backup plans should be. You should consider creating a backup for any work that would be difficult or time-consuming to re-create, especially if the project has significant value to you or your clients.

Whenever creating a backup or archive copy, be sure to include any media files (audio and video) that are referenced by the project. Keep in mind that these files may not be included in the original project folder.

Saving a Project Copy

You can create a copy of your project and all related files using either the **SAVE AS** command or the **SAVE A COPY AS** command. With either command, you can choose to save all project media, allowing you to create a self-contained project folder in a separate location, such as on another drive.

- The **SAVE AS** command saves a copy of your current project under a new name and/or in a different location, allowing you to continue work in the newly saved copy.

- The **SAVE A COPY AS** command saves a copy of your current project in its current state without closing the original project, meaning that as you continue to work, any subsequent changes are made in the original and do not affect the copy.

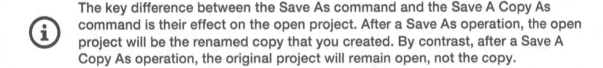 The key difference between the Save As command and the Save A Copy As command is their effect on the open project. After a Save As operation, the open project will be the renamed copy that you created. By contrast, after a Save A Copy As operation, the original project will remain open, not the copy.

Including Project Media in a Backup Copy

The Save As and Save A Copy As commands are both available under the File menu. The dialog box for each includes a variety of configuration choices.

To back up a project and its media, do the following:

1. Choose **FILE > SAVE AS** or **FILE > SAVE A COPY AS**. The associated dialog box will open.

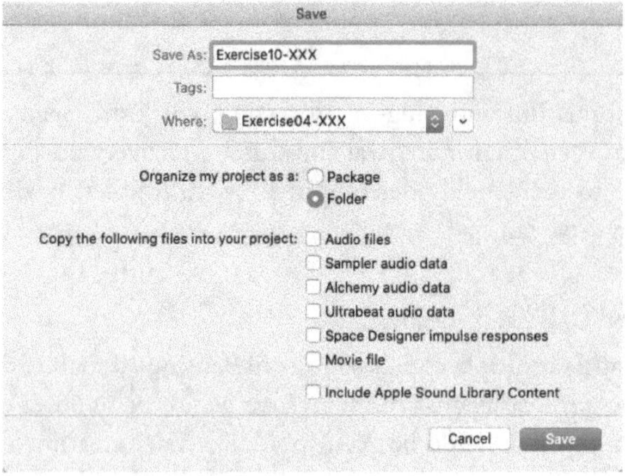

Figure 10.17 The Save As dialog box

2. Rename the project backup as desired, and navigate to an appropriate save location.

3. In the bottom of the dialog box, next to **Copy the following items into your project**, enable additional options as desired.

> (i) The Save A Copy As function works similar to Save As; however, You may notice some options greyed out in the dialog box when using this command.

When creating a backup archive, be sure to enable the **AUDIO FILES** option here to include copies of all the audio files used in the project. If the project includes a movie track, you may also want to enable the **MOVIE FILE** option to include a copy of the video file in the backup project location.

4. Click **SAVE** when you are finished configuring the options as desired. The new project and any selected media files will be saved in the selected directory location.

Creating a Stereo Mixdown

Mixing down is the process of recording the output from multiple tracks to a stereo file. This process is also commonly referred to as *bouncing* the project. Mixing down is often the last phase of music production, although you can create a bounce at any time to create a complete mix as a stereo file.

Considerations for Bouncing Audio

When creating a mixdown from Logic Pro, the bounced file will capture all audible information in your mix just as you hear it during playback.

Basic Principles

The following basic principles apply to the mixdown file:

- **The file will include only audible tracks.** What you hear during playback is exactly what will be included in the mix. Any tracks that are muted will not be included. Similarly, if any tracks are soloed, they will be the *only* tracks included.

- **The file will be a rendered version of your project.** Plug-ins, sends, and external effects will be applied permanently. Listen closely to your entire project prior to bouncing the mix to ensure that everything sounds as it should. Pay close attention to levels, being sure to avoid clipping.

- **The file will be created based on the active selection.** If you have an active selection when you bounce your project, the mixdown file will last for the length of the selection only. If you do not have a selection, Logic Pro will create a bounce from the start of the project to the end of the longest track.

 You will have the option to adjust the start and end points for the bounce in the Bounce dialog box, as discussed below.

Considerations for Bit-Depth Reduction

If you need to create a CD-ready mixdown from Logic Pro, or any other 16-bit bounce, you will need to perform a bit-depth reduction: Logic Pro uses 24-bit audio files by default.

 The Red Book audio CD standard requires audio files that are encoded with a sample rate of 44.1 kHz and a word length of 16 bits. Audio for video, on the other hand, typically uses a sample rate of 48 kHz with a word length of 24 bits.

As discussed in Chapter 1, lower bit-depth audio also exhibits a reduced dynamic range. To help preserve the dynamic range when reducing bit depth, you can add *dither* during the bounce. Dither is a form of randomized noise used to minimize signal loss when audio is near the low end of its dynamic range, such as during a quiet passage or fade-out.

Bouncing an Audio Mix

When you are ready to create your mixdown in Logic Pro, you can use the **FILE > BOUNCE > PROJECT OR SECTION** command. You can alternately use the shortcut **COMMAND+B.** The Bounce command provides a fast and easy way to create a mixdown to a stereo file, requiring little to no setup.

Selecting Bounce Options

The Bounce command combines the outputs of all currently audible tracks to create a new audio file on your storage drive. You can select options for the bounced file using the Bounce dialog box.

To bounce all currently audible tracks and select bounce options, do the following:

1. Verify that the project plays back as desired, as discussed above.

2. Choose **FILE > BOUNCE > PROJECT OR SECTION**. The Bounce dialog box will display.

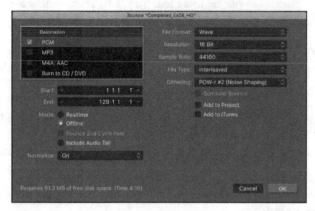

Figure 10.18 The Bounce dialog box

3. Select one or more formats in the **DESTINATION** section. Bounce options for the selected format(s) will appear to the right of the Destination area.

4. Double-check the **START** and/or **END** fields. These represent the entire length of your Bounce. Adjust the Start and End fields with the up/down arrows, as desired.

5. In the **MODE** section, select Realtime or Offline. Offline provides faster than Realtime bouncing; however, it cannot be used with External MIDI sounds. Make sure to select Realtime if you're using any External MIDI sounds routed into the Mixer via Auxiliary channel strips.

6. Configure the **MODE** checkboxes for additional control over effect tails:

   • **Bounce 2nd Cycle Pass**—This option is designed for bouncing selections. It requires two cycle repetitions, with the bounce starting on the second pass. This allows time-based effects in your project to bleed into the start of the bounce.

   • **Include Audio Tail**—This setting extends the end of your bounce to let any time-based effects ring out until they decay into silence.

7. Choose a Normalization setting from the **NORMALIZE** pop-up menu.

   • **Off**—No normalization is applied to the bounce.

   • **Overload Protection Only**—Normalization is applied for any levels that exceed 0db, but no normalization takes place for lower levels.

- On—The project's audio is scanned for the highest amplitude peak, then the level is increased so that the peak is at the maximum possible level before clipping.

8. Select a **FILE FORMAT** for your destination file (Wave, Aiff, CAF).

9. Choose the desired bit depth for the bounce from the **RESOLUTION** pop-up menu.

   - Choose 16 Bit if you plan to burn your bounce to CD without further processing.

   - Choose 24 Bit or 32 Bit (float) to create a final mix that will be mastered separately.

10. Choose the desired sample rate for the bounce from the **SAMPLE RATE** pop-up menu. Higher sample rates will provide better audio fidelity but will also increase the size of the resulting file(s).

> (i) If you plan to burn your bounced audio directly to CD without further processing, choose 44100 as the sample rate for the bounce.

11. Choose the file type for your stereo bounce from the **FILE TYPE** pop-up menu.

    - Interleaved—Creates a single file containing both channels of a stereo mix. Interleaved files are compatible with most online services and music applications, including SoundCloud and iTunes.

    - Split—Creates two separate mono files for a stereo mix: one for the left channel and another for the right channel. This file format is required by certain media applications.

12. Use the **DITHERING** pop-up menu to select a dither option, as needed. (See "Adding Dither to a Mixdown" below.)

13. If desired, enable the **ADD TO PROJECT** checkbox. This option will import the bounced file as a new track in your project.

> (i) The Add to Project option is available only if the target sample rate for the bounce file matches the sample rate of your project.

14. After confirming your settings, click **OK** to complete the bounce. A dialog box will display, allowing you to specify a file name and destination for your bounced file.

> (i) By default, bounced files will be named after the project and will be placed in the BOUNCES folder inside project folder.

15. Specify the file name and location for your bounce; then click **BOUNCE** to complete the action.

Adding Dither to a Mixdown

Proper use of dithering allows you to obtain better subjective performance out of 16-bit or 8-bit audio when performing a bit-depth reduction.

To add dither to your mix during a bounce, do the following:

1. Select **FILE > BOUNCE > PROJECT OR SECTION** as described above.

2. Click the **DITHERING** pop-up menu to choose the type of dither noise shaping to apply.

Figure 10.19 The bounce project window (left), and Dithering options (right)

Dither Noise Shaping Options

Noise shaping is a method of improving the signal-to-noise ratio of dither. POW-r Dither noise shaping improves audio performance and reduces the perceptible noise in the dither by shifting it into a less audible range.

None: No dithering is applied during bounce.

POW-r #1: A dithering curve is utilized to minimize quantization noise.

POW-r #2: Additional noise shaping is used over a wide frequency range. This can extend the dynamic range of the bounce file by 5 to 10dB. This is suitable for most genres of music.

POW-r #3: Even more noise shaping is used. This can extend the dynamic range by 20dB in the 2- to 4kHz range. This option features psychoacoustically-optimized noise-shaping designed for full-spectrum, wide-stereo field material; it is recommended for material with a broad dynamic range, such as classical and orchestral music, but can also be effective for rock and pop music.

UV22HR: Allows for the best possible sound resolution when bouncing 24-bit recordings down to 16-bit files.

Monitoring Bounce Progress

When performing an offline bounce, Logic Pro processes the bounce without audio playback. A progress window will appear, displaying the processed amount against the total Timeline duration. (See Figure 10.20.)

Figure 10.20 The bounce progress window

Locating the Bounced File

After the bounce completes, you can retrieve your mix file from within the **BOUNCES** folder in the Project's main folder or other location where you directed the bounce.

To locate your bounced mix, do the following:

1. Using any method of your choice, switch from Logic Pro to the Finder.

 The Mac Application Switcher lets you toggle through open applications by pressing COMMAND+TAB.

2. Navigate to the **Bounces** folder in your project folder.

Review/Discussion Questions

1.   What term is used to describe an audio patch point that applies a signal processor directly into the signal path on a track? How many of these patch points does Logic Pro provide on each track? (See "Inserts" beginning on page 272.)

2.   What term is used to describe a signal path carrying a mix output of one or more tracks routed for parallel processing? (See "Sends and Returns" beginning on page 272.)

3.   What menu would you use to display or hide the Mixer panel in the Main Window? What keyboard shortcut can you use for this process? (See "Working in the Mixer" beginning on page 273.)

4.   How can you display or hide channel strip parameters the Mixer? (See "Showing and Hiding Mixer Parameters" beginning on page 274.)

5.   What two types of inserts are available in the Mixer in Logic Pro? (See "Effects Slots and Send Slots" beginning on page 275.)

6.   What are some plug-in options that are available for EQ and dynamics processing? (See "Plug-Ins Provided with Logic Pro" beginning on page 278.)

7.   Which Logic Pro automation mode writes new automation for all parameters whenever the transport is rolling? (See "Selecting an Automation Mode" beginning on page 280.)

8.   What is the difference between Read mode and Off mode? Which mode allows you to play back existing automation on the track? (See "Selecting an Automation Mode" beginning on page 280.)

9.   What track control can you use to display automation curves? What window are automation curves displayed in? (See "Viewing Automation Curves" beginning on page 282.)

10. What are some ways of editing automation points with the Pointer tool? With the Pencil tool? (See "Editing Automation Points" beginning on page 283.)

11. Why is it important to back up your Logic Pro projects? (See "Backing Up Your Project" beginning on page 285.)

12. How is the Save A Copy As command different from the Save As command? (See "Saving a Project Copy" beginning on page 285.)

13. How can you create a project backup that includes all of the project media files? (See "Including Project Media in a Backup Copy" beginning on page 285.)

14. What are some considerations for bouncing audio in Logic Pro? How is the bounce affected by soloed or muted tracks? How is it affected by the active selection? (See "Considerations for Bouncing Audio" beginning on page 286.)

15. What command lets you mix your entire project directly to a stereo file? What are some supported file types for the bounce file when using this command? (See "Bouncing an Audio Mix" beginning on page 287.)

16. What bit depth and sample rate should you use when bouncing if you plan to burn the file to CD without further processing? (See "Selecting Bounce Options" beginning on page 287.)

 To review additional material from this chapter and prepare for certification, see the Logic Pro 101 Study Guide module available through the Elements|ED online learning platform at ElementsED.com.

Automating Shared Effects and Exporting a Stereo Mix

🎧 Activity

In this exercise, you will finalize your project. You will start by creating a shared effect using a delay plug-in on an Auxiliary channel strip. Then you will automate the delay effect using send automation on the **Noise Sweep** track. Next you will set basic levels for your mix, and you'll finish by bouncing the mix to a stereo file.

🕐 Duration

This exercise should take approximately 35 to 45 minutes to complete.

⊕ Goals/Targets

- Add a send to an Auxiliary channel strip to create a delay effect

- Use automation to set levels for your mix

- Use a limiter to maximize output levels

- Export your final mix

Media Files

To complete this exercise, you may need to use various media files included in the **Media Files 2021-Logic101** folder. You should have downloaded the media files in Exercise 4.

If needed, you can re-download the media files by going to www.halleonard.com/mylibrary and entering your access code (printed on the opening page of this book). From there, click the **Download** link for the **Media Files 2021–Logic101** listing in your **My Library** page. The Media Files folder will begin transferring to your Downloads folder.

Getting Started

You will start by opening the project you completed in Exercise 9. If that project is not available, you can use the Ex09 Sample file in the 01 Completed Exercises folder within the **Media Files 2021-Logic101** folder.

Open the project and save it as Exercise 10:

1. Do one of the following:

    *   Open the project file that you created in Exercise 9 (**Exercise09-XXX.logicx**).

    *   Alternatively, you can use the Ex09 Sample file (**Media Files 2021-Logic101 > 01 Completed Exercises > Ex09 Sample.logicx**).

2. Choose **FILE > SAVE AS** and name the project *Exercise10-XXX*, keeping the file in the same drive location. (Move the project to your selected save location, if working from the sample file.)

Creating a Delay Effect

In this part of the exercise, you will create a send to an Auxiliary channel strip. Then you will assign a delay plug-in on the channel. Finally, you will use the send controls on the **Chords** and **Noise** tracks to introduce a delay effect for the audio from those tracks.

Adding the Send and Return

Use the following steps to add a send to a new return channel and place a delay plug-in on the channel.

Create a send to an Auxiliary channel strip:

1. If necessary, press **X** to pull up the Mixer.

2. Click on an open Send Slot on the **Chords** channel.

3. Choose an available bus from the send menu, such as **BUS 2**. This will automatically create a new stereo Auxiliary channel and route the bus to its input.

Figure 10.21 Clicking on a blank Send Slot (left) to create a bus path to a new Auxiliary channel (right)

4. Double-click on the name field for the newly created Auxiliary channel to rename it. Change the channel name to **Delay** and press **RETURN** to commit the change.

5. Add a second send on the **Noise** channel, also routing to the same bus (such as Bus 2).

Next, you'll apply the Tape Delay plug-in on the **Delay** channel.

To configure the delay plug-in on the Auxiliary channel:

1. Click on the first Audio FX Slot on the **Delay** channel strip.

2. From the plug-in dropdown menu, select **DELAY > TAPE DELAY > STEREO**.

3. After adding the plug-in, click near the center of the Audio FX Slot (where the left-right sliders appear) to open the plug-in window, if not already displayed.

Figure 10.22 Clicking on the sliders icon in the Audio FX Slot to open the plug-in window

4. Click on **Factory Default** to pull up the preset pop-up menu, and select **1/8 Note Dotted**. The Delay window will update to show the settings from the preset.

Figure 10.23 Selecting the 1/8 Note Dotted preset for Tape Delay plug-in

5. Click on the **FEEDBACK** control and set the Feedback amount to **30%**.

6. Use the **DRY** and **WET** sliders to set the Dry signal at **0%** with the Wet signal at **100%**. (See Figure 10.24.)

Figure 10.24 The Tape Delay effect with the Feedback and Dry/Wet parameters set

7.   Close the plug-in window when finished.

Set the Send Levels

Use the following steps to set appropriate send levels from the source channels in your project.

Raise the send levels on the Chords and Noise tracks:

1.   Locate the **SEND LEVEL KNOB** on the Send Slot for the **Chords** channel in the Mixer.

2.   Click and drag on the Send Level Knob to raise the level to around **-10.0 dB**. (See Figure 10.25.)

3.   Locate the **SEND LEVEL KNOB** for the **Noise** channel.

4.   Click and drag on the control to raise the Send level to around **-3.0 dB**.

Figure 10.25 Setting send levels in the Mixer for the Chords and Noise channels

5.   Play the project to hear the delay effect from the **Chords** and **Noise** channels. Adjust the send levels on each channel to taste.

Recording Automation and Setting Levels

In this part of the exercise, you will record automation during playback. Then you will set basic levels from the Volume sliders for all the tracks in your mix.

Record Automation

In this series of steps, you will automate the volume for the **Delay** return channel so that the echoes from the delay do not extend past the end of the song. You may need to practice the timing a few times to get the desired results.

 To practice the timing without recording Automation, you can simply move the Volume control while playing through the project. After each practice pass, Option-click the Volume slider to reset the value to 0.0.

To get started, you'll need to display the Auxiliary channel in the Tracks Area. This will make it easier to view changes on the Volume automation curve as you work.

Enable the Auxiliary channel in the Tracks Area:

1.   Control-click on the **Delay** channel in the Mixer and select **CREATE TRACK** (see Figure 10.26) or press **CONTROL+T**. The **Delay** track will appear in the Tracks Area.

2.   If needed, drag the **Delay** track to position it at the bottom of the Tracks Area, as the last track.

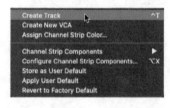

Figure 10.26   Using Create Track (left) to add the Delay track to the Tracks Area (right)

Display automation graphs in the Tracks Area:

1.   Press the **A** key on the computer keyboard to activate the Show/Hide Automation button.

Figure 10.27   The Show/Hide Automation button active in the Tracks Area

2. Click to position the playhead in the last few bars of the project, where the final chord region plays.

Record volume automation for the Delay track:

1. Verify that the **Delay** track's Volume is currently set to **0.0**. This is displayed above the Volume Fader in the Mixer section.

2. Click on the track's **AUTOMATION PARAMETER POP-UP MENU** and select **Latch** mode. This can be done from the Mixer or from the Tracks Area (with Show/Hide Automation enabled).

Figure 10.28 Selecting Latch automation mode in the Tracks Area

3. Click a few bars before the end of the song in the Ruler to set the playhead position and begin playback.

4. As the playback position approaches the end of the song, fade out the **Delay** return track by gradually moving the Volume slider control to the left so that the echoes do not extend past the one-minute mark. (Start the fade around Bar 29 and complete it before you get to Bar 31).

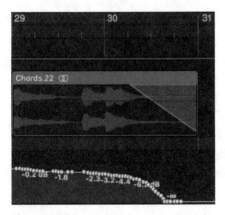

Figure 10.29 Track Volume automated on the Delay track

5. Continue recording automation for a few seconds with the volume set to -inf.

6. Press the **SPACEBAR** when finished to stop playback.

7. Reposition the playhead as needed and press the **SPACEBAR** again to audition the automation that you recorded. If you are not satisfied with the results, you can try again while still in Latch mode, overwriting the previous automation.

8. When finished, use the track's **AUTOMATION PARAMETER POP-UP MENU** to return to **Read** mode.

Set Relative Levels for the Tracks

In the next series of steps, you will adjust the levels for individual tracks using the tracks' Volume Faders.

Set levels for your mix:

1.   Press **X** if needed to display the Mixer window.

2.   Begin playback and adjust the levels of each track to achieve a clear, intelligible mix with appropriate levels from the Audio tracks and Software Instrument tracks.

     Following are some suggestions:

     • Start by lowering all of the Volume Faders to around **-6 dB**. This will give you room to increase the levels on tracks that are too quiet.

     (i)   An easy way to change the levels of all tracks in the project is to select them all and then move the Volume Fader on any one track.

     (i)   You will not be able to affect the volume on the Delay track, since it has been automated. The Volume slider will return to the automated levels on playback.

     • The melody may be a bit too prominent in the mix. Try lowering the Volume Fader on the **Melody** track by an additional 3 to 4 dB.

     • The **Drums** and **Noise** tracks are a bit too quiet. Try raising the Volume Faders on these tracks by 3 to 6 dB.

Bouncing the Mix

In this part of the exercise, you will maximize the output levels for the mix using a limiter plug-in on the **Stereo Out** channel strip. Then you will use the Bounce function to create a stereo file from your mix.

Add a Limiter

Use the following steps to add a limiter to the project.

Apply a limiter to the mix:

1.   Click on an Audio FX Slot on the **Stereo Out** channel strip.

2.   Locate the Limiter plug-in (**DYNAMICS > LIMITER > STEREO**). The Limiter plug-in window will open.

3.   Press the **SPACEBAR** to begin playback.

4. In the Limiter window, set the **OUTPUT LEVEL** knob to around −0.1 dB. This sets the maximum allowable level for the limiter's output and is used to prevent clipping.

5. While listening to the mix, adjust the **GAIN** knob to achieve a healthy output level without artificially compressing the dynamic range. A setting of around 3 to 6 dB will likely be adequate for this mix.

Figure 10.30 The Limiter on the Stereo Output with the Output Level set to -0.1 dB and Gain set to +3.0 dB

6. Close the Limiter plug-in window when finished.

Create a Stereo Mixdown

Use the following steps to create a stereo mixdown file for your project.

Bounce the mix to a stereo file:

1. Click the **HORIZONTAL AUTO ZOOM** button in the Tracks Area to get a view of the entire project.

2. Set a cycle area extending from the start of the project to just after the last region.

3. Choose **FILE > BOUNCE > PROJECT OR SECTION** or press **COMMAND+B** to open the Bounce dialog box.

4. Verify that the start and end locations match the start and end of your project.

5. Select the following options for your bounce:

   - File Format: **Wave**
   - Resolution: **16 Bit**
   - Sample Rate: **44100**

6. Leave the other options set to their defaults (or as directed by your instructor) and click **OK**. A Save dialog box will appear.

7. Name your file **Ex10-FinalMix-YourName**.

8. Navigate to the desired save location; then click **BOUNCE** to create your mix. (The default location is the **Bounce** folder within the Project folder; use this unless you have a reason to choose otherwise.)

Finishing Up

Congratulations! Over the course of these exercises, you have created a Logic Pro Project from scratch, imported and edited audio, recorded audio and MIDI, added effects, recorded automation, and bounced the result to a stereo file.

1. When your bounce completes, save your project and quit Logic Pro.

2. Navigate to the location of your bounced file and verify that it plays back as intended.

In classroom settings, your instructor may require that you copy the bounce file and/or your Project Folder to a learning management system, flash drive, or shared network location to submit it for a grade.

For more hands-on experience, see the Final Projects in the last two chapters of this book.

Creating a Musical Arrangement

🎧 Activity

In this hands-on project, you will complete a project featuring a roughly 90-second musical arrangement. To complete the project, you will create Software Instrument tracks, import audio regions, create playable instruments using the Drum Machine Designer and Quick Sampler instruments, create MIDI regions, record from the Live Loops Grid into the Tracks Area, and bounce an audio file from the project.

🕐 Duration

This project should take approximately 90 minutes to complete.

⊕ Goals/Targets

- Customize the appearance of your project and your tracks

- Work with the Drum Machine Designer and Quick Sampler instruments to create MIDI-based drum and bass parts

- Import and work with audio files

- Record from the Live Loops Grid into the Tracks Area

- Add a Limiter to enhance your mix

- Bounce your final mix and archive your finished project

The media files for this project are provided courtesy of the artists Haak and Siddhant Bhosle:

- **Song**: The Fall (excerpt)

- **Performed by**: Haak and Siddhant Bhosle

- **Written By**: Haak and Siddhant Bhosle

- **Produced By**: Haak and Siddhant Bhosle ©2018

The audio files provided for this project are strictly for use to complete the exercises contained herein. No rights are granted to use the files or any portion thereof in any commercial or non-commercial production or performance.

Powering Up

To get started on this project, you will need to power up your system. It is important to power up properly to avoid problems that could possibly damage your equipment.

When using audio equipment, you should power up components in the order that the audio signal will flow through them.

The general process for starting up Logic Pro is as follows:

1. Power up external hard drives, if used.

2. Verify connections and power up any audio and/or MIDI interfaces.

3. Start the computer.

4. Launch Logic Pro.

5. Power up your monitoring system, if applicable.

Getting Started

You will start by opening the Music Project Starter file. The project file is located in the **03 Final Project Media > Project 1** folder within the **Media Files 2021-Logic101** folder.

Accessing the Media Files for this Project

To complete this project, you will use various files included in the **Media Files 2021-Logic101** folder. You can download the media files by going to www.halleonard.com/mylibrary and entering your access code (printed on the opening page of this book). From there, click the **Download** link for the **Media Files 2021-Logic101** listing in your **My Library** page.

The Media Files folder will be downloaded and placed in your Downloads folder by default.

Open the Final Music Project:

1. Do one of the following:

    -   Choose **FILE > OPEN**.

    -   Press **COMMAND+O**.

2. Locate and open the Music Project Starter file (**Storage Drive/Folder > Media Files 2021-Logic101 > 03 Final Project Media > Project 1 > MusicProject-Starter.logicx**).

3. Choose **FILE > SAVE AS** and name the project *FinalProject1-XXX*, where *XXX* is your initials. Save the project to an appropriate location on your system. You can save this project as a package or a folder.

Adjust the Project Display

When the project opens, you will see the starter template in the Live Loops Grid view. You will start here, but eventually you will record your work from the Live Loops Grid into the Tracks Area. You can switch between the two views or see them in a split view using the **SHOW/HIDE** buttons in the Tracks Area menu bar.

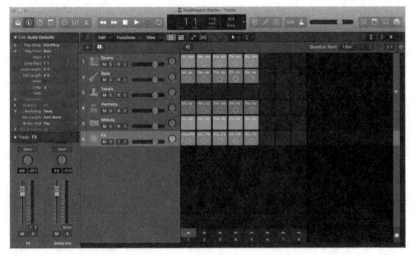

Figure 11.1 The starter template, as seen in the Live Loops Grid view

You may want to adjust the Live Loops Grid view track widths before continuing.

Change track width using one of the following methods:

-   Press **COMMAND+UP/DOWN ARROW** to zoom in incrementally.

-   Use the **VERTICAL AUTO ZOOM** button in the Tracks Area menu bar to make all tracks fill the workspace area. (In the Live Loops Grid, this method will also perform a horizontal zoom to preserve the cell dimension ratios.)

- Hover your mouse pointer over the lower edge of a track's header and resize individual tracks by clicking and dragging with the Resize Pointer (double-headed arrow).

Figure 11.2 Adjusting the height of the Bass track in Track Header

You may also want to expand or contract the Track header area width. This is a horizontal adjustment that can reveal additional mixer features, as well as add resolution to each track's volume meter.

Expand or contract the width of the Track header area:

1.   Hover your mouse pointer over the right-edge of the Track header area. The mouse pointer will change to a Resize Pointer (double-headed arrow).

2.   Click and drag horizontally to expand or contract the header area section.

Figure 11.3 Adjusting the Track header area width to show mixer features (left) or hide features (right)

Connect Monitoring Devices

If you have a monitoring system connected to the left and right outputs of your audio interface, you will use that to listen to the project playback. If you do not have a monitoring system, you can listen to the playback using headphones on a compatible interface or on your computer (if using onboard sound output). Plug in your headphones to an available headphone jack and test the output and playback level.

Creating New Tracks

In this section of the project, you will create the new tracks needed for the project.

Create, Name, and Color-Code Tracks

You will need to create two new tracks for the project. Both tracks will play back MIDI information using software instruments, so both will be Software Instrument tracks.

The first track you will create will be a Snare Drum track to accompany the existing drums and percussion. The second will be a Bass Instrument track, which will be played during the Intro and Verse scenes.

Create new Software Instrument tracks:

1. Select the Drums track by clicking on the Track header area.

2. Choose **TRACK > NEW SOFTWARE INSTRUMENT TRACK** or press **OPTION+COMMAND+S**. A new Software Instrument track will be added below the currently selected track.

3. Select the Bass track by clicking on it in the Track header area.

4. Press **OPTION+COMMAND+S** to insert a second Software Instrument track below the selected track.

Logic Pro will apply generic names, colors, and icons to the tracks you create. This is a good time to customize these qualities to help keep your project organized.

Name the new Software Instrument tracks:

1. Do one of the following to rename the tracks:

   - Right-click the first new Software Instrument track and select **RENAME TRACK**. (See Figure 11.4.)

   - Double-click the track name in the Track header area.

2. Type Snare Drum as the new track name.

3. Press **RETURN** to commit the change.

4. Repeat this process to rename the second new track. Name this track Bass Instrument.

Figure 11.4 Right-click pop-up menu for renaming and configuring the Track header

To show Color Bars for tracks, do the following:

1. Right-click anywhere in the Track header area to display the pop-up menu.

2. Select **TRACK HEADER COMPONENTS > TRACK COLOR BARS.**

Color-code the new Software Instrument tracks:

1. Select the **Snare Drum** track.

2. Select **VIEW > SHOW COLORS** or press **OPTION+C.** This will open the color palette window.

3. Click on a color to select it. The color will be applied to the **Snare Drum** track.

4. Repeat this process to select a color for the **Bass Instrument** track you created.

5. Close the color palette window when finished.

Choose a track icon for the new Software Instrument tracks:

- Right-click each track icon and select an icon of your choice for each track from the pop-up menu.

Save Your Project

After making any significant changes to a project, it's a good idea to save your work. Doing so will minimize any rework that you might have to do in the event of a disruption.

Save your progress up to this point:

- Choose **FILE > SAVE** or press **COMMAND+S.**

Working with MIDI Data

For this section of the project, you will add the Drum Machine Designer and Quick Sampler instruments to your Software Instrument tracks, add audio samples to each instrument to make them playable, and program or record MIDI data using the Piano Roll Editor.

Add the Drum Machine Designer to the Snare Drum Track

Here, you will add a Drum Machine Designer instrument to the Snare Drum track. This will allow the Software Instrument track to play back audio drum samples that are triggered by MIDI data.

Insert Drum Machine Designer on the Snare Drum track:

1. Select the **Snare Drum** track by clicking on it in the Track header area.

2. Show the Inspector (if it isn't already visible) by selecting **VIEW > SHOW INSPECTOR** or by pressing **I.**

3. Select the **INSTRUMENTS** slot from the Snare Drum channel strip in the Inspector.

4. Choose the **Drum Machine Designer** instrument from the pop-up menu. The Drum Machine Designer instrument window will open.

By default, the Drum Machine Designer does not contain any drum samples, so you will need to add a snare drum sample to it in order for MIDI information to trigger sound. This project includes the original snare drum samples used in the song.

Add a snare drum sample to the Drum Machine Designer:

1. Show the **All Files Browser** by clicking the **BROWSERS** button or pressing **F** and selecting the **ALL FILES** tab.

2. Navigate to the **Media Files 2021-Logic101 > 03 Final Project Media > Project 1** location.

3. Open the **Instrument Samples** folder in the Browser to display the audio files it contains.

4. Click on each of the snare drum samples individually (**Snare Drum 1.wav** and **Snare Drum 2.wav**) to audition them and evaluate them for use in the project.

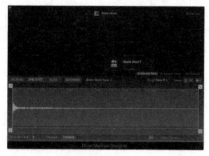

Figure 11.5 Auditioning snare drum samples in the Browser

5. Click and drag the snare drum sample of your choice to a cell in the Drum Machine Designer. (See Figure 11.6.) Note that each cell is triggered by a specific MIDI note, so pay attention to the note corresponding to the cell where you drop the sample.

Figure 11.6 Snare Drum 1.wav mapped to MIDI note D1 in a Drum Machine Designer

 You can also put each of the two snare samples in their own cell and trigger them separately from their respective MIDI notes.

You can now play the snare drum sound of your choice using MIDI information. You can experiment with this by selecting the **Snare Drum** track and playing the associated note with a MIDI controller. You can also trigger MIDI from your computer keyboard with the Musical Typing feature by selecting **WINDOW > SHOW MUSICAL TYPING** or use the keyboard shortcut **COMMAND+K**.

  See Chapter 6 for details on using the Computer MIDI Keyboard function.

You will create a MIDI performance for the **Snare Drum** track in a later section of this project.

Add Quick Sampler to the Bass Instrument Track

Next, you'll insert a Quick Sampler instrument on the **Bass Instrument** track. By dragging and dropping an audio sample over a track drop zone, you can select an instrument to be inserted, and the audio sample will import and be mapped automatically.

Add a bass sample to create a Quick Sampler:

1. Show the **All Files Browser** by clicking the **BROWSERS** button or pressing **F** and selecting the **ALL FILES** tab.

2. Navigate to the **Media Files 2021-Logic101 > 03 Final Project Media > Project 1** location.

3. Open on the **Instrument Samples** folder in the Browser to display the audio files it contains.

4. Click on the bass sample (**Bass Pluck.wav**) to audition the sound.

ⓘ This sample may be difficult to hear when played using the built-in outputs on a computer or laptop. You may need to temporarily increase your computer's speaker volume to adequately hear the low-frequency audio.

5. Drag the **Bass Pluck.wav** file over the **Bass Instrument** track in the Track header area. A menu overlay in the Track header will show instrument and import options for the file.

Figure 11.7 Drag and drop options on the Bass Instrument track

6. Select **Quick Sampler (Optimized)**. This will insert a Quick Sampler instrument to the **Bass Instrument** track and map the sample to the MIDI note with the correct pitch. Other optimizations include setting the sample volume to better match the project.

> (i) In certain cases, you may need to determine the pitch of an imported sample and adjust its transposition in the sampler as necessary.

7. Select the **ONE SHOT** mode button located above the sample waveform in the Quick Sampler. This allows even very short MIDI notes to cause the entire sample to play back, which will work best for this short, percussive bass sound.

Figure 11.8 An instance of Quick Sampler with the provided Bass Pluck.wav sample loaded in One Shot mode

You can now play back the bass sound of your choice using MIDI information. You can experiment with this by selecting the **Bass Instrument** track and playing the sound with a MIDI controller or your computer keyboard with Musical Typing.

  See Chapter 6 for details on using the Computer MIDI Keyboard function.

You will create a MIDI performance for the **Bass Instrument** track in a later section of this project.

Create a Snare Drum MIDI Region

Now that your two instruments are capable of playing sounds, you can use them to round out this piece of music. You will start by creating a pattern of MIDI notes for the **Snare Drum** track.

Create a MIDI region on the Verse scene:

1. Find the empty cell on the **Snare Drum** track that corresponds to the **Verse** scene.

2. Right-click the empty cell and select **INSERT MIDI CELL**. A new cell will be created, named **Snare Drum**.

Figure 11.9 Creating a MIDI cell on the second scene of the Snare Drum track

3. Open the Inspector by pressing **I** and expand the Cell Inspector by clicking the disclosure triangle, if not already visible.

4. In the **Play From** section of the Cell Inspector, set the **CELL LENGTH** to 8 bars (8 0).

Figure 11.10 Setting the Cell Length parameter to 8 bars in the Cell Inspector

5. Double-click the **Snare Drum** cell to open the cell in the Editor.

6. Add MIDI notes using the Piano Roll Editor. Each note will cause the Drum Machine Designer to trigger the snare drum sound. For a simple, straightforward snare drum presence, add MIDI notes at the third beat of each of the 8 bars, as seen in Figure 11.11 below.

(i) You can use the Pencil tool to manually create MIDI notes in the MIDI Note Editor. To activate the Pencil, hold the COMMAND key while clicking in the editor.

(i) You may need to scroll the piano roll to find the Snare Drum note. You will see the instrument name listed in the column next to the piano key for the mapped note.

(i) You may want to set the Snap value to BEAT to make placing notes easier.

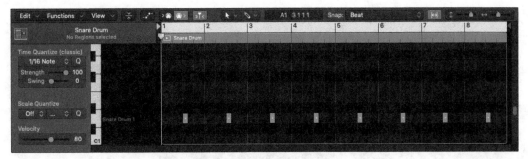

Figure 11.11 MIDI notes at the third beat of each bar

7. When finished, click the **SCENE** trigger on the **Verse** scene to audition your **Snare Drum** track in context with the arrangement.

8. If necessary, adjust the placement and velocity of the MIDI notes to your liking.

Duplicate the Snare Drum MIDI Region

To save time, you can copy your snare drum MIDI cell to both the **Pre-Chorus** and **Chorus** scenes of the Project. That will allow your snare drum pattern to play across all of the applicable parts of the song.

Use one of the following methods to duplicate the **SNARE DRUM** cell to additional scenes:

- Press **COMMAND+R** to repeat the pattern in the subsequent cell.

- Right-click the cell and select **EDIT > REPEAT** to add it to the subsequent cell.

- While holding **OPTION**, click and drag the cell to duplicate it in another empty cell.

(i)   Rather than simply duplicating the SNARE DRUM cell, feel free to create unique snare drum patterns for different parts of the song in this project, as time allows.

Create a Bass Instrument MIDI Region

Next, you will create a MIDI sequence for your **Bass Instrument** track by importing MIDI files that contain the song's original bass line.

Import existing MIDI files for the bass line:

1. If needed, show the All Files Browser by clicking the **BROWSERS** button or pressing **F** and selecting the **ALL FILES** tab.

2. Navigate to the **Media Files 2021-Logic101 > 03 Final Project Media > Project 1** location.

3. Open on the **MIDI Regions** folder in the Browser to display the MIDI files it contains.

4. Click and drag the Intro Bass Region.mid file to the empty cell that corresponds to the Intro scene of the Bass Instrument track.

5. Click and drag the Verse Bass Region.mid file to the empty cell that corresponds to the Verse scene of the Bass Instrument track.

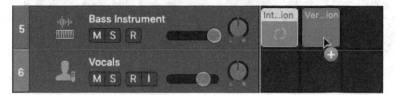

Figure 11.12 Dragging MIDI files from the Browser to empty cell

Alternatively, you can program your own bass line (using the Piano Roll Editor) or record a bass performance (using a MIDI controller). Be sure to work in the key of C minor using the notes of the scale: C, D, E-flat, F, G, A-flat, and B-flat.

For details on creating MIDI performances, see Chapter 6 in this book.

6. Click the **SCENE** trigger on the Intro scene to audition your Bass Instrument track in the context of the arrangement. Repeat this process on the Verse scene.

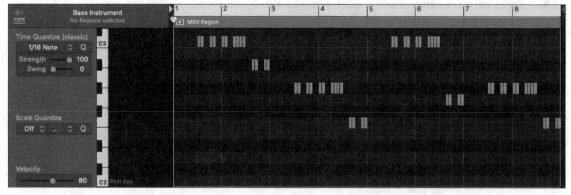

Figure 11.13 The provided MIDI notes, after being imported and displayed in the Piano Roll Editor

7. If necessary, edit the MIDI notes to your liking.

If you find that your new bass line is too quiet, turn up the Volume of Quick Sampler. The default volume is set at -6.0dB. Try increasing that value to 0dB.

Save Work in Progress

As you complete each main portion of the project, you should save your work in progress. This will protect your work while the project is open.

Save your progress up to this point:

■   Choose FILE > SAVE or press COMMAND+S.

Working with Audio Data

In the next section, you will use the Browser to import several audio files to an existing audio track.

Import an Audio File to a Track

The Logic Pro Browser is great for locating, auditioning, and importing instruments and audio files. For this part of the project, you will use the Browser to import audio files containing the vocals for the song.

Locate and import the audio files:

1.   Click the BROWSERS button or press F and select the ALL FILES tab to show the All Files Browser.

2.   Navigate to Media Files 2021-Logic101 > 03 Final Project Media > Project 1 > The Fall Stems.

3.   Open the Vocals folder in the Browser to display the audio files it contains. In this folder, you'll find the vocal files, separated into sections for the verse, pre-chorus, chorus, and outro.

Chorus Vocals.wav	1/1/19, 10:...	9.2 MB
Outro Vocals.wav	1/1/19, 10:...	1.2 MB
Pre-Chorus Vocals.wav	1/1/19, 10:...	4.6 MB
Verse Vocals.wav	1/1/19, 10:...	4.6 MB

Figure 11.14   The vocals are separated into four audio files, as seen in the Logic Pro Browser.

4.   Drag the Verse Vocals.wav file to the empty cell on the Vocals track corresponding to the Verse scene. Repeat this process for the remaining audio files: Pre-Chorus Vocals.wav, Chorus Vocals.wav, and Outro Vocals.wav.

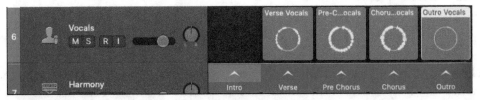

Figure 11.15   After importing the audio, you will have cells on the Verse, Pre Chorus, Chorus, and Outro scenes.

5.   Audition each scene to confirm that the vocal cells play back as intended.

When importing audio files, Logic Pro may automatically flex the audio regions it creates. Before continuing, you should check the FLEX & FOLLOW settings and CELL LENGTH of the regions in the CELL INSPECTOR and make any needed changes.

Verify the flex, cell length, and loop settings for imported files:

1.   Start by clicking on the Verse Vocals cell of the Vocals track so that its cell information displays in the Inspector.

2.   In the Cell Inspector, verify that FLEX & FOLLOW is enabled (status will show ON). Repeat the process for the other regions.

3.   In the Play From section, verify that each CELL LENGTH matches the following:

   •   Verse Vocals.wav (8 0)

   •   Pre-Chorus Vocals.wav (8 0)

   •   Chorus Vocals.wav (16 0)

   •   Outro Vocals.wav (2 1)

4.   Next, click on the Outro Vocals cell. Since this scene occurs at the end of the performance, the cells in this scene should not be set to loop.

5.   Uncheck the LOOP checkbox to disable looping. (You can also repeat this for all cells in this scene)

 You can also experiment with disabling the Flex & Follow setting on the Outro Vocals cell. Since this region has no rhythmic material, it may not need to match the tempo.

Save Work in Progress

You have now imported the audio files needed for the project. Take this opportunity to save your work.

Save your work by doing one of the following:

■   Choose FILE > SAVE or press COMMAND+S.

Recording from the Live Loops Grid to the Tracks Area

While the Live Loops Grid is a useful environment for live performances and sketching out song ideas, you will often want to record what you have created in the Live Loops Grid into the Tracks Area as a linear piece of music. In this section of the project, you will complete this process.

Prepare for Recording into the Tracks Area

Before recording the five scenes—Intro, Verse, Pre-Chorus, Chorus, and Outro—as a linear arrangement, take a moment to play through the scenes. When each scene is about to end, press the play button on the following scene. This is the process you'll use when recording to the Tracks Area, so it will help to get some practice in advance.

 When launching cells and scenes in the Live Loops Grid, your timing doesn't have to be perfect. The Quantize Start value ensures that cells only trigger at the specified increment. This will keep your cells and scenes in sync with one another by aligning their start and stop points to a global grid.

 You can change the Quantize Start value on the right side, above the grid area.

If you want to get creative, you can make changes to the scenes or experiment with having certain scenes play for longer periods of time. For instance, you might want a 16-bar intro rather than an 8-bar intro. If you want to take things further, you can add tracks and instruments to create your own version of the song. Working in Logic Pro means it's never too late to make changes; this is a good time to experiment with additional creative choices.

Record into the Tracks Area

When you are ready to proceed, use the following general steps for recording from the Live Loops Grid to the Tracks Area. Although the steps will largely be the same even if you've chosen to modify the project, you can vary the process as needed or desired for your own composition.

Record from the Live Loops Grid to the Tracks Area:

1. Before starting a record pass, press the **STOP** button in the control bar twice or press the **[0]** (zero) key on the numeric keypad twice to place the playhead back to 1 1—the very beginning of Bar 1. This will ensure that your recording begins at the start of the arrangement.

2. Before recording, set the **QUANTIZE START** value to **1 Bar**, if not already selected, as seen in Figure 11.16 below. This will help avoid rhythmic errors when recording from the Live Loops Grid to the Tracks Area.

 Additionally, make sure the Count-in is enabled and set to the same length as the Quantize Start value. Otherwise, recording might start from an unintended location.

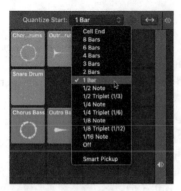

Figure 11.16 Setting the Quantize Start value to 1 Bar

3. Click the **ENABLE PERFORMANCE RECORDING** button in the Tracks Area menu bar. The button will turn red and the project will be primed for recording, but it will not initiate recording just yet.

Figure 11.17 The Enable Performance Recording button set to record

4. Right-click the **SCENE** trigger on scene 1 (Intro) and select **QUEUE SCENE**. This will queue the Intro scene to trigger playback when recording begins.

Figure 11.18 Queuing the Intro scene

5. Click the **RECORD** button in the control bar or press **R**. This will trigger the recording and begin playback of the cells in the Intro scene.

6. During the final measure of the Intro scene, click the **SCENE** trigger on scene 2, Verse. To gauge the timing, watch the circular indicators in the middle of the cells (see "Playback Indicators" below).

7. During the final measure of the Verse scene, click the **SCENE** trigger on scene 3, Pre Chorus.

8. During the final measure of the Pre Chorus scene, click the **SCENE** trigger on scene 4, Chorus.

9. During the final measure of the Chorus scene, click the **SCENE** trigger on scene 5, Outro.

10. At the end of the Outro scene, click the **STOP** button in the Divider column to conclude the recording at the next downbeat. This ensures the recording doesn't end abruptly.

    If you turned off **LOOP** for the cells in the Outro scene, they will stop when they reach the end of the cell.

Playback Indicators

When playing and recording from the Live Loops Grid, it can help to watch the playback indicators (shown in Figure 11.19) for the currently playing cells. This will guide you when switching scenes, as you can see how much time remains in each cell. Looping cells display circular indicators, while non-looping cells display linear indicators.

Figure 11.19 Playback indicators active in cells of the Chorus scene

Verify Your Results

Having completed the recording, it's time to switch to the Tracks Area and listen to the results.

Verify your recording in the Tracks Area:

1. If the Tracks Area is not already visible, click the **SHOW TRACKS AREA** button in the Tracks Area menu bar. Logic Pro gives you the option to show the views individually or simultaneously.

2. Click the **TRACK ACTIVATION** button (two triangular arrows) at the top of the Divider column. (See Figure 11.20.) This will switch to playing regions in the Tracks Area instead of cells in the Live Loops Grid. Regions in the Tracks Area will switch from inactive (no color) to active (colorized). The **TRACK ACTIVATION** button will show a solid arrow pointing at the active view.

Figure 11.20 Track Activation with Live Loops Grid active (left) and Tracks Area active (right)

3.   Press the **STOP** button in the control bar twice or press the **[0]** (zero) key twice on the numeric keypad to position the playhead at the start of the project.

4.   Press the **PLAY** button in the control bar or press **SPACEBAR** to begin playback.

If you are not satisfied with your recorded arrangement, you can use **COMMAND+Z** to undo the recording, or you can delete the regions. Then repeat the recording from the Live Loops Grid as described above.

Clean Up the Recorded Arrangement

You may want to fine-tune your arrangement once you've recorded it from the Live Loops Grid. For instance, if you've extended a section of the song, you might need to smooth out the transition as the section repeats.

Here are some techniques you can use to clean up the arrangement you've created.

■   Set the cycle area to a 4-bar range at the start of the arrangement and choose **EDIT > CUT/INSERT TIME > INSERT SILENCE AT LOCATORS** or press **OPTION+COMMAND+Z**. This will insert 4 bars of silence on the front end of the arrangement.

■   Delete, mute, or edit certain regions so that they play back only when you want them to.

■   Trim the end of the arrangement of any unnecessary tails on your audio and MIDI regions.

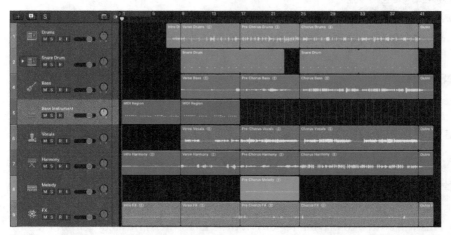

Figure 11.21 An example of an arrangement that has been edited and simplified after recording

Save Work in Progress

You have now created an arrangement for your project. Take this opportunity to save your work.

Save your work:

■   Choose **FILE > SAVE** or press **COMMAND+S**.

Finishing Your Work

To finish the project, you will add final processing on the **STEREO OUT** track, bounce your arrangement to a stereo audio file, and archive your work. The archive process will allow you to create a backup of your work without consuming excess disk space.

Add a Limiter

First, you will add a Limiter audio effect to the **STEREO OUT** channel strip. This will help maximize the overall level of the mix, while simultaneously limiting peaks to prevent clipping.

 The Logic Pro Limiter performs "look-ahead" analysis, anticipating audio peaks and preserving attack transients during reduction. This helps provide transparent results and maintain the character of the original audio signal while preventing clipping.

Insert the Limiter effect on the Stereo Out channel strip:

1. Show the Mixer by pressing **X**.

2. Click on an available Audio Effect slot in the **STEREO OUT** channel strip to open the pop-up menu.

3. Select **DYNAMICS > LIMITER** to insert a limiter onto the Audio Effect slot.

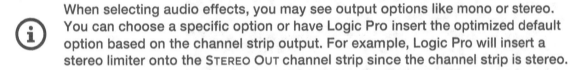 When selecting audio effects, you may see output options like mono or stereo. You can choose a specific option or have Logic Pro insert the optimized default option based on the channel strip output. For example, Logic Pro will insert a stereo limiter onto the STEREO OUT channel strip since the channel strip is stereo.

4. Set the **OUTPUT LEVEL** parameter in the Limiter to **-0.3 dB**. This will ensure that your output will never exceed -0.3 dB and will safeguard the mix against clipping.

5. Increase the **GAIN** parameter to around **6.0 dB**. During louder parts of the song, you should see some light to moderate activity on the Gain Reduction meter. This indicates that the Limiter is preventing the signal from exceeding the -0.3 dB ceiling and protecting against clipping.

Figure 11.22 The Limiter audio effect on the Stereo Out channel strip

Be careful not to increase the Gain too much, as this can introduce distortion.

Bounce the Song

You can now proceed to bounce your song as a single stereo audio file.

Bounce the song:

1. Select the bounce range by doing one of the following:

    *   Make a Marquee selection spanning the entire length of the arrangement on at least one track.

    *   Use the Select All command by pressing **COMMAND+A** to select all regions in the arrangement.

    *   Enable Cycle and select a range spanning the length of the arrangement, as illustrated below.

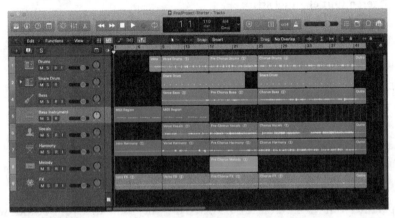

Figure 11.23 The cycle area range covering the full arrangement

2. Select **FILE > BOUNCE > PROJECT OR SECTION** or press **COMMAND+B** to open the **BOUNCE** dialog box.

3. Verify that the **START** and **END** values are an accurate representation of the arrangement start and end. Check the box to **INCLUDE AUDIO TAIL**. This will help you avoid exporting silence and/or abruptly cutting off audio in the bounced file.

4. Choose the following settings in the Bounce dialog box:

    *   Destination: PCM

    *   File Type: WAV

    *   Bit Depth: 16

    *   Sample Rate: 44100

- File Type: Interleaved

- Dithering: POW-r #1

 You should always add dither when bouncing to a lower bit depth.

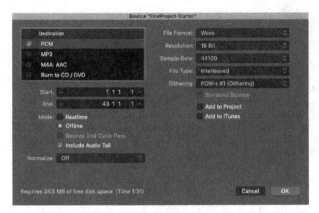

Figure 11.24 The Bounce dialog box

5. (Optional) Set the Bounce Mode to **OFFLINE**.

6. Click the **OK** button. A Save dialog box will display.

7. Navigate to the Final Project directory where your project is saved. The default location is the **Bounce** folder within the Project folder.

8. Name your file and click **BOUNCE**. The mixdown will be saved as a .WAV file in your project directory.

Archive Your Work

Now that your project is complete, you have the option to back it up for storage. On a real-world project, you might also need to deliver the work to a client. If you are completing this project in an academic classroom environment, you may be required to submit your work to your instructor for grading.

In this section, you will use the **CONSOLIDATE** command to collect all of the project's media files into the current project directory. This will ensure that your archive includes all of the files needed for the project.

Archive your project:

1. Choose **FILE > PROJECT MANAGEMENT > CONSOLIDATE**.

2.   When prompted to specify the files that will be included in the project, check the boxes for the following settings (See Figure 11.25.):

- Copy audio files

- Copy Sampler audio data

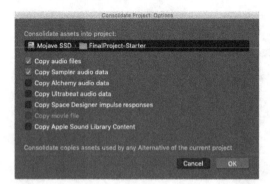

Figure 11.25 The Consolidate Project dialog box

3.   Click the **OK** button. This will copy the audio files used in the project into the current project directory.

Save your work and close the project when finished:

1.   Choose **FILE > SAVE** to save the project.

2.   Choose **FILE > CLOSE PROJECT** to close the project.

3.   If desired, press **COMMAND+Q** to quit Logic Pro.

This concludes the project. If you are completing this work in an academic environment, please check with your instructor for submittal requirements; be sure to include the bounced audio mixdown file with your project archive, as appropriate.

Creating a Mix

🎧 Activity

In this hands-on project, you will mix a music project from the artist King Dream. You'll work with a set of stems, organize the project for mixing, and create a quick rough mix with Logic's channel strip and plug-in presets. You'll configure the sample rate and tempo settings to match the stems, organize different tracks into stacks, then apply processing and complete the mix before creating a bounce.

🕐 Duration

This project should take approximately 75 minutes to complete.

⊕ Goals/Targets

- Configure a project to match the supplied stems
- Import and work with audio files
- Organize your project for mixing
- Add markers for quick navigation
- Add and work with various audio effects
- Create a bounce of your final mix

The media files for this project are provided courtesy of the artist King Dream:

- **Song**: Living Like a Teenager
- **Performed by**: King Dream
- **Written By**: Jeremy Lyon of King Dream
- **Produced By**: Jeremy Lyon ©2020

The audio files provided for this project are strictly for use to complete the exercises contained herein. No rights are granted to use the files or any portion thereof in any commercial or non-commercial production or performance.

Powering Up your System

To get started on this project, you will need to power up your system. It is important to power up properly to avoid problems that could possibly damage your equipment.

When using audio equipment, you should power up components in the order that the audio signal will flow through them. The general process for powering up a Logic Pro system is as follows:

1. Power up external drives, if used.

2. Verify connections and power up any audio and/or MIDI interfaces.

3. Start the computer and launch Logic Pro.

4. Power up your monitoring system, if applicable.

Getting Started

You will start by creating a new project file and importing stems into the project.

Accessing the Media Files for this Project

To complete this project, you will use the audio files included in the Media Files 2021-Logic101 folder. You can download the media files by going to www.halleonard.com/mylibrary and entering your access code (printed on the opening page of this book). From there, click the Download link for the Media Files 2021-Logic101 listing in your My Library page.

The Media Files folder will be downloaded and placed in your Downloads folder by default.

Create the Final Mix Project:

1. Choose FILE > NEW FROM TEMPLATE or press COMMAND+N.

2. Select EMPTY PROJECT in the CHOOSE A PROJECT dialog box and click CHOOSE to proceed.

3. Add any track to get started (you'll be deleting this after importing the media for this project).

4. Choose FILE > SAVE AS and name the project *FinalProject2-XXX*, where *XXX* is your initials. Save the project to an appropriate location on your system. You can save this project as a package or a folder.

Set Project Parameters

With the project created, you'll next need to set up your project to match the tempo and sample rate of the audio you'll be importing. The tempo of this song is 125 bpm, and the audio files have a sample rate of 48 kHz.

Configure the project:

1. Set the project tempo to 125 bpm by doing one of the following:

   • Double-click in the tempo area of the LCD and type **125**.

   • Click and drag the tempo value in the LCD, changing from **120** to **125**.

2. Choose **FILE > PROJECT SETTINGS > AUDIO** and adjust the sample rate to 48 kHz before file import.

Figure 12.1 Navigating to the Audio section of Project Settings (left) and changing sample rate (right)

 If you don't change the sample rate in advance, you'll be prompted by a dialog box when you drag in the media (see below). Clicking CHANGE PROJECT will switch the sample rate to 48 kHz.

Figure 12.2 Changing the sample rate to 48 kHz during file import by clicking Change Project

Import Audio Stems

For this project, you'll be working with *stems*, a set of tracks sub-mixed down to mono or stereo files. Outside of composing/producing your own projects, mixing previously recorded stems is one of the most common situations you'll encounter as an engineer.

To import the final project stems, do the following:

1. In the Finder, locate the Living Like a Teenager Stems folder, which contains all the media (Media Files 2021-Logic101 > 03 Final Project Media > Project 2 > Living Like a Teenager Stems).

2. Click and drag all 16 audio files from the folder into the Tracks Area.

Figure 12.3 Dragging from the finder to import all the media in the Living Like a Teenager Stems folder

The **ADD SELECTED FILES TO TRACKS** dialog box will display.

3. Select Create new tracks and enable the checkbox at the bottom for All selected files are stems from one project.

Figure 12.4 The Add Selected Files to Tracks dialog box

You're now ready to start organizing your project for mixing.

Getting the Project Ready to Mix

You should now see 16 audio tracks in your project, and they should be perfectly synced up with your project's tempo. The tracks are ordered as follows: drums, bass, keyboard instruments, guitars, percussion, lead vocals, and background vocals (BGVs). The tracks are essentially organized by frequency going from low to high by instrument category.

Before continuing, press **SPACEBAR** to take a listen to what you just imported. You can also delete the track you initially added during project creation.

Add Track and Region Color

Initially, all the tracks and regions will be the same shade of blue. Color-coding will help organize the project and make it easier to navigate. You'll start by displaying the mixer and giving different instruments their own colors.

To assign track and region colors, do the following:

1. Display the Mixer by pressing **X**.

2. Press **OPTION+C** to bring up the color palette.

3. Assign a distinct color to each group of tracks by selecting the track or tracks to colorize and clicking on the desired color in the color palette. You may want to use a unique color for the **Lead Gtr** track, as well as the **Lead Vocal** track, to make it easier to quickly pick them out as you're working.

Figure 12.5 Color-coding tracks by instrument group in the Mixer

4. Close the color palette when finished.

5. In the Tracks Area, Control-click on any track header and select **ADD TRACK COLOR** to add the associated colors in the Tracks Area. (See Figure 12.6.)

Figure 12.6 Adding color to the Tracks Area

Next, you'll match your region colors to your track colors.

6.   In the Tracks Area, press **COMMAND+A** to select all regions.

7.   To give regions the same color as your tracks, do one of the following:

- Control-click on one of the selected regions and choose **NAME AND COLOR > COLOR REGIONS BY TRACKS**. (See Figure 12.7.)

- Use the keyboard shortcut **OPTION+SHIFT+C** to color regions by tracks.

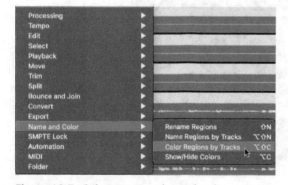

Figure 12.7 Coloring regions by track color

Use Track Stacks to Create Submixes

In this section, you'll arrange some of these instrument groups into submixes using track stacks to further clean up the visual presentation.

Arrange instruments into track stacks in the Mixer or Tracks Area:

1.   Select the keyboard instruments (tracks 3 through 5) and press **COMMAND+SHIFT+G** to place them into a track stack. (This shortcut creates a Summing stack for submixing.)

2. Name the stack **Keys** by double-clicking on its name and entering the new name.

3. Repeat this process to create track stacks for the guitar tracks (6 through 10) and the background vocals (13 through 16). Rename the track stacks **Guitars** and **Background Vocals**, respectively.

4. Press **OPTION+C** to bring up the color palette, and color the Main Tracks for each stack to match the tracks inside.

Use the Track Stack disclosure triangles to show or hide each set of tracks as needed. This collapsed view simplifies the track display, while the expanded view let's you work with the individual tracks.

Figure 12.8 The Tracks Area after organizing with track/region color and Summing stacks

Add Markers

In this section, you'll add some marker locations for easy navigation. To get started, you'll configure the global tracks to display only the Marker track.

■   To configure the global tracks, press **OPTION+G** and de-select everything except the **Marker** checkbox.

Now you can add markers to all of the key areas in the song for quick navigation.

Add markers to your project:

1. Position the playhead at Bar 1.

2. Click on the **ADD MARKER** button (plus sign) on the Marker track or use the shortcut **OPTION+'**. A marker called **Marker 1** will be added at the start of the project.

3. Double-click on the marker name and rename it as **Start**.

4. Repeat the process, adding markers at each of the following locations and renaming them as shown:

    •   Bar 3 (**Verse 1**)

    •   Bar 15 (**Verse 2**)

- Bar 27 (Bridge 1)

- Bar 41 (Chorus 1)

- Bar 49 (Verse 3)

- Bar 61 (Verse 4)

- Bar 73 (Bridge 2)

- Bar 87 (Chorus 2)

- Bar 105 (Outro Riff)

- Bar 113 (End)

You can optionally include the marker number in each marker name. This can help you jump to any marker using the shortcut **OPTION+/**, as you will need to enter the marker number in the resulting dialog box.

 Typing "##" in the marker name will add automatic numbering based on the marker position in the Marker List.

Figure 12.9 The Marker List showing marker names and locations

 You can add color to any markers in your project using the color palette. To color multiple markers at the same time (such as all the verses), you can SHIFT-CLICK to add more markers to your selection before coloring.

Mixing in Logic Pro

In this section, you'll delve into the creative aspects of mixing. You'll set volume and pan on the tracks to create static settings, then browse channel strip and plug-in presets for some tracks to quickly get a rough mix.

As you go about auditioning your mix, you can try out the following techniques:

- To navigate the markers, press **OPTION+/** to jump to a specific marker by number.

Figure 12.10 A color-coded and numbered Marker track showing song sections

- To jump to the previous marker, press **OPTION+,** (comma).

- To jump to the next marker, press **OPTION+.** (period).

- To listen to different sections of the song using cycle behavior, select any marker or markers, then use the shortcut **COMMAND+U** to create a cycle area based on your selection.

Set Volume and Pan Levels

To get started with the mix, you'll set initial levels and panning and for all the tracks in the project. As you work, listen to each element in isolation as well as in context. Try to find the loudest sections and quietest sections for each instrument.

Use the volume faders and pan knobs in the Mixer to give each track a specific location in the stereo field. Panning is particularly important for the mono tracks in the project.

Here are some suggestions to get a baseline; feel free to tweak and adjust at your own discretion.

- **Drums** – Fader -2dB, Pan N/A (Stereo)

- **Bass** – Fader -1.5dB, Pan N/A

- **Keys (main track in track stack)** – Fader N/A, Pan N/A (Stereo)

- **Piano** – Fader -1dB, Pan N/A (Stereo)

- **Organ** – Fader 0.0dB, Pan N/A (Stereo)

- **Synth** – Fader -1dB, Pan L -10

- **Guitars** – Fader -2.5dB, Pan N/A (Stereo)

- **Gtr 1** – Fader 0.0dB, Pan L -47

- **Gtr 2** – Fader -5.5dB, Pan L -64

- **Gtr 3** – Fader -2.5dB, Pan R +40

- **Gtr 4** – Fader -4.5dB, Pan R +63

- Lead Gtr – Fader -4.5dB, Pan R +15

- Shaker – Fader 0.0dB, Pan N/A

- Lead Vocal – Fader 0.0dB, Pan N/A

- **Background Vocals (main track in track stack)** – Fader N/A, Pan N/A (Stereo)

- Vocal Harmony – Fader -1.5dB, Pan L -15

- **BGV Low** – Fader -5dB, Pan R +22

- **BGV Mid** – Fader -2.5dB, Pan L -32

- **BGV High** – Fader -3.5dB, Pan R +46

> (i) Audio effects can change how things sound, so you may want to continue adjusting these settings as you add effects to the mix.

Add Effects

Next, you'll go through each track and browse effects for that track. A good way to go about auditioning effects is to solo a single track and then try out effects on it. Once you have a sound you like, un-solo the track and see if it sounds good in the context of the mix with other tracks.

As discussed in Chapter 6, you can add multiple effects to a track at one time using Logic's channel strip presets in the Library.

Open the Library:

- Click on the Library button, or by press the **Y** key.

Add punch to the drums using the Squeezed Kit preset:

1.   Select and solo the **Drums**.

2.   Press spacebar to begin playback.

3.   In the Library, click on **DRUMS AND PERCUSSION > STEREO KIT > SQUEEZED KIT**. (See Figure 12.11, below.)

The Squeezed Kit preset adds a compressor, EQ, and limiter effects to the **Drums** track. A couple different Auxiliary channels are also created with reverbs on them.

Figure 12.11 Adding the Squeezed Kit patch from the library to the Drums track

Place the Modern Stack preset on the Bass track:

1. Select and solo the **Bass** track.

2. In the Library, click on **ELECTRIC GUITAR AND BASS > CLEAN BASS > MODERN STACK**.

It is typically helpful to solo the Bass and Drums together to make sure they blend nicely. Notice that other bass patches might sound good when soloed, but blended with the drums can be muddy in the low-end.

Adjust the Piano track with slight EQ boost and added reverb:

1. Select and solo the **Piano** track.

2. In the Library, click on **STUDIO INSTRUMENTS > KEYBOARDS > GRAND PIANO**.

This preset gives the piano a bit of a lift in the mix so your ear can pick it out easier. It also routes the piano to the reverbs that were added with the drums preset (bus 5 and 7). You can adjust the amount of reverb to taste using the send level knobs.

Add effects to the Lead Vocal:

1. Select and solo the **Lead Vocal** track.

2. In the Library, click on **VOICE > CLASSIC VOCAL**.

This preset adds EQ, compression, delay, and reverb to the lead vocal, helping it sit more comfortably in the mix.

Remove low-end from Background Vocal tracks:

1. Click on the first Audio FX Slot on the Vocal Harmony track (track 13).

2. Choose **EQ > CHANNEL EQ > MONO** or click on the EQ display to place an EQ plug-in on the track.

3. Solo the Main track of the background vocal stack to hear all the background vocals in isolation. As you make adjustments, you can un-solo periodically to hear the tracks in context with the mix.

4. Configure the EQ as follows:

   • Enable Band 1 by clicking the graphic at the top left of the plug-in to engage a high-pass filter. This will cut all frequencies below the specified point.

   Figure 12.12 Clicking the Band 1 button to enable the high-pass filter

   • Drag the red dot to the right until you hear it thinning out the vocal too much; then adjust by moving it left. To thin out the background parts a bit, shoot for around **240 Hz**.

   • Click on Band 5 (the green center band around 1 kHz) and decrease the gain by dragging down on the dot or the middle set of numbers beneath the frequency readout. Try a setting of around **-2.5dB**.

   • Use Band 7 (high shelf) to boost from a set point and above on the frequency spectrum. Try setting the frequency around **7500 Hz** with the gain around **3.5dB**.

   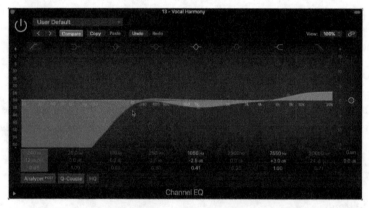

   Figure 12.13 Setting the Background Vocal EQ

5. Once you're satisfied with the sound of this vocal track, close the plug-in window. Then in the Mixer, **OPTION-DRAG** the plug-in from the track to the first Audio FX Slot for each of the remaining three BGV tracks. (See Figure 12.14.)

 Remember that Logic's effects provide several presets to use as starting points. If you want to audition other sounds, click on an effect like the EQ or Compressor and browse the settings pop-up menu.

Figure 12.14 Copying Vocal EQ settings to another background vocal track in the Mixer

Add Reverb to the Background Vocals

Using the Summing stack for the background vocals, you'll now route all of the background vocals using a Send Slot. Adding a bit more reverb on the background vocals will make the lead vocal stand out.

Configure the reverb:

1. Click on a blank Send Slot on the **Background Vocals** stack and select Bus 5, which routes to the Long Ambience effect. (See Figure 12.15.)

2. Begin playback and increase the send level knob to taste. A starting point could be **-8 dB**.

3. Click on the next Send Slot on the **Background Vocals** stack and select Bus 7, which routes to the Prince Hall One. (See Figure 12.15.).

4. Increase the send level knob to taste. Try setting this between **-16** and **-12 dB** as a starting point.

Figure 12.15 Adding a bus send to a reverb

Continue Experimenting!

You can continue adding effects to the remaining tracks to taste, as time allows. Check out some of the many patches and presets in Logic Pro's arsenal for Guitars. Try out different settings on the remaining tracks and see if you find a new effect you like. You can also add sends to a reverb on any of the other tracks. For example, you could add some room ambience on some of the guitar tracks.

Save Work in Progress

You have now created a basic mix for your project. Take this opportunity to save your work.

Save your work:

■   Choose **FILE > SAVE** or press **COMMAND+S**.

Finishing Your Work

To finish the project, you will add final processing on the Stereo Out channel strip and bounce your arrangement to a stereo audio file. You can also optionally use the Consolidate command to create a backup of your work without consuming excess disk space.

Add a Limiter

First, you will add a Limiter audio effect to the Stereo Out channel strip. This will maximize the overall level of the mix, while simultaneously limiting peaks to prevent clipping.

 Logic Pro's Limiter device performs "look-ahead" analysis, anticipating peaks in audio material and preserving attack transients during reduction. This helps the results sound more transparent and maintains the character of the original audio signal without clipping or distortion.

Insert the Limiter effect on the Stereo Out channel:

1.   Show the Mixer, as needed, by pressing **X**.

2.   Click on a blank Audio Effect slot on the Stereo Out channel strip and select **DYNAMICS > LIMITER > STEREO**.

3.   Set the **OUTPUT LEVEL** parameter in the Limiter to **-0.5 dB**. This will ensure that your output will never exceed -0.5 dB and will safeguard the mix against clipping.

4.   Increase the **GAIN** parameter to around **+3.0 dB**. During louder parts of the song, you should see some light to moderate activity on the Reduction meter (the middle meter). This indicates the Limiter is working to prevent the signal from exceeding the -0.5 dB ceiling and protecting against clipping, while raising the overall level of the Logic Pro Project by 3.0 dB.

Figure 12.16 The Limiter audio effect on the Stereo Output channel strip

  Be careful not to increase the Gain too much, as this can introduce distortion.

Bounce the Song

You can now proceed to bounce your song as a single stereo audio file.

Create a stereo bounce:

1.   Select the bounce range by doing one of the following:

 • Make a selection spanning the entire length of the project on at least one track. This can easily be done in this case by selecting a region.

 • Select the **Start** marker, then **SHIFT-CLICK** the **Outro Riff** marker on the Marker track.

Figure 12.17 A selection made to define the bounce range

2. Press **COMMAND+U** to set a cycle area.

3. Select **FILE > BOUNCE > PROJECT OR SECTION** or press **COMMAND+B** to open the Bounce dialog box.

4. Verify that the **START** and **END** locations line up with the project's start and end points, and check the box to **INCLUDE AUDIO TAIL**.

5. Choose the following settings in the Bounce dialog box:

   - File Format: Wave

   - Resolution: 16-bit

   - Sample Rate: 44100

   - File Type: Interleaved

   - Dither Options: POW-r #1

 You should always add dither when bouncing to a lower bit depth.

Save your work and close the project when finished:

1. Choose **FILE > SAVE** to save the project.

2. Choose **FILE > CLOSE PROJECT** to close the project.

3. If desired, press **COMMAND+Q** to quit Logic Pro.

 You can also consider making a back up of your work for archiving. You can use the **CONSOLIDATE** command to collect all of your project's media files into the current Logic Pro project directory.

 See "Finishing Your Work" in Project 1 for details on using the Consolidate command in Logic Pro.

This concludes the project. If you are completing this work in an academic environment, please check with your instructor for submittal requirements; be sure to include the bounced audio mixdown file with your Logic Pro project archive, as appropriate.

Index